WOMEN
WHO
ignite

WOMEN
WHO
ignite

A COLLECTION OF ENLIGHTENING
STORIES TO RECONNECT, UPLIFT
& INSPIRE YOUR SOUL'S JOURNEY

kate butler
BOOKS

This book is dedicated to every woman who has
had a fire in her belly, a burning in her heart, and an
unquenchable desire to get more out of life. We see you,
we feel you, we are you. May you find the spark that
ignites your soul. The answers you need lie
in the pages ahead. It is ALL possible.

enjoy the unfolding ...

FOREWORD

Dina Proctor

Breaking through. Transformation. Healing. Miracles. Overcoming obstacles. Beating the odds. Transcending circumstances.

So many of us are yearning for change, for new ideas, for inspiration, for new and better ways to improve the quality of our health, our relationships, our financial situations, our lives. We try, we strive, we aim for better, we seek the missing piece—the thought or idea that will be the catalyst that launches us through to the lives we dream of living.

What I have found through my own struggles was that it was not the paid experts who coached me through the biggest breakthroughs and healings in my life, it was connecting with other people who understood how I felt on the inside, who had felt that way too, and who had overcome exactly what I was looking to overcome.

They were just like you and me. Sharing their raw and real stories from the deepest corners of their hearts.

When I was navigating the darkest times of my life, I spent years going to different therapists and doctors and trying different medications to fix myself. I suffered from clinical depression for more than a decade and felt like I tried everything to fill the emotional black hole inside of myself. The doctors and therapists were all wonderful people—very knowledgeable and well-meaning, but as I shared my feelings and struggles with them, I could also tell that, though they sympathized, they had never felt the way I did.

Much of my struggle was in feeling completely misunderstood. I hated feeling like even trained professionals couldn't relate to what I was experiencing. In addition to my clinical depression, this bewildering inner anguish made me question what was wrong with me. Why was I so different from normal happy people? This spiraled me into feeling desperately hopeless. As my emotional black hole grew, I sought different ways of self-soothing. I ended up becoming heavily addicted to alcohol for several years and eventually became suicidal.

I hid my drinking and didn't tell anyone how I felt because I thought if my clinical depression was not fixable, how could anyone ever understand the extent of my drinking and the depth of my despair? Feeling like no one understood me was the major factor in deciding to plan a date to take my own life. I thought that if no one could help me fix the way I felt and I had tried everything I could think of in order to help myself, I just wanted out.

And that's when it all changed for me.

When I (quite unintentionally) began attending meetings at an addiction recovery center, I sat quietly in the back and didn't tell anyone my name. I found myself crying silently, unable to suppress the emotion I felt as one person after another shared their feelings of hopelessness, desperation, and desire to be loved and understood. I didn't expect to identify so deeply with these people but, for the first time, hearing people share themselves with raw vulnerability and understanding them so deeply helped me to feel like I could be understood if I shared my feelings, too.

Women that I'd never met held my hands, brushed my tear-stained hair back from my face, looked into my eyes, and enabled me to believe that it could get better. I felt a level of connection with these strangers that I'd never felt before. It surprised me and helped ease my inner suffering. I finally felt understood by people who had once been where I was. From there, one day at a time, my life began to improve.

That is the power of sharing ourselves. That is the power of sharing our stories. That is the power of Women Who Ignite—the women who participated in writing this book get it. They have been there, struggling in the trenches, each in her own way. And one by one, each of these women has found her inner source of power, peace and wisdom.

If you have ever yearned to read about someone who has gone through what you're now going through, or you felt like no one understood you, this book is for you. I hope you find the depth of resonance and inspiration as I did when I read these pages.

With so very much love,
Dina Proctor

table of contents

TRUST IS A PRACTICE

Kellie Adkins

I walked up the slight hill toward the tiny grove house, a patchwork quilt of a building crafted from half-thought-out renovations and situated in a steamy Florida swamp-turned-grove. Behind me, the lake's surface had become a looking glass, reflecting an ochre sunset tinged with fuchsia and lavender. The gilded reflection was broken, only occasionally, by the circular maw of a hungry fish.

The heavy heat was finally fading and the autumn evening promised to be cool, a sweet reprieve from the muggy daytime hours.

I kept walking, making straight for the orange trees at the side of the house, as my mind swirled with questions. "What am I supposed to do?" rose to the surface above the rest. It was more of a rhetorical wail than a direct request, and I recognized that. But an unexpected reply resounded in my mind: trust.

Trust is not an easy practice.

That autumn marked the first year after my step into the wild unknown of balancing a mission-driven business with an equally weighty commitment to living a conscious lifestyle. I was already a "success" in many ways—I'd built a successful yoga studio and eco-boutique in a small town, was a graduate-trained Wellness coach specializing in behavior change with a full list of clients, and had introduced thousands of people (ranging in age from 5 to 95) to integrative wellness, yoga therapy and meditation—but my lifestyle and my business had been at war with each other, and my health and happiness were paying the ultimate price. The demands of running a yoga studio while also holding down the role of primary instructor, teaching yoga training on the weekends, and having a full private coaching practice had hijacked my time, strained my marriage, and taken a toll on my mental and physical health. The passion that fueled my business caused me to over-give to clients and over-work—and since I genuinely believed my work was a service and an offering, I frequently gave too much for too little compensation.

I believed my work was my calling, but lately it'd been calling collect.

In retrospect, I can see that my journey followed a narrative arc that is incredibly common among ambitious women committed to building meaningful, mission-driven businesses. Too many gifted female entrepreneurs have struggled to move past behavioral blockages to ease and abundance—over-working, money struggles, perfectionism, people-pleasing, overachieving, and busy-ness, to name a few. And I found myself grappling with them all as I searched for my true career path.

I've made a few mistakes in business, but failing to prioritize my own energetic needs was the biggest learning lesson of all. As a mission-driven entrepreneur, I believe your business is a reflection of your dharma—your sacred purpose. I took that to heart and I did the work. But it wasn't until I'd burnt myself out that I realized I needed to balance "doing the work" with some essential self-care.

In my first solo endeavor—the Jeweled Lotus Yoga Studio and EcoBoutique—I intentionally created a conscious business model designed to share the message of integrative yoga lifestyle and wellness with all comers. The studio was the first of its kind in a town where yoga was new, revolutionary, and completely foreign. I frequently fielded questions like "Can I practice yoga if I'm a Christian?" "Do I have to chant in Sanskrit?" and (my personal favorite) "What flavors of yogurt do you sell?"

Amid the fog of community confusion about what yoga and "conscious lifestyle" practices entailed, I hustled, networked, and educated. I taught workshops on breathing, posture, and mindful movement in local schools and businesses. I lectured on balanced nutrition and the seasonal approach to meal planning. I offered classes on mindfulness in the moment to change high risk health behaviors like disordered eating, smoking, and substance abuse. I worked with individuals in my role as a wellness coach and developed online programs and resources to support anyone outside my immediate community seeking an integrative approach to health and well-being.

Basically, I marketed my quiet-loving, introverted socks off. I was patient, persistent, pragmatic, and gritty, even when I didn't want to be. I did the work for the work, not for the money or the recognition. I was completely devoted to improving a small corner of the world with my mission-driven business, and I loved the services I was creating and providing. I'm wildly passionate about the juxtaposition of business and transformation, and believe that when world-changing work meets strategic business principles, everyone benefits. That's why I started a business grounded in conscious lifestyle, integrative wellness, and a commitment to making a difference; I wanted to help people.

That desire to support, educate, and inspire others is quite literally in my blood. Yoga, conscious lifestyle, and spiritual inquiry are the primary themes in my life, but business is a force that's shaped my past, present, and future. I come from a long line of entrepreneurs—in service-based spiritual enterprise, at that—and have a lion's share of American entrepreneurship and service-minded motivation. My eyes were wide open to the reality of running a business because I watched my parents' and grandparents' entrepreneurial endeavors ebb and flow. They began their business journey with a faith-based music and drama business, traveling all over the United States, Europe and parts of Asia. My father traded a high school diploma for an education on the road, earning his GED as he drove the tour buses all over the nation. My mother was one of the costume makers, sewing elaborate outfits for both men and women, while my grandmother Alice was the visionary maven that organized and directed the productions, wrangling hundreds of American youths into top shape in the dramatic and musical arts. Later, the family business expanded and they bought a turn of the century hotel in Lake Wales, Florida, to act as a home base, complete with a fabric shop, an ice cream parlor open to the public and lodging for the tour groups between shows.

That wasn't the first or last business, either. Next, came a summer camp, then a carpet business, and more. Entrepreneurship is in my DNA and I grew up listening to stories of business ups and downs. I was no stranger to hard work—in a family business it's all hands on deck, even if those hands belong to a 10 year old—and since all the entrepreneurs in my family also believe that business is a vehicle for sharing world-changing ideas and solving important problems (preferably for the greater good), mission-driven business was a natural career path for me.

My entire family legacy told me, "Do what you love and the money will follow." I never thought to ask, "What happens when the money *doesn't* follow?"

But I found out the hard way: Although the yoga studio was a financial success according to the books, I was the rate-limiting factor for growth. My skill set, unique in the area, was the driving force of the business. Each time I tried to optimize, outsource, hire staff or train others to fill roles, the money didn't follow. And my business instincts told me that was a very bad thing.

So I had to suck it up and change my ways. I had to put some energy toward the nitty-gritty, wholly unglamorous aspects of business-building or be prepared to walk away and sling lattes at a coffee shop. I had to nail down the strategies for conscious business growth so I could earn a living while making a difference—and working reasonable hours, too. Even though I started out with a lifetime of entrepreneurial experience and plenty of practical and tangible support from my family, I struggled to find balance between work and life, passion and profit. I spent far too long with my head down, pushing my way through week after busy week, frustrated by my lack of growth.

Especially since that lack of growth wasn't from lack of trying. I taught 20 hours each week on top of the full-time responsibilities of managing the studio and eco-boutique. I also lectured in a yoga teacher training program on the weekends, so 60 hour work-weeks were normal.

Though I had many joyful moments introducing my tiny hometown to therapeutic yoga, integrative wellness, and meditation, I eventually realized that the life of a studio owner was not for me. Teaching is a true passion of mine and I love people, but the forced extroversion drained me. Having to be constantly "on" was an unsustainable effort for this lover of solitude and silence. I craved a return to the studying, writing, and deepening of wisdom that first drew me to yoga, meditation, and conscious lifestyle studies.

Then, in the third year of the business I became a new mom, and in the blink of an eye, the world shifted. I found myself wading through the postpartum stage feeling completely unprepared for the intensity of my "baby blues." I was on a terrifying roller coaster with no end in sight. Naïvely, I believed my yoga and meditation practices were enough to sustain me, so I resisted support and kept pushing through with all of my responsibilities. I taught 15 or more classes per week until three days before I delivered, and was back to teaching two weeks after giving birth. I nursed my daughter between classes, doing my best to cope privately with the emotional fallout.

In addition to forcing me to ride waves of strong emotion, becoming a mother added a whole new set of priorities and needs to my life. Now, on top of feeling like my work consumed every drop of available stamina and strength, I longed for the freedom to be home with my husband and daughter, and to be more available for my little one overall. But how? How was that even possible with a brick-and-mortar business that required me-energy to run effectively? Although by that time I had systems and limited part-time support staff, the additional talent—well-trained instructors—needed to fuel the studio's growth was nowhere to be found.

As the first year of motherhood progressed, I sunk into a severe depression and eventually acknowledged that this was a very bad sign. The irony of my postpartum experience was that, as a yoga therapist and integrative coach, I taught clients and students the value of self-care and well-being at all levels. These principles of conscious lifestyle were the threads that bound my business together, but I couldn't seem to use them to mend my own holes. The startup phase had depleted my inner resources, the challenges innate to business were intensified by the transition to motherhood, and all the ups and downs that come with running a business from the heart drained me. Even when I was able to acknowledge all of those truths, it took a while to realize that self-care was the missing piece of my personal puzzle. That I needed to start practicing in my life what I preached to my students.

My rock-bottom moment became a universal wake-up call,

and that wake-up call brought me to a moment of intense clarity. I resolved to prioritized my own self-care at all levels, from the physical to the financial. I sought out support for strategizing my next steps in business so I could work less and earn more. I made time for my own self-care even (and especially) when it felt I had no time to give. And I did some deep soul searching around my business plans. Motherhood had shifted my perspective in a good way and I explored alternative business models to accommodate my commitment to family. I began piecing my life—and business—back together with a newfound respect for and attention to aligning my values with my actions. That meant making some big changes, but I felt ready. I accepted that I was exhausted, depleted, unfulfilled, overwhelmed, and underpaid. I could no longer fit my life around my business. In order to remain in integrity, I needed to fit my business around my life.

So I took a hard look at what I wanted more of in the world and how I could bring that forward in my business; I asked what the business needed, and how I wanted to reshape my work-life rhythms. I knew I needed to apply all the tools in my arsenal to shift my mindset and circumstances, and I wanted to do just that. But the reality was that at that moment I was tired, overwhelmed, and questioning whether my business was worth everything I was putting into it. I knew something had to change. I knew I needed to change course so that my past didn't dictate my future. I needed to break the cycle. But the question was … how?

I pondered that question as I made my way up that small hill, on that fateful autumn day, begging the Universe for a sign. And as I crested the hill, I entered a broad grove where bright globes of ripe oranges were hanging heavy on the trees. I remembered that oranges represent new beginnings and good fortune, that the fruit symbolizes the infinite abundance of the Universe.

Trust.

The message echoed in my heart and mind.

Looking back now, I realized all of the stressful, painful, draining experiences that led up to this moment were all necessary growing pains. Those pains were pointing me to a new path. Yes, taking the first step on that new path was also a huge leap of faith into the unknown and that meant I needed to honor my deeper wisdom and choose to trust the unfolding of my life's path.

Embracing trust enabled me to get really clear on the life I wanted to live—and how I wanted to bring my life's work to the world. I focused on finding ways to leverage my skills, gifts, and experiences to live my purpose, while also taking better care of my family in the process. For instance, I'd made an unspoken promise to my daughter to give her a life of stability and security, a life that included plenty of afternoon adventures, nature walks, and time for creative play. Bearing that promise in mind, I was able to look at my career path through new eyes. I embraced the idea that resting and relaxing with my family was essential to re-fueling my creativity tank, and that time off was not a luxury but a necessity. If the current business model didn't afford me that necessity, it had to shape-shift. I accepted the role that my preconceived notions of purpose, business, creativity, and money were playing in my decision-making process. With that clarity, I was able to take strategic actions to shift those business-limiting beliefs and change the self-sabotaging habits.

I began again.

And what I created was a cohesive blend of the core tenets of meaningful life and business.

I went back to the primordial questions: Why am I here? What is the best use of my sacred gifts and signature strengths? How can I share those gifts in service to a higher good? I aligned the inner and outer, and set my intention to make the practice of building a business feel like a devotion. But this time, I remembered to include the essential art of enjoyment, prioritizing the conscious lifestyle and family values that I also wanted to be a consistent part of my life.

A few short years later, I'm infinitely happier. I am doing more meaningful work on a larger scale, I am financially secure, and I have a much healthier relationship with my own self-care.

Nowadays, I use my own life lessons to teach others how to grow and expand businesses that reflect their brilliance. I work mainly with holistic entrepreneurs, helping them design and expand purpose-fueled businesses that give them the freedom to do more of what they love, and do it more profitably. Through coaching, classes, and writings, I work with individuals to design or expand sustainable, values-centric businesses grounded in their own strengths, skills, and powerful work in the world.

And I can do so effectively because of the hard-won wisdom I gained through my own struggles. When I first entered my entrepreneurial life, I worked hard ... then I fell hard. I was no stranger to burnout and overwhelm and I spent a long time putting on a happy face and pushing through the discomfort. But I learned amazing lessons as I hauled myself back up, and later chose to share my lessons with others in hopes that they might soar without falling. Or, at least, fall a little softer and get up a little quicker.

If you're searching for ways to do business in alignment with your ethics, unsure of how to bring your practice to the next level, or feeling overwhelmed by the "business side" of your heart-centered business, I sympathize and I can help. I faced the same struggle, and though it took me time to figure out how to do business in a way that aligned my ethics with my income, I finally found a system that worked for me. And for my amazing clients.

And those primordial questions? I kept asking them and kept answering them. In fact, I expanded those questions until they crystallized into four core components of a meaningful life and business: enjoyment, purpose, service, and prosperity.

ENJOYMENT

People like us—heart-centered independents, creatives, healers, and helpers—have good work to do in this world. The work that we do is important and needs to be shared. We must do this work because we see the need, we see how we can help, and we step up. But we also need to find enjoyment in the day-to-day act of showing up and serving, rather than resorting to the self-sacrificial patterns so common in the healing and helping fields: lack of self-care, burnout, overwhelm and overwork.

Since my self-care had suffered in service to my business, I made changes by beginning with the element I had the most control over: my level of enjoyment in life. I made a non-negotiable commitment to work-life balance that restored my body, mind, and spirit and that included the simple pleasures that result in a rich and artful life. Forcing this shift in thinking gave some much-needed clarity as I remembered that each day is precious and irretrievable.

In the spiritual traditions I follow, we believe that how you spend your days is how you spend your life. So, leading a more meaningful life begins with designing a more meaningful day. I call this concept the "Ideal Day," and it was here that I began translating conceptual work-life balance into tangible action. I asked myself, if I could choose a perfect day, one from past experiences or one from future dreams, what would that day look like? What would I do? Who would I be with?

And from that template, the truth of my next steps became clear. To be fully authentic, I needed to create beauty every day, to preserve time for the people and relationships that mattered, to practice the art of sacred self-care, and to share the wisdom that made a huge impact on my wellbeing in business and in life. Over time, I began piecing together these elements into the current flow of my days, bringing more intentionality, focus, and divine connection into my work and non-work activities.

PURPOSE

I believe in *dharma*, the concept that everyone has a sacred purpose in this life. Instead of asking children what they want to be when they grow up, I wish we would ask them *what they think they should do* and encourage them to do it, whatever it may be. Can you imagine if the focus was on your inner passions and desires instead of pre-determined career slots? What if you'd grown up believing you could create your own path instead of being forced to tread the well-worn ones laid out before you? We'd probably have far fewer mid-life crises, and many more world-changing entrepreneurs.

Discovering your dharma is resonant work that ripples out into your relationships, your community, and your world. It is purpose PLUS service, in action. And if you are an entrepreneur, I believe it should be the cornerstone of your business.

And yes, discovering your purpose is deep, introspective work … but it isn't hard. You already have the answers and, indeed, your entire life has been a training ground for the divine work of dharma. But before you can unearth those answers from the lessons of your past, a shift in thinking may be necessary. Try to view the events in your life as a necessary education, rather than positives, negatives, detours, failures, successes, or mistakes. Thinking and believing that everything has happened for you, not to you, will bring incredible clarity to your dharmic musings. You can choose to accept that the twists and turns in your life contributed to the natural path of your journey rather than throwing unwanted speed bumps onto your life's intended route. By tuning in to your intuition, you can use the past as a roadmap to set yourself on the new path before you.

Connecting with dharma is learning how to be 100% authentic and 100% ourselves—letting go of "shoulda, woulda, coulda," and constructs like "I need to," "I have to," and "I must," so we can make room for "I want to," "I love to," and "I am energized by." This existential housecleaning is the opposite of selfishness. When you make these mental-emotional changes, you aren't abandoning responsibility or prioritizing yourself above others. You are stepping into the You-shaped hole in this Universe and standing firm just as you are: unapologetically unique, precious, and irreplaceable.

Uncovering your purpose is altruistic, not selfish. In fact, standing in your truth, sharing your gifts, and being 100% authentic liberates those around us to do the same. It opens the doorway to possibility, deeper meaning, and connection.

As I embraced this process, my purpose became clear: To be the person I needed, I had to show up and share my experience, then translate that experience into solutions for the people who needed me most.

SERVICE

The heart of business is service, and as I embraced that message, I also accepted that the best way for me to serve was to identify and connect with the people who needed me most. When I shifted my attention from "What am I going to do?" to "Who am I here to serve and what do they need?" my next steps became clear. I went back to the drawing board in my business and highlighted the skills I could share that were in alignment with my higher purpose.

I asked myself: "What are the skills, services, or products in my business that allow me to do my best work, and that I can leverage in the marketplace?" And later on, I would ask those same questions of each of my coaching clients.

Because every one of us, including you, has a set of talents and traits that comprise, in my lingo, our Unique Magic. When you do the deeper work of knowing yourself by asking and answering these questions, you unlock your Unique Magic, and you can't help but make yourself visible! Then the people who look at you and see reflections of themselves will want nothing more than to know, learn from, and support you.

For me, undertaking this process of discovery resulted in an abundance of opportunities to show up and serve. If you choose to focus on business as service, you'll undoubtedly encounter similar abundance yourself.

PROSPERITY

Once I began to shift my business around the balance points of enjoyment, purpose, and service, prosperity gradually followed. My husband and I spent our money in shops and with organizations that shared our sacred set of values, we connected with people who had similar experiences and backgrounds, and we were attracted to people who valued what we valued.

When you are clear on the values you treasure, the "why" of your work in the world, and the core of business as service, prosperity is a natural evolution. You attract the right people by design, and the types of clients you most want to work *with* and work *for* can find you, connect with you, and buy from you.

It is in this personal zone of alignment where your profits lay—both monetary AND at a soul level. But to tap that fantastic, productive, and prosperous zone, you first need to identify and tap into the deeper wisdom behind what I call, "life and business alignment." Put simply, life and business alignment is bringing your life's work and values forward in every aspect of your business—from the focus of your business (actualizing your purpose) to how you run the business (aligned with your core values) to the rates you charge (rates that support your desired lifestyle) to the customers and clients you serve (the people who will most benefit from your work.)

Pull on the threads of these four components—enjoyment, purpose, service, and prosperity—and you'll tease out one essential question: What do you want the pinnacle of your life's work to be?

That autumn day, I asked that question of myself and listened to my soul's response. I acknowledged the inner whispers. I accepted the message of trust. Then ... I acted. I built a newly evolved business centered around the premise of awakening insight and sharing my gifts with the people who needed them most. The best part is that, although I was doing remarkable similar work in my business evolution, I had more freedom, more impact and more time.

And the prosperity did follow ... and is still following.

But building a mission-driven business is much more than just doing what you love and hoping the money will follow. It requires a commitment to evolution and the courage to take scary steps into the unknown. When I took those steps into the unknown I had no idea where the path would lead. I honestly had no idea how to do what I did ... but I took one tiny step, then another and another and the how came later.

If you have that commitment and courage coursing through you, you'll take those steps with your head held high and move swiftly down your unique path toward success. But before you begin that journey, I do have one more tidbit to share, one more insight I've gleaned from all my years of honing and fine-tuning my own work practices: Living a fully-awake life and walking your talk—in business and non-business life—is not for the faint of heart. You need a warrior spirit because many people won't understand your decisions. You need a thick skin because some people will judge you. You need a boatload of self-confidence because a few may be disappointed, angry, or hurt by the direction that your commitment to life- and business-alignment takes you.

But when you choose trust and commit to what is truly important for your own meaningful life and business, the lessons arrive, the path reveals itself, and the prosperity does follow.

Keep trusting and keep listening to what others can't hear.

ABOUT KELLIE ADKINS

Kellie Adkins is a holistic business mentor for conscious entrepreneurs who want to grow their influence and do more of what they love, more profitably. Kellie believes in a values-centric approach to business design and growth, and she loves to work with the individual to align both business and lifestyle goals. Kellie believes business is a vehicle for sharing world-changing ideas—and solving powerful problems—preferably for the greater good. Wildly passionate about the juxtaposition of business and transformation, Kellie provides personalized mentorship, on-demand training programs and an elite society for women entrepreneurs who want to expand their message and their mission.

Through business design courses, coaching practice, and mentorship offerings, Kellie teaches holistic entrepreneurs how to design and expand purpose-fueled businesses that allows them the freedom to do more of what they love, more profitably.

Kellie is a master Yoga Therapist and holds a B.A. in Religions and Gender Studies, New College of Florida, as well as a Master of Sciences in Nutrition and Food Science from Florida State. Kellie has presented at the Yoga Alliance's Business of Yoga conference, guest lectured at New College of Florida, and is a passionate speaker on the topics of business, conscious lifestyle and transformation.

Connect with Kellie at:
www.KellieAdkins.com
www.Facebook.com/KellieIAdkins
Visit:
www.KellieAdkins.com/free-gift/
to get immediate access to the guide "Path to Prosperity as a Conscious Entrepreneur".

LEARNING TO DANCE IN THE RAIN

Lucette Beall

got married in February of 1995, nine months after graduating from veterinary school. I had our daughter, Hallie, five days before my 36th birthday in May of 1997. I built and opened my own veterinary practice in May of 2001. In 2006, a year after we had purchased a house, a little barn and a large shop on 26 acres, I found out that my husband had run up over $100,000 in credit card debt, and he had been making numerous 1-900 sex calls, and he had also been watching many pay-per-view porn movies. Although it was devastating, I stayed and tried to work it out for three more years before finally realizing I had to leave. What follows is an excerpt from the time period starting just before the divorce was final. I learned some of the most valuable lessons about myself, about my daughter, and about the choices we get to make in life. I hope you will find lots of hope and inspiration in this story.

As soon as I filed for divorce I made an appointment for Hallie and myself with the same counselor. In evaluating our marriage, and the failure of our marriage, it was very clear to me that the dysfunction of our marriage was a clear indication that neither of us were the parents my daughter deserved and needed. I very much wanted to take responsibility and learn to be the parent that I always wanted to be—even when I didn't know how—and to be the parent that my daughter, whom I loved with all my heart and was so grateful to have, deserved. I also knew that 12-year-old Hallie, who already had plenty on her plate, was starting seventh grade and was now for the first time really struggling in school. She needed the help and support a good counselor could give her. Our counselor had been our marriage counselor and had also counseled Hallie's father.

Hallie's father and I made an agreement: He would not go after half of my veterinary practice and he would keep the promise to me he had made three years prior, when he said I would not have to pay his debt. In return, I would not ask for child support or for any help in paying for any of Hallie's expenses or health insurance.

I remember clearly the day of the divorce. The court was in Sherman, Texas, and I met my lawyer there. Hallie's dad did not show up, so it was a simple matter of the lawyer presenting our case to the judge and the judge agreeing to what was in the papers and signing off on it. I remember walking out to seeing softly falling snow out of the huge windows in the Sherman courthouse and taking a deep breath, feeling grateful to be moving onto the next phase of my life. That was December 3rd, 2009.

Saturday, December 5th, I found the lump in my left breast. A week prior to finding the mass, Hallie had come to me at home one day and said, "Mom, if something happens to you do I have to live with Dad?" The words came back to me immediately when I found that lump in the shower that Saturday. I was scared for both of us.

A month prior to finding the mass in my left breast I had been taking a shower and found firm swelling in my left arm pit. I had immediately scheduled a doctor's visit. She said they were lymph nodes, she checked both breasts thoroughly, and found nothing. She told me that sometimes the lymph nodes would do that if you shaved with a dull razor and to take some Advil and see if they went down (which they did and never became enlarged again.) Something kept drawing me to continue to check that left side, and I finally found the mass on that day. I strongly believe that God led me to "know" and to find that mass. I have never before or since had any lymph node inflammation or enlargement, and after the doctor didn't find anything I should have felt "safe", but there was a feeling I just couldn't let go of. Ultimately it saved my life.

I managed to see the same doctor on Monday afternoon, December 7th. When I showed her the lump, she felt it and, without saying anything, left the room and came back with a sheet with breast surgeons on it with one circled that she recommended.

My tumor did not show up on the diagnostic mammograms but was clearly visible on ultrasound. The next appointment was with a breast radiology group that were in the same office as the breast surgeon. The radiologist who did the ultrasound told me I would have to schedule another appointment to come back for an ultrasound guided biopsy, which meant waiting another weekend. It was then that the fear hit me in my gut and I began to cry. I was so scared and I had come to the office alone without thinking. Over the weekend I was determined to be optimistic and believe it was all going to be fine. I even found some Peanuts (Hallie's favorite) Christmas cards to send out. I did take a friend with me for the biopsy, and by then I had gathered a little strength and optimism and watched with interest on the ultrasound as she did the guided biopsies on the mass.

When Dr. Malone called the practice for me that afternoon the receptionist had no idea that she was my radiologist and came back to tell me that Dr. Malone was on the phone for me. I immediately knew I had cancer. It was December 15th, less than two weeks since my divorce was final. The words that flew out of my mouth were,

"Oh my god I have cancer!" Unbeknownst to me, my daughter was behind me in the hall, having just been picked up from school. I was in tears. I had to gather my voice and get on the phone. I really don't remember the conversation. I just remember how I felt—devastated and terrified! After the phone call I told my employees and we all were in tears. Then my receptionist said, "Dr. Beall, we still have two clients here. Should I tell them and reschedule them?" I said, "No, we need to go ahead and finish the day." Because I was having trouble keeping myself together, I mentioned the cancer diagnosis to one sweet client, Rhonda Snyder. She gave me the most wonderful pep talk and told me I was strong and I could absolutely do this. Her pep talk gave me so much courage that day, and I was and am so thankful that God put her there for me.

On the way home (we lived 30 minutes from the clinic) with Hallie, my mind was in turmoil. Part of me wanted to curl up in a ball in bed and cry myself to sleep, and the other part of me knew that such a choice would only lay more on Hallie's twelve-year-old shoulders. I absolutely did not want to do that. In discussions with her it seemed that she was really not worried that anything was going to happen to me. Since my mother had breast cancer about six years prior to that and had recovered, Hallie's viewpoint was that I was going to have treatment, go bald, wear a wig and be fine. I was absolutely determined to not show her my own fears and add to the difficulties she faced. I never got those Peanuts Christmas cards sent.

The next few weeks were a blur of working as much as I could between the diagnostics and appointment after appointment. Blood work, breast ultrasound with surgeon, breast MRI, CAT scan, cardiac ultrasound, liver MRI after CAT scan—on and on it went. It was like suddenly stepping onto a conveyer belt at a high rate of speed that someone else had the controls for; you are desperately trying to stay on it and hold on to your stuff that just seems to be going everywhere.

In the middle of this was Christmas, my favorite holiday and Hallie's first Christmas since the divorce. Christmas was a four day weekend that year because Christmas Eve fell on a Thursday. I decided that once we got to Christmas Eve I was going to suspend all thoughts of the cancer and just enjoy every part of that weekend. It snowed that year and it was beautiful. After doing some shopping on Christmas Eve, we stayed home and enjoyed the peace. I cooked a large Christmas dinner and enjoyed my time with Hallie and my parents. On Christmas night, Hallie came and sat next to me on the couch after my parents had gone to bed, shoulders touching, and we talked for such a long time. My heart was so full of love and peace. On Sunday, reality came back and I knew the next day would start the continuous diagnostics for the cancer. It was back to the real world.

The first step in my treatment plan was to surgically remove my ovaries and immediately start on a potent hormone suppressant to shrink my tumor prior to surgery to remove it.

I was terrified. Hallie and I were already struggling at home. She was angry so much of the time. She had learning disabilities that we were just beginning to touch the surface of during this time, and she had so much anger towards both her dad and me. The counselor said that, because she was afraid of her dad, all of her anger towards him was directed at me (along with her anger at me.) I could not imagine how I was going to manage all of that and be the parent she so desperately needed me to be if I was in a major hormonal rage or depression.

I begged the doctors for help in managing the side effects that I knew could be huge—from an immediate and aggressive drop into raging menopause. It took two tries but they were able to find an antidepressant that I could start prior to the surgery to help min-

21

imize the emotional side effects from the sudden and severe drop in hormones.

At the same time that I was working with the doctors on the plan for my treatment and upcoming surgery, I also realized that (with the recent divorce) all of my life insurance policies and my will needed to be updated immediately, and it needed to be completed before my surgery on January 7th. I had to do everything in my power to protect my daughter as much as possible at every turn. I literally left the lawyer's office from signing all of the paper work to go to the hospital the day before the surgery for my pre-surgical blood work. Of course I was still working full time, so I was constantly racing back and forth from work to appointments, knowing that every time I was not at work we were not earning any income.

Money was tight and I quickly learned that I needed to concentrate on what needed to be done. I would have to trust the Lord with the rest of it. Worrying all of the time would get in the way of making sure everything that needed to be done was taken care of. Another beautiful life lesson: Trust in the Lord and leave your worries to him. Sometimes I forget, but when I look back to that time in my life the reminder is clear. It guides me to move away from worry and towards belief and trust in this amazing life we are given!

The surgery was done out-patient on a Thursday morning. After your ovaries are removed, if you still have a uterus (as I did), you begin your last menstrual cycle. As fate would have it, Hallie started her first menstrual cycle the same day I started my last one. I really questioned the Lord about his sense of humor here.

Several awesome veterinary friends covered my practice during the days that I took off to have surgery. I returned to work for a half day on Monday, and by Tuesday I was back at work full time. Thankfully, I did not "wake up on fire" from the surgery as I had heard some people do. But within a few days I began to have many,

many hot flashes both day and night. The night ones woke me up long enough that it was hard to go back to sleep and I had seven or eight of them a night. I remember feeling like I was going to pass out at work from having a hot flash—while doing surgery in a surgery gown, under the very hot surgery lights. I would wear tank tops underneath my lab coat to be as cool as possible and sometimes had to stand in the freezer side of the refrigerator in the treatment area to cool off. Although my body had physically recovered from the surgery procedure, the huge and immediate changes to my hormones were taking their toll.

After some research and reading up on things, I found that acupuncture could be used to help my body deal with the stress of the major changes it was undergoing. I discussed this option with my oncologist and she gave her blessing. I found a wonderful acupuncturist trained in Chinese acupuncture and began sessions with her. She was absolutely wonderful and I began to get some relief from the intensity and just sheer number of hot flashes I was having each day. My body began to feel stronger and I felt much better and more energetic again.

I was so very thankful on a daily basis that I did not have to start chemotherapy right after the surgery to remove my ovaries. This gave Hallie and me time to go to counseling and learn and grow through the difficult transitions we were dealing with. Hallie was active in our youth group at church and was playing in band. She played the drums as well as the electric and acoustic guitar. I put my house and twenty six acres on the market in February, shortly after the divorce was final. We lived twenty-five minutes, including several miles of dirt road, from Hallie's school and our church. I was another seven to ten minutes from there to my clinic. All of my doctors and our counselor were in Denton, another fifteen to twenty minute drive south and a little west of the clinic—that much further from where we lived. We spent hours upon hours driving to and from appointments, church, youth group, counseling, etc. Music became our connection. Hallie introduced me to all kinds of music and we sang together in the car all of the time.

The purpose in selling my house was to downsize as I certainly didn't need or have the resources to take care of twenty six acres. We also needed to move closer to all of our activities. It would also decrease the mortgage payments, fuel expenses, and reduce much of our driving time. We had a very large shop on our land, and in the divorce agreement I gave my husband extra time to move all of his stuff out of the shop. Once I put the house on the market, he began to show up unannounced whenever he wanted to in order to get things out of the shop. I was doing my best to keep the peace and not do anything that would cause Hallie any further stress.

One Saturday morning, I was in the kitchen and had just noticed that he was at the shop, loading stuff, when Hallie came around the corner, saw him, screamed, and ran to her bedroom and hid. That absolutely broke my heart!

She did not see her dad on a regular basis because he traveled a lot. But when she did see him she always came home upset and, unfortunately, I still had not mastered the situation as well as I would have liked. We often got into arguments when she came home. God blessed us with an amazing counselor who helped us both to develop better coping skills and communication skills. This was the beginning of so much growth in my relationship with Hallie. It wasn't magic, but more and more often we could find laughter and humor to get us through the hard times, and we began to have fewer hard times. Love is definitely always the answer. We spent many hours in the car, driving to and from school and work, counseling and church, and we began to grow our bond with music and humor.

All of the driving, Hallie's activities, work, counseling and treatment, and keeping the house in condition to be on the market was just too much. So, although finances were tight, decreasing our stress level was more immediately important. I took the house off of the market. Looking back, I can see how important waiting to sell the place was to our relationship and stability. In retrospect, I don't think Hallie (or I) could have handled a move at that time, and all the time spent in the car did much to grow and heal our relationship. God's timing is always perfect. And it was all perfect because putting it on the market got her dad to remove all of his stuff which was healing for both of us. Taking it off the market allowed us to slow down the many changes going on in our lives all at once.

The original plan was for the tumor to be removed after shrinking in August, and then chemotherapy would start three weeks after the surgery. In late April, the doctor decided that the tumor had shrunk quite a bit and she really wanted to go ahead and do the surgery. I asked her if I could still wait until fall to start the chemotherapy, as that would not affect my prognosis, and I really needed to work through the busy summer months for financial reasons.

She removed the mass and took three sentinel lymph nodes. After the surgery, they intially thought there were no cancer cells in my lymph nodes. I was super excited! However, two days later I got call saying that there were, after all, a few tumor cells in the first two lymph nodes, and she also had not gotten all of the tumor.

Great! Now I needed more surgery, and I was in danger of losing all of my lymph nodes on my left side. I needed to work through the busy summer months, and I was scheduled to go as a chaperone on a mission trip with Hallie and her youth group. For Hallie it was very important that I go on this mission trip, and I was determined to make it happen—as long as it did not jeopardize my health or treatment.

I was able to convince the surgeon and oncologist to wait until

August to continue to the next surgery. The radiologist had put wire markers in my breast, marking the exact spot of the mass prior to surgery, so the markers were still there to use when they went back in. I was still on the hormone suppressant and the tumor had responded excellently to it.

I was so grateful to have the opportunity to go with Hallie, the youth group, and three other wonderful women on that mission trip. We made lasting friendships on that trip. One of the moms became the next youth leader, and she and her husband and kids became such amazing, loving, and important support for Hallie. Their home was such a wonderful place of unconditional love and acceptance along with fantastic fun and humor. As always, God was leading me to make choices that ultimately brought so many fantastic people and experiences into both of our lives. That time period between May and August gave Hallie and I some much needed time to just be. She was going to Sylvan three days a week and we were still going to counseling, so we had lots of time in the car but less pressure than during the school year, which really helped us find more joy and less anger. It was truly a blessing.

Every step of the way there choices to be made and chemotherapy was no exception. The original recommended protocol called for three chemotherapy agents. Of course all of them would have some nasty side effects, but one in particular concerned me the most. It could cause a leukemia that is always fatal. It only happens in 1% of cases, but Hallie was going through so much and I wanted so much to make sure I would be there for her. I asked my doctor for another option and what she would do if she were in my shoes. She gave me another option and said that if she were me, she would choose the second option as well.

Thankfully, during those summer months, a published report came out that would allow me to keep my lymph nodes. I was ecstatic; not having them would make my job much riskier due to many opportunities for scratches or abrasions that could be life threatening without those lymph nodes.

Shortly after we returned from the mission trip, Hallie started high school band camp, which she absolutely loved. As an eighth grader, she was not yet marching, but she got to play in the pit at every high school game and all of the band contests.

The surgery to remove the rest of the mass was scheduled on a Friday two weeks before the first high school football game. My plan was to have the surgery on Friday and be back at work on Monday, which worked out well. Dad came down to drive me to and from the hospital and stay the first night with me. Unfortunately, my tumor was tricky and the report on Tuesday said that they still had not gotten all of it. Now the mad scramble was on. I needed to find someone to cover my practice in three days and make a plan for Hallie so that she could get to school that Friday.

Then the really unthinkable happened. They still did not get all of the tumor cells. At that time, I had the option to let them go in one more time to try to get it all or have a double mastectomy. Because of the type of cancer I had, a mastectomy did nothing to improve my chances for survival. While another surgery to remove the rest of the cells would be a minor surgery, a double mastectomy would be a really major surgery with major recovery time (and I had no sick days because I was self-employed.) It would require at least one more major surgery six months after radiation was completed for reconstruction.

I opted for one more lumpectomy procedure. Again, I was in a mad scramble to cover my practice with three days notice (you usually need month to schedule a relief veterinarian), find a place for Hallie, and get all of the details in place. Hallie was upset because this surgery would again be on the very next Friday—yes, three

Fridays in a row. This was the Friday of the first high school game with the band, thankfully a home game. I told her, "No worries, I'll be there". Daddy was again by my side. This surgery ended up being a little later than the other three, and we were getting ready to head to the OR at 10 am. I told the anesthesiologist, "No pressure, but I HAVE to be at a high school football game tonight." He took good care of me and I was up and out of there in no time. Daddy and I made it to the football game to watch Hallie play with the high school band for the first time!

The next day, one of my clients, who had also been through breast cancer, and some friends threw me a "hat party". Everyone brought hats, blankets, and all kinds of useful things that one needs during chemotherapy. Hallie and Daddy came with me, and I modeled hats and scarves and we had a blast, except for the half hour or so I got stuck in the bathroom. There is no surgery without some price to pay. I think I got pretty lucky! Besides wonderful hats, scarves, and tons of support, I also received all kinds of things one needs to get through chemo, including a beautiful nap blanket that I still have to this day. What a blessing to have such wonderful people around me!

One Saturday, Hallie and I met with two of my receptionists/ friends and we went "wig shopping" at a wig boutique that had been recommended to me. The guy who owns and runs it is very, very good and very compassionate. After a fun time playing around with wigs, we narrowed it down and made our final selection. Then he put it on my head and tailored it for me. It was wonderful to have my daughter and friends to laugh and joke with while making this choice. I felt very, very blessed. His wig was so good that there have been people that never knew I lost my hair. At his recommendation I had my hair cut fairly short instead of having my head shaved before starting chemotherapy.

One of my dear college friends made a ten hour trip to be with me for my first chemotherapy treatment and she stayed with me the following weekend. The nurses advised us to go eat immediately afterwards while all of the anti-nausea medications were working and before my taste buds took a total nose dive for the next few weeks. That started a tradition that continued after every chemotherapy session. I was so grateful to have Darlena there that first weekend. The doctor said that usually people developed a pattern of their worst day after chemotherapy. After that, you could be prepared. It didn't work out that way for me; each time it was a different day. But on that first weekend it was Saturday. I was trying to take a shower that morning and thought, "No wonder all of your hair falls out. You don't have the energy to wash it!" It was all I could do to finish the shower. I kept leaning against the wall, and when I finally got done I had to sit down a bit before I could go dry my hair. But by Monday I felt great.

The next weekend I attended a large veterinary conference in Ft. Worth. My hair had not started falling out yet when I arrived on Thursday, but when I woke up Saturday morning it was everywhere. On my pillow, in my bed, in the shower, in the sink when I brushed my teeth. I plopped my wig on for the first time before heading off to continuing education classes (mainly so everyone, including me, wouldn't see my hair falling out everywhere.) It was such a good wig that several veterinary friends took most of the day to realize my hair was different. The best thing about not having shaved my head was that, though most of my hair did fall out, I had a little fringe along the sides and back, just enough that I could wear a cap and not look like I was going through chemo. It was really nice to be a little incognito from the cancer!

One of my employees teamed up with a group of men in Aubrey who did fundraisers for local cancer patients and people who experienced a tragedy or were in need. She organized an incredible fundraiser for me and enlisted the help of many clients and local businesses. Although I had good insurance because I was self-employed, the expenses of having to leave work all the time were adding up, along with all of the things that insurance doesn't pay for.

At the fundraiser there was a silent auction, a live auction, a pink fire truck, and barbecued briskets with all of the fixings. They sold over 500 meals to go and ran out of containers. They sold whole briskets individually, and they sold a huge number of meals to those who came and stayed and bid on the many items in the silent and live auctions. I tried to talk to everyone there, but there were so many! All of my friends, clients, and church members from both Pilot Point and Aubrey were there. There were so many volunteers. The men that cooked the brisket and beans set up on Friday night for the Saturday event, and some stayed out there all night tending to the brisket and beans. It is so amazing how small towns come together to support their own, and I believe Pilot Point and Aubrey, TX are some of the best! The money was a HUGE help, but more than that, the feeling you get when so many people go out of their way to help you is phenomenal. It changes you in ways you can't even explain.

Soon after the diagnosis, one of my high school classmates who had already been through breast cancer herself gave me some of the very best advice. She said when people ask how they can help, TELL them. She reminded me that allowing people to help who want to help is just as much a gift to them as it is to the receiver. When I was exhausted from chemo and working and something would come up—like Hallie needing a ride to an appointment or an activity—I would send a prayer up asking for someone who could take care it. Someone always showed up or called, asking how they could help, and if they couldn't do what I needed they would find someone who could! It was wonderful to learn to trust and be secure that the help would arrive, and it always did! I have forgotten those lessons a few times, but each time I go back to it, it works just as well as it did back then. "Ask and you shall receive, seek and you shall find, knock and the door will be opened unto you."

Hallie and I were never ones to arrive early. We were always scrambling out of the door at the last minute. I would put on my wig last, after I was dressed and my make-up was on. One day I went racing back through the house from the car just as Hallie was headed to get in, and I shouted back at her, "Oh my god, I almost forgot my hair!" We had a good laugh over that. Humor was a huge part of our relationship and she is incredibly funny, so we often found ourselves laughing, no matter the situation.

There were three couples with daughters who were Hallie's age that she had known since she was very small. All three couples offered that Hallie could stay any time she needed to, and Hallie was comfortable in all three of their homes. This was such a huge blessing since we had no family nearby and her dad traveled a tremendous amount. One of the couples had an RV and they offered to drive it to the away games if I should need it to rest after chemotherapy. I rode with them to every away game, and I never needed the RV, but I so appreciated the rides and the offer of the RV.

The only football game I missed that year was the one while I was in Ft. Worth at the veterinary conference.

Each chemo session, a different friend would go with me. I had one special friend, June, who went with me twice. It was nice to have someone with me and after that first session together, we always went to lunch afterwards, before heading home. When you go to the oncologist and when you go into the chemotherapy room, it is always an eye-opening and humbling experience. You see many people who have "chronic cancer" and for the rest of their lives they will be in treatment of some sort. You see and meet people who know they don't have very long to live. When you know you have a really good chance of remission and a really good chance to lead a normal life afterwards, it is extremely humbling to look around you and talk to these people, to know how much they would love to be walking in your shoes. I had a young client, a friend of one of my employees, who had a fifteen-year-old daughter and a three-year-old daughter. She was diagnosed with breast cancer after I was (a very aggressive form of breast cancer) and died before I finished chemotherapy. I also had a cousin who was eighteen months older than me, and she died of lung and brain cancer while I was going through chemotherapy. We all know many people who have lost their battle with this terrible disease. I was extremely grateful to have a very treatable form of the disease and to have good insurance.

One Sunday, after one of my chemotherapy treatments, Hallie was going to play her guitar in church for the very first time. I was so excited and couldn't wait to watch her. However, for that particular treatment, Sunday turned out to be my worst day. I tried so hard to get ready and it was just so difficult. Finally, I realized that even if I could get ready I was never going to make it through church and youth group. (That year our youth group met shortly after church for the express purpose of Hallie being able to attend, since we lived so far from the church. We were so blessed in so many ways.) Finally, I just put on some sweats and drove Hallie the half hour to church and dropped her off and came home. I told the man who Hallie was playing guitar with what was going on, and I knew that everything would be taken care of. I knew she would be fed, gotten to youth group, and gotten back home again. Though I missed Hallie playing, I could rest at home with such peace knowing that she was loved and taken care of, and that she got to have a wonderful day, even if I wasn't up to it at that moment.

One of the ladies from our church, with the occasional help of another dear lady, brought us one meal a week, EVERY week for a year! It was SO helpful! One of their meals would usually make at least three or four for us, and trust me, there wasn't a lot of cooking going on for a good part of that time.

My last chemotherapy session was December 29th, 2010. Hallie had requested to go with me. She was out for Christmas break at that time, so she got to be with me for the last round of chemotherapy celebration and "graduation". The sweet nurses in the chemotherapy treatment area gave me balloons and a certificate, and they took a picture of Hallie and me with the certificate, balloons, and a graduation cap perched on my wig. It was definitely a great feeling to be DONE with chemotherapy! I was so very glad that it was available and I had the chance to beat cancer, but it is not something one would ever choose to go through. All that was left now was seven weeks of daily radiation—Monday through Friday.

I finished radiation therapy in early March of 2011. I put my house back on the market in January of 2011 and sold it, and I bought a house in Pilot Point where Hallie was attending school, which was less than 10 minutes from work.

Fast forward to May of 2016. I am now five years cancer-free, and Hallie and I are both doing very well. I love my funny girl with all of my heart and I enjoy her tremendously. While I would certainly never choose to have cancer, I can say that I learned some of the most profound, life changing, joy-bringing lessons of my life during that time period. I would not trade anything for all that God has given me through the amazing life lessons I learned during that time of my life.

ABOUT LUCETTE BEALL

Lucette Beall is a veterinarian, cancer survivor, single mom, and a passionate advocate for high functioning autism. When Lucette's daughter was 15, after an entire life time of confusion and searching, she was finally diagnosed with high-functioning autism. This happened right after Lucette went through a divorce and survived cancer, all while running her own business. Two years later, she brought her brother home to live with her. He had survived a traumatic brain injury but was struggling and in a mental hospital at the time. He is now successfully living independently. She would not trade anything for all that God has given her through the life lessons on her journey. If you would like to know more about Lucette, you can visit her website at www.adjustingsails.com.

FINDING FABULOUS AT 52

Donna Nudel Brown

Doesn't it sound fabulous to walk around all day buzzing and vibrating with high energy? Well it is! I am lucky enough to experience this daily and perhaps you may be wondering how or why I do! The reasons are two-fold. I work with crystals in my business so, physically, I vibrate and buzz from being surrounded by them and holding them. I also vibrate and buzz on a soul level because of the major life transformation I recently experienced.

It hasn't always been like this, nor did I know what it felt like or even what it meant to vibrate. I also never imagined I would have a story worth telling or the ability to inspire others, but I do know the exact moments that my life began to shift. Once those shifts occurred, I realized one of my passions was to help other women identify and release what was holding them back from stepping into the lives they desired and deserved. I want you to know that no matter where you are in your life, you have the power to create the life of your dreams. I am going to share with you the shifts necessary to live the life you are seeking.

I have always been drawn to all things beautiful and sparkly, but I experienced a time in my life when I could no longer see beauty.

After my children were born, I had a tough time because I did not know or understand what my purpose was beyond diapers, carpool, and soccer games. I felt I was going through the motions and the daily to-dos without a sense of direction. I am eternally grateful that I had the privilege of being home with my children as they grew, but I knew I needed more. I struggled with who I was as a person beyond being my children's mother. I did not have a career to return to since I made the choice to leave college before graduating. That choice always left me feeling inadequate and as though I wasn't enough. I knew I needed something to feel fulfilled, but I had no idea what that would look like. I am extremely blessed to be the mother of my three amazing children and am so grateful I was able to be there for all the moments in their lives. These feelings were completely separate from the love I felt for them. This struggle was about understanding my purpose and the importance of knowing how I would impact the world and the legacy I would leave. I wanted and needed something to define me that would make me and my family proud.

Because of my love of beautiful things, I had been drawn to creating beauty in many areas ever since my oldest daughter was born in 1995, over 21 years ago. While I was bonding and nurturing her during some of our 24-hour nursing marathons, I watched the creative shows on television and felt compelled to create much of what they demonstrated. After having two more children, I played with many different materials and functions and then decided to create mosaics. This was my first creative failure. No one was buying what I created. I translated the lack of public interest and low sales into a lack of talent. As a result, my self-esteem plunged to a very low point and it stayed there for many years. Proof that I was not good enough.

Once all my children were enrolled in school full time, I immersed myself in volunteering in their schools, at my synagogue, and in my community. My husband worked hard to provide for our family while I took care of the house (not always that well), the children, and all the logistics that accompanied their endless activities. When I didn't have obligations during the day, I was able to exercise and spend time with friends. Still, I felt there had to be something more to my life, and yet I felt badly thinking that way since I had a life others dreamed of. Only, to me, it felt empty and lacked direction. I had a hard time opening up and talking about these feelings with others. I found that my "non-working mom" friends thought I was crazy for wanting more and my "working mom" friends thought I was crazy because I had the life they desired. But I was miserable and I felt stuck. I needed something that would help me find my purpose *so* badly!

After yearning for something more for so long, I was introduced to a group of female entrepreneurs. There was a desire deep down for something more in my life and I owed it to myself to try again. With the help and support of my team, I was able to build a business with a health and wellness company around my family's schedule. This business would allow me to still be there for the soccer games, field trips, and volunteer duties but would also allow me to help women look and feel better about themselves. Earning my own money was empowering. My husband was generous and I was fortunate, but it was very satisfying to earn an income. Frankly, I enjoyed spending my own money to shop without providing an explanation, buying something 'just because' or feeling the need to sneak packages into the house when my husband wasn't looking. I was also able to contribute by helping with some of our household expenses. It was quite liberating!

I also found satisfaction in helping other women address health and personal care issues that became transformative for them, and knowing that I was really making a difference for them filled me with joy. Through my involvement in that business along with my commitment to personal growth and development, I began to see my self esteem rise. It was during that time that my creative spirit and artist in me was asking, no *begging*, to come out. The feelings I experience when I am creating art feeds my soul, and I so missed having that feeling. It just so happened a short time later that I needed a headpiece for a family event and I couldn't find anything that suited me, so I made my own. Everyone loved what I had created from wire and Swarovski crystal beads, so I began to make them for others and give them away. My sister encouraged me to stop giving them away and to begin selling them. My second business was born: DonnaBrownDesigns. Over time, I expanded my line to include jewelry and accessories, received positive feedback, and it felt amazing! Most importantly, my self-esteem continued to flourish.

In August of 2014, my husband, three children (ages 19, 17, and 13) and I embarked on our annual summer vacation to New England. We stopped in Massachusetts at my in-laws for a long weekend before going to Maine. The conditions that weekend were absolutely perfect in every way. The weather, the brilliant blue color of the sky, the water temperature (it is usually too cold for me), and the tide (since the beach is only accessible to us at low tide) were all simply breathtaking and beautiful. While there, we enjoyed being in the water, playing on the rocks and jumping off of a cliff at high tide. I volunteered to be the designated photographer because there was *no way* I would jump! Photo after photo, jump after jump, I captured their memories. After I was asked repeatedly if I would join them, and repeatedly insisted that I would not, I was struck by the fact that if I left that day without at least trying to jump, I would go on to regret it.

As I made my way over and around the crescent-shaped rock

formation toward the cliff, a memory came flooding back. I remembered what I believe to be the last time I took a risk; I mean really took a risk. I had jumped out of an airplane. At the time, I was in college, and at 19 I didn't think about consequences or all that could go wrong because I was infallible! So on that day in 1982, I drove from my campus to a small town in Pennsylvania. I spent five hours learning how to inspect my parachute, jump, land and roll. And it was exhilarating! Finally, at the end of the training, and racing against the clock as darkness approached, we were fitted with our parachutes and boarded a tiny plane without seats. I was crouched on my knees and I was to jump first. We were assigned positions in the plane based on our weight in order to balance the plane —the heaviest was to jump first. The fact that I was the heaviest made me feel uncomfortable, especially since I was always so self-conscious about my weight and appearance. But I knew this was definitely not the time to lie about my weight! So there I was in the first position. I heard mumblings about wind and positioning but I was too distracted by my loud, overpowering, pounding heartbeat to really hear what anyone was saying. The next thing I knew, I was standing on the support strut of the wing of the plane! The instructor yelled, "JUMP!" several times before I actually leapt. And then I did it, I JUMPED! I did not need to remember to pull my parachute cord since I was fitted with a static line that would automatically deploy the chute once the strap was fully extended and separate from its attachment.

With a jolt, the parachute opened, and thankfully, as I was trained to check, it was a perfect circle. Once I recovered from the panic of falling, I was able to relax for a bit and enjoy the beauty and silence as I drifted down. To this day, I remember how quiet, beautiful and peaceful it was floating down over the farmland as I occasionally pulled on the toggles to adjust my direction. The sense of peace

I felt was interrupted when I realized I could not see the landing target. I had made the decision not to wear my glasses for fear of them falling off and losing them. Well *I* got lost instead, missed the target and landed in a bank of trees with my parachute tangled in the branches and my feet dangling approximately eight feet above the ground. I was close enough to the ground so I could free myself from the parachute and safely jump the rest of the distance. I landed on the ground using the roll technique I was taught earlier that day. I struggled to remove the parachute from the tree, eventually gave up and walked to the nearby road to wait, hoping someone would drive by since I had no idea where I was in relation to the airport. Soon after, a yellow VW bug pulled up and the driver asked if I had seen a jumper. I replied "Yup, that's me!" He rescued my parachute and drove me back to the tiny airport. I was graded on my jumping technique (good) and my distance from target (TFFTM'—too flipping far to measure.) The memory of that day still makes me chuckle and brings a smile to my face.

Although it was under completely different circumstances, I thought of my day of parachuting as I approached the top of the cliff. It occurred to me that I hadn't taken many risks since my children were born because of the enormous responsibility I felt in being their mother. I felt as though I always needed to play it safe. Like I always needed to put my own oxygen mask on first in order to take care of my family. As I approached the top of the cliff, I suddenly got excited, knowing I would feel the powerful rush of adrenaline once again. It took several minutes for me to prepare—all the while watching my children and other family members leap continuously and hearing the squeals and laughs as each took their turn. Slowly, I inched closer to the edge, mustered all my courage and reached the jump off point as far forward as I could with my toes hanging over the edge. My daughter gave me encouraging words. The wind provided a comfortable breeze that helped keep my perspiration at bay. Again, I looked down at the water below to assess whether it would be safe. I heard my husband yell from below in a kayak (the rescue boat), "You can do it but don't wait too long, the tide is going out!" So with that, I took several deep breaths to calm my nerves, inhaled the beautiful salt air, and then finally made the decision—and I JUMPED! As the wind blew through my hair and against my face, falling through the air felt amazing. The water was cool and refreshing as I entered, and as my feet touched the sandy bottom I pushed up to propel myself to the surface. I emerged out of the water exhilarated.

I came up out of the water, fist in the air, and screamed "I DID IT!" I had conquered my fear and it felt amazing! And this time I hit my target!

The following morning we left for our favorite vacation destination in Maine. We stayed at a house on the coast with gorgeous mountain and water views and the most spectacular sunrises and sunsets. We truly enjoyed the peace and beauty of our surroundings. We experienced all of our favorite activities—sailing, boating, kayaking, hiking, picnicking, searching for sea glass, eating lobster, late night card games, and so much more. During our time there I often recalled my jump and felt so proud that I had made the leap off the cliff! Then on our last night of vacation, we took one final trip to the dock and my husband slipped on wet grass and broke his ankle badly. I took him to the local hospital and they told us we needed to come back the next morning for surgery. The doctors told me I was to be sure that his toes did not turn purple during the night. Clearly, I did not sleep at all that night!

We decided it would be best to have the surgery in Baltimore, our hometown. We made the very long drive home with him in extreme pain and fortunately, I was able to schedule an appointment with a specialist for the next day. After one of his three surgeries, the doctors were giving me instructions on how to care for him and the erector set attached to his leg. I was trying my hardest not to vomit or pass out since, typically, any mention of blood or medical details makes me nauseous and squeamish. Knowing this, my husband, in his anesthesia-induced fog, lifted his head and said, "You won't be able to do that!" As tears streamed down my face, I responded "I jumped off a cliff, I can do anything!" In my heart, I was wondering how in the world I was going to take care of him. As is generally the case when caring for a loved one, you put your fears and hesitations aside and do whatever is necessary in order to make them comfortable. As it turns out, I was able to follow the instructions and took very good care of him and his wounds. While he was recovering, I served him three meals a day on a tray, gave him sponge baths (not as sexy as it sounds), and once he was cleared to return to work, I drove him to and from work each day for six weeks.

In the middle of that ordeal I met Kate Butler, my mentor and coach …

I met her at a retreat she hosted at a friend's home that August, just a few days after returning from Maine with my husband and his broken ankle. I went because I had seen the businesses of my colleagues flourish after they had worked with her and I wanted that success as well. When I arrived that day, I was frazzled and overwhelmed.

Our first exercise required us to repeatedly answer the question, "Who are you?" As Kate gave us instructions, I recalled an experience from several years before when I participated in a personal growth program that included a series of workshops and seminars. I remembered one exercise where we had to stand face to face with a partner and silently stare into their eyes for several minutes. It brought me to tears and I had to look away almost immediately. I imagined my partner, who had been randomly selected, staring into my soul and uncovering the truth, the truth that I wasn't good enough. I imagined he would see all of my flaws and I could not hold his gaze. So as a way to help the others at Kate's retreat, I shared how this exercise may bring up surprising thoughts and feelings. Kate then asked me to be her partner for that exercise. She immediately and intuitively found a way to pinpoint the support I needed that day by providing me with useful tools and techniques.

Shortly thereafter I began to coach with her privately. What she helped me uncover was that my passion lay in the process of designing and creating my accessories. Through our work together, we began to focus on growing my accessories business alongside my health and wellness business that I had started years before. We also spent time discussing my relationships, finances, spirituality, environment, and several other areas of my life. I incorporated the practices of meditation, reciting affirmations, and detailed future visualization, all of which were outside of the scope of any personal development work I had ever done before.

Feeling inspired and with Kate's guidance on the best way to grow my accessories business, I bought a domain name, built a new website, and began to share my accessories on a larger scale. Though this felt amazing, something was still missing. I still wasn't completely fulfilled even though I was enjoying positive shifts in many areas of my life. I was open-minded, I continued to meditate and say affirmations daily and some of my visions were beginning to manifest. In fact, during one of my calls with Kate, I shared some of my affirmations regarding my husband: wanting to spend more time with him, wanting to feel valued and appreciated by him, and the desire for him to have some additional time off work to enjoy being home. And then it struck me that I had manifested all of that as a result of his broken ankle. What?! At that moment, I thought to myself that I had superpowers even before I learned about affirmations or fully understood that each of us has the ability to manifest through visualization! Clearly, I wanted all of those things but while we were all healthy! Remember, the 'how' is not up to us or within our control. The Universe conspires to turn our thoughts into reality in some form. Knowing this, it is important to only think positive thoughts!

Over the course of the following year, I continued to coach privately with Kate. I participated in group coaching and attended more retreats. Each time something new would develop and I would learn even more about myself and my purpose. I was experiencing growth in many areas of my life and as a result, my relationships were stronger and money was flowing easily and effortlessly from many sources (one of the affirmations I say multiple times per day). I was noticing shifts everywhere!

In September of 2015, I attended the Success in the Sand retreat with Kate and 10 other women in Myrtle Beach, SC where many shifts occurred. On the second night of the retreat, we were to identify our most limiting belief so that we could burn it with the intention of releasing it. Many thoughts came to mind but we were instructed to select only one. I wrote down several in my journal and pondered each one carefully in the hopes of uncovering which one would give me the most freedom after I eliminated it. After several moments, I selected the belief that had the biggest impact on my life. For me, that belief was that I was not smart enough. I had held that belief for so long because I never graduated from college. I had attended three universities over five years, studied several majors, experienced a few failed classes and I finally decided to leave before graduating. The decision to leave without graduating translated into me believing I was not smart enough. At the time, I felt that was my only choice—to leave before finishing the necessary courses. I believed I lacked the ability to complete the required classes in a timely manner and did not want to face the possibility of failing another class and so I left school. I realize most people don't equate not graduating from college with not being smart, but that was my belief. There were such high expectations for me after graduating from high school and I felt I had disappointed myself and my family. The decision to leave school affected so many areas of my life for over 30 years—until that moment. While digging a hole in the sand, I ripped the page from my journal and ceremoniously burned it in a fire pit in Myrtle Beach that weekend at the retreat. The TRUTH was I didn't graduate from college because academic excellence was not my goal. My goal was to be on my own and have a good time. I did that! The TRUTH was I missed a lot of classes and didn't spend a lot of time studying. The TRUTH was that I hadn't tried very hard! The TRUTH was I went to more concerts than classes. THAT was the truth, but I held the belief that it was all because I was not smart enough, and it affected me for over 30 years. So that Saturday night, after tossing the piece of paper into the fire, watching it turn to ashes and smoke, I burned and released that belief forever!

The following morning my crystal business was born. We were having a discussion about crystals and the energy they possess when my friend looked at me and had a vision that would become my new business: Energy Infused Crystals. She suggested that I use the same technique I had been using in my accessories business and wire wrap the crystals after I infused them with energy. I would also apply an intention designed specifically for the recipient. A short time after I began working with crystals, I became certified in Reiki—a healing energy that I infuse into my crystals to provide a more intense energy, which in turn heightens their properties. I had to give up the belief that I was not smart in order to make space for what was waiting: my crystal business.

45

Before I left Myrtle Beach, I had registered for my first event where I would have a display and share my crystals. I had two weeks to learn, prepare and purchase everything I needed for the conference where my crystals would make their debut. A few days after returning to Baltimore from Myrtle Beach, I walked into a local crystal shop for the first time to purchase crystals, and my life changed forever without my realizing it. I was overcome by the variety of all of the beautiful crystals, large and small, in a rainbow of what seemed like hundreds of colors. There were crystals that were smooth and polished and others that were rough and jagged. Some were dull and others sparkly; some were small enough to curl into my hand and others large enough that they would need a piece of furniture of their own to hold them and a designated space to display them. I took a few moments to look around and take it all in. I had never seen anything so magical before and the energy I felt standing in the center of it all was quite literally intoxicating for me. I did not know where to begin so I explained to the shop owners what I was seeking and what my intention was. They recommended I first fill my bowl with the crystals I was attracted to. On that visit I was immediately drawn to all blue crystals, so I filled my bowl initially with only blue crystals. The first stone I reached for was Blue Kyanite. Following the owner's recommendation I then selected many other stones in a variety of colors.

As I began to learn more information about crystals—how they can help us and how to use them—I was amazed and surprised how each crystal has different properties to support and heal. The crystals immediately began to change my life on many levels. Blue Kyanite, the first crystal I reached for on my first visit, has several properties, including assisting in problem solving, breaking negative cycles, and aiding in the opening of telepathic communications. Wearing or holding that crystal daily has made such a difference mostly because it has allowed me to feel a much stronger connection to my father who passed away in 2004. He was a huge supporter of mine and always saw my potential when I did not. As one might recall, I had a low opinion of myself. But my father was always one of my biggest champions and believed I could accomplish anything, even when I did not see the possibility. While wearing that crystal and feeling his presence stronger than I had before, I felt so much closer to my dad. I also felt supported, as though I was headed in the right direction to fulfilling my purpose. Those feelings helped me believe more in myself and know that I could achieve anything, including successfully growing my crystal business, which was now an extension of my already established accessory business. So not only did the Kyanite help me feel the stronger connection to my father, it also had a huge impact on me having the confidence to grow my business.

I often tell people when they are searching for a crystal to notice which ones seem to speak to them and want to be picked up. Most often the crystals that attract them hold the properties they need. Energetically, your body knows what it needs and will be drawn to the stone that holds those properties. I often share the story of my first crystal shopping experience, but it had not occurred to me that the selection process applied to me as well! It finally dawned on me that *that* Blue Kyanite crystal was exactly what I needed at the time—that crystal and all the other blue crystals helped me find my voice. Blue is the color associated with the throat chakra which is one of our seven energy centers. The throat chakra is linked to our creativity and our ability to communicate. Finding my voice allowed me to share my story so that I could impact others. It enabled me to communicate my life lesson of finding my worthiness and show others that they already have everything inside of them they need, they just need to let go of what isn't serving them so they can step into what is waiting. We all have amazing gifts and we just need to identify and realize what they are so we can share them with the world. I encourage you to look inside yourself and see what gifts you possess and to identify what is keeping you from living your best life. What gifts do you have that can empower even just one person? That person could be you! I encourage you to uncover what brings you joy because when you do, you will find fulfillment. And if you choose, you can use your newfound awareness, strength and courage to serve others.

In March of 2016, I was invited to speak and share my crystals at a women's conference in NYC. Since I had a difficult time believing I had a story worthy of sharing, this experience caused me anxiety. I was completely terrified and overwhelmed at the thought of speaking in public. It took a huge amount of courage for me to stand in front of a group of women and speak about my life lessons. Just before I took the stage, I actually stood in the ladies room in the 'Wonder Woman' position (my favorite power pose)—standing tall with hands on hips and legs spread. I truly believe that helped me focus my intention and provided me with the insane courage I needed that day. I spoke of things that I had never shared before with anyone, especially in a public forum, but I knew that by being brave I could inspire others.

Think about what you may be holding on to that isn't serving you. What can you release that will allow you to step into your greatness and be the best version of you that you can possibly be? I am proof that it is never too late! I was 52 before I figured out that my life's purpose was in serving others through my energy work with crystals and using my story as an inspiration for others. As a result of the amazing gifts and growth I received from working with a coach, I pursued my certification and am now able to help others through coaching so that they can uncover what their true gifts may be. Your gifts may be hidden but strive to identify them. I am so grateful that my journey has led me to this point where I can help others uncover the gifts that lie within them. I have never felt more fulfilled in my entire life!

My work with crystals has been so well received and I know this is what I am meant to do. Interestingly, I knew nothing about crystals prior to that life changing retreat in Myrtle Beach. My massage therapist had given me my first crystal, a Rose Quartz, just two weeks before that retreat. I know there are no accidents in life and I am meant to be on this path. I get truth bumps (chills) each time I recall the moment when the idea of me working with crystals was mentioned. Each time I hold a crystal and feel its power it feels so right! It's as though I have always had the power inside me, much like Dorothy's ruby red slippers. My hope is that you experience your own version of feeling the energy that I feel when I hold crystals in my hand.

Remember that artist who was begging to come out? She is now filled with so much joy and a soul filled with love! Creating pieces of art with my crystals and using my artistic talent of turning the crystals into wearable art has excited a deeper passion within me that I didn't realize I had. Each time I wrap a crystal with wire, I envision the twists and turns and journey of life where the curved wire represents the journey and the stones are the stops along the way. Each time someone selects a crystal, learns its meaning, and finds that it is exactly what they need, I know this is my path. Through sharing the energy of my crystals, I have helped so many find the support they need in areas of healing, strength, protection from negative energy, and so much more. This is so incredible because over the years the voices were telling me I was not good enough and not smart enough. Who was I to start a business? I was not an expert. It wouldn't work. I should quit! Some of the voices were mine and some were from others. I often worried what other people would think of me but I now know what other people think of me is none of my business. I used to let that stop me. Not anymore! I know that I need to live my life to fulfill my own needs and pursue what is best for me and for my family.

Another huge shift occurred once I stopped comparing myself to others—to their appearance, to their intelligence, to their careers, to their homes. All of those comparisons made me feel inadequate and reinforced my belief in myself that I wasn't enough. Once I let go of those feelings—and it took my being grateful for all that I had instead of focusing on what I didn't have—I was finally filled with a sense of peace. I could stop chasing what I thought was a perfect life. My life was already perfect. I want what I already have. No amount of searching for external 'things' would make me happy. I had to find the happiness within. I had to come from a place of abundance and not a place of lack, and this is achieved through gratitude. Gratitude, in my opinion, is the secret sauce of life.

So I choose to continue to manifest my visions and dreams. I know I have the power to manifest because I have proof. After all, I actually manifested my being on stage at the women's conference in March 2016. The previous month at Kate Butler's Ignite Your Inner Magic retreat, I had learned of the NYC conference. The organizer had just spoken about it and shortly after, we were doing a future vision exercise to imagine our lives five years ahead. Without any forethought, I said I would be a speaker at the conference … in five years. Within the hour, I was committed to participating and speaking at that conference.

As I was preparing my speech for NYC, I found a piece of paper that had my very first affirmation written on it from six years earlier. Prior to receiving this affirmation, I had not heard of them and did not know how to incorporate them. During that time,

I had participated in a series of coaching calls by a leader in our business. These calls were designed to build belief in ourselves in order to grow our businesses, because you cannot have one without the other—you cannot build a business without confidence. One of the exercises was to state the following daily: "I am smart, I am beautiful, I am worthy, and I am enough." I remember clearly that I COULD NOT SAY those words because they did not define me. I was not even open to the possibility that they could. That piece of paper remained face down, hidden on my desk.

When I held the belief that I was not smart, I found evidence everywhere. As soon as I declared that I was smart, I found evidence of that everywhere. Remember, your thoughts create your reality, and the Universe will continuously give you signs to support whatever your thoughts may be. I was 52 when I experienced that incredible shift and stepped into my greatness. As I look back on the weekend in Myrtle Beach, I remember I had referenced my age at least three times, and that is not something I typically do. It was as though it was important for me to comprehend its significance. I am here to tell you that no matter what your age, you can live your dream. I share this message to be a role model for others. It is especially important that my daughters, who are presently in college, know that they can create their own path and design their own life in order to have and achieve whatever they want in this life. There is so much pressure in going to college, earning a degree, and making a good living. Many believe that is the *only* path. Yes, that can be true for many, but there is so much more that is possible when we believe that ANYTHING and EVERYTHING is possible!

After having the incredible experience of sharing my story in NYC and knowing that I inspired many people, it became important to me to touch as many lives as possible. I am passionate about helping others step into their greatness. We all have that power inside, no matter our age. Perhaps you are in a job or relationship that is not serving you, or in a situation that does not feel right. Whatever it is, if you feel in your gut that it just does not suit you and it is not in alignment with your true purpose, you can take inspired action right now to change it in order to live the life of your dreams—the life that you desire and deserve. What are you waiting for? Make the decision and do it.

You are destined to live your best life and the Universe will bring to you whatever you think and believe. I ask you again, what are you holding on to that isn't serving you? Let it go, release it so you can make room for what is waiting. You deserve to live a life of joy. I challenge you to dream and dream BIG. Believe BIG, believe that you are amazing, believe that you are worthy, believe that you are deserving of a life of joy! If needed, repeatedly tell yourself you are amazing, worthy and deserving. Act AS IF and BELIEVE that you already have the life you desire. Our thoughts become things, so think expansive, beautiful, deserving thoughts!

Once you define your dream, meditate on it, visualize it, and say your affirmations daily so that you can manifest it. Remember, you are enough just the way you are. The first time I heard those words (perhaps even the first 10 times), I had no idea what they meant. I now know what they mean and I know with certainty that I AM ENOUGH!

We can all have everything we want and you can manifest anything you can dream. The moment you do that, your cliff will appear so you can jump. And when you surface, you too can yell, "I DID IT!"

"I am smart, I am beautiful, I am worthy, and I am enough." So are you!

ABOUT DONNA NUDEL BROWN

Donna Nudel Brown is an inspiring speaker and certified Ignitor Coach, specializing in mindset work where she is passionate about helping others uncover their true gifts. In her Crystal Clear Coaching programs she works 1:1 with her clients, guiding them in identifying and releasing limiting beliefs. She is able to uniquely incorporate her Energy Infused Crystals and Reiki healing energy to help her clients live their best life they desire and deserve.

Each of Donna's crystals are charged in the full moon and infused with Reiki energy and then set with an intention created specifically for the recipient. She especially loves sharing her crystals with her Crystal of the Month Club members around the world.

Donna lives in Baltimore, MD with her wonderfully supportive husband and three amazing children. Her favorite things in life include spending time with her family, traveling, enjoying a delicious meal, laughing until her belly hurts, being on the water, surrounding herself with close friends, and reveling in the amazing beauty Mother Nature provides, especially when observing incredible sunrises and sunsets. Witnessing a full moon rising takes her breath away.

To learn more about Donna, please visit her websites at: www.donnabrowndesigns.com and www.donnabrowncoaching.com.

WHILE YOU WERE NAPPING

Kate Butler

As your head hits the pillow, I lie next to you and gently rub your back until you float off to dream land. I stay there just long enough to soak in the smell of your innocence. I begin to think about all the things you will dream about as you sleep, and I begin to dream for you, too. I dream that you will always know how incredibly brilliant you are. I dream that your heart is protected but doesn't harden. I dream that you are always able to connect to your guidance within, so that you may know your way.

I always cherished these quiet moments of nap time. It was a time of solace amidst a normally busy and chaotic day. This was my chance to soak it all in, to take a step back and reflect, even if just for a moment. But today was different. I found myself staying longer than normal in that little pink room. I found myself connecting at a much deeper level and questioning these dreams I was envisioning. The dream for my children was so clear. But I began to ask myself, *What do you dream for your own life?*

On this day, during nap time in my daughter's room, I found myself next to her bed, on my knees, praying to God. The reality had hit me. It all came crashing down in an instant. This life I had been living was not my dream. It was good. I was blessed. My husband was wonderful and supportive; my children were healthy and beautiful. My home was pretty close to the one I had always envisioned. But I was looking around at this white picket fence life saying, *Now what?* The voice followed up with … *You made a commitment. You made a deal. You are here to DO more. You are here to give more. You are here to SERVE more.*

I picked myself up off the floor and opened my eyes. I could no longer hide behind my busy life or pretend that inner knowing was not there. I knew my time had come.

You see, six years earlier, at the age of 27, I was diagnosed with a fatal heart condition. By this point in my life, I had successfully worked my way up the corporate ladder. I was running multiple offices as a career, life, and business coach. The offices were yielding millions of dollars in revenue and I was blessed to be earning well over six figures. It felt like everyone was winning. Along with this high powered position came a massive amount of responsibility. I was responsible for the operations and P&L 's of multiple offices as well as the livelihood of the employees that worked in those offices. It was a heavy weight to carry and the stress began to seep into my life. There were signs along the way that I was getting off course, but I refused to see them. This was everything I thought I wanted. I had an amazing career. I was making a lucrative income. My job was actually centered around helping people. I was certain I was on the right path.

So when the stress poured in, I did not acknowledge it as a sign that I was off course, I just made a decision that I would handle it just like I handled everything else in my life. I was not eating properly, I was drinking too much, and I was simply not making my well-being a priority. Work was the focus and there just weren't enough hours in the day for two priorities.

My heart was full of business success, monetary success, and career achievements. But in those quiet moments that, admittedly, were few and far between, I knew there was something missing. My heart was beginning to break for more meaningful work, a life with more balance and more fulfilling moments.

I began waking up in the middle of the night with panic attacks. I would think, *Did I remember to send that email? Did I ever get back to that client? How am I going to let this person go for not meeting their sales goals?* My mind would race all night long. It was overwhelming and exhausting. I felt like I could not get it under control.

In the mornings, when I was getting ready for work, I would often have to sit down on my bed for several minutes just to catch my breath. I would get myself so worked up over the upcoming events that day that I would literally have to catch my breath.

I would randomly burst into tears for no reason. I would overreact to situations that, rationally, I knew were not a big deal. I found myself in the middle of drama everywhere I turned. I was spiraling. It all felt like too much. But yet, I felt like this was what I was supposed to be doing. I felt like I had achieved so much success at such a young age. How could I possibly stop now? I couldn't.

And then that fateful Tuesday hit and it hit hard. I was driving home from work and I had to pull over to the side of the road. I couldn't breathe. I couldn't speak. I was holding my chest. The pain was excruciating. This was beyond a panic attack. This was very different than the stress symptoms I had felt in my body up until that point. This was unbearable.

Over the course of the next few days, I went through a series of doctor's appointments, evaluations, and tests that normally take many months to complete. I knew by the medical professional's sense of urgency that something was seriously wrong. Within a few days, I was diagnosed with Ventricular Tachycardia. This basically meant that my heart was beating too much, too fast, and if not operated on immediately it was at risk of bursting. This was a fatal condition. Within weeks I was scheduled for surgery.

I was in shock. I was scared. I was uncertain for the first time in a long time. But more than this, I had an inner knowing that this was happening to get my attention. And so I acquiesced.

"I'm ready to listen," I told God.

I began to divinely download His messages. The series of messages He sent me instructed me to get back on course, to connect with my God-given gifts, and that by traveling on my highest path to purpose I would find true life fulfillment. I took it in and said, "Yes." I made a promise to God that day. If I was graced with a second chance and he was able to fix my broken heart, I would fulfill my mission.

Thankfully, the doctors were able to fix my broken heart. Leading into the surgery, during the surgery, and post-op, every administrator, nurse, doctor, or medical professional that I came in contact with made a production over my age and my stats. They said that there was no indication on my records that should have led to this condition. I was, otherwise, completely healthy. They would bring other doctors in to view my "case." I was an anomaly.

But I knew something they didn't. I knew God was trying to get my attention. I knew that there were many signs along the way that I could have acknowledged but chose to ignore. And, as a result, this was the only way to get me to pay attention, to get me to listen, to get me back on my path and back to my life's mission. To me, this all made perfect sense. I was eternally grateful for the break and the mending of my heart, because now I could clearly see my life's purpose.

Over the next few years I followed my heart and it led me to love. So much love. I met my handsome husband; we got married, had two beautiful daughters, and settled into our cozy home to begin our life together. My heart was happy. I felt joy and love each day. I did not realize, however, that I had replaced my obsession with work with an obsession for my family. I was pouring my energy, time, heart, and soul into them. It was my greatest joy to do so. Unbeknownst to me, however, in showing up for everyone else, I was stepping away from my life's mission. And I had made a commitment.

So that day in the nursery, when I began dreaming, it all became so crystal clear. There was space for my husband, there was space for my children, there was space for my family and friends, and there was space for my work. But…there was also space for my dreams. I was missing a few links of this chain and, in turn, I was not being true to myself or my commitment to God.

With my daughter still napping and this new awareness, I walked

Image A: The Ignite Your Future tool Kate uses for this practice.

out of my daughter's room, down the stairs, and into my home office. I cleared off my desk and for the first time in too many years, I gave myself permission to dream again. I began honoring that inner voice that I had been pushing aside. I began tapping into the gifts that I always knew were there. I began putting as much time, energy,

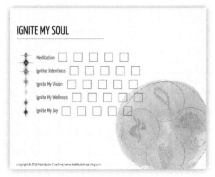

Image B: The Ignite Your Soul tool Kate uses to track her daily disciplines.

heart, and soul into myself as I was putting into everyone and everything else.

So each day during nap time, I would carve out time to connect with my inner guidance. Upon connecting to this guidance, I decided to take it one step further and journal about what I desired for my future.

This act of forward thinking began to activate strong feelings of joy and excitement about what my future had in store. I knew that honoring my inner guidance always led me to experience more joy, but it was also clear to me that I would need to do some more work if I was going to truly understand what my life's mission entailed. Daily meditation was the key element that brought me extreme clarity on my next steps. I still could not see the entire path, but I was certain of the inspired action I was being called to take, one step at a time.

My inspired actions consisted of taking complete responsibility for my life. I stopped blaming others for my circumstances, and I stopped blaming my circumstances on the things I did not have in my life. Through meditation, I began to clearly understand that if I desired something, I had the power to

Image C: The Winks & Whispers tool Kate uses to record daily signs that she is on the right path.

create it. But taking responsibility involved more than that; it was also about seeing the role I played in everything in my life, even the things that were displeasing. This new awareness truly empowered me to begin showing up differently, in every single encounter. With each thought, word, and action, I was literally creating the script for my life.

In addition, I began to notice the miracles that were all around me. Some were small miracles and some giant miracles, but all were equally significant ... they were winks from God telling me that I was on the right path. The more I noticed and acknowledged these miracles, the more they occurred. Truly proving to me that what we focus on grows.

Since I was a child, I had been creating vision boards ... actually they were vision books back then. This was before vision boards had a name, before I really knew what I was doing. I felt called to different pictures that captured my dreams, and I would keep them in a book. This process had always proved to be successful for me in the past, so I started it again. One vision board became two, and before I knew it, my office walls were covered with images of my dream life. And amazingly, things began to manifest! Some things quickly, other things not in the way that I expected, but there was no doubt things were changing and shifting. I could *feel* it.

As my way of living began to change, I began to attract more peace, harmony, and happiness into my life. The people around me began to notice and ask what was different. At first, I wasn't sure I could articulate it. But as I became more comfortable with my shift in perspective, I began to share my new awareness and techniques with the women in my life. To my amazement, these women's lives also began to transform before my eyes! Before I knew it, they were referring me their friends and co-workers, I was hosting retreats and group calls ... and my coaching practice was born. I went on to become a Certified Professional Success Coach (CPSC), primarily focusing on the intuitive downloads I receive for my clients. Most of which have proven to be life changing.

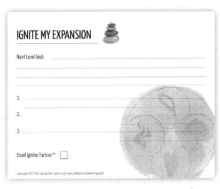

I not only wanted to share this with my clients, I had a strong desire to teach my children the power of mindset. I began to feel a strong pull to write a children's book. I thought that if I desired

Image D: The Ignite My Expansion tool Kate uses to put her dreams into action.

to have a book that taught my children how to view life from a new angle, then there must be other mothers out there looking for this type of children's book as well. As a result, my idea for my first book was born. I was dreaming again, and I was dreaming big.

I was dreaming big, though still with an infant and toddler in tow. And so now during nap time, I continued my daily disciplines including meditating, writing my future intentions, and engaging my vision board. But now, I would also spend time taking action towards writing my book, researching printers, and figuring out how I was going to get this book out to the world.

Once I committed to the dream, the people, circumstances, and resources that I needed effortlessly fell into my lap. I was amazed. In my corporate position, it seemed as if we worked so hard for a sale. We hustled to meet our goals. But this, it just came so easily.

When I developed the dream of writing an inspirational children's book on the power of a positive perspective, I did not know anyone who had ever written a book before. By the time I had completed my book, I was endorsed by Jack Canfield, creator of the *Chicken Soup for the Soul* Series™, Peggy McColl, NY Times Best Selling Author, Kidorable™ Children's Brand, Miriam Laundry, Guinness World Record Holder, and the Garden State Discovery Museum ... just to name a few. These were nothing short of miracles granted by God because I was honoring my inner gifts and I had decided to show up for my life's mission.

My children's books went on to become #1 Best Sellers, remaining best sellers on the Amazon charts for over 100 weeks straight. They have been showcased in schools, turned into plays and performances, and have inspired children all over the globe. I was recently featured in Jack Canfield's newest book, *Living The Success Principles*. And I will go on to publish my 5th book this year. All of this in just a few years time because I decided to show up for my life's mission.

My work is now being honored in 11 countries around the world. It takes my breath away as I step back and take it all in. Daily, I receive hand-written notes, emails, or messages from clients all around the world who have been positively impacted by my work in some way. I just learned that I have my first client in Serbia! Many of these clients have the opportunity to work with me one-on-one, some have read my books, while others have participated in my online programs. Many have attended one of my live events, which truly have transformational and life impacting results. This is the person I want my daughters to see when they look at their mom. This is what I want them to believe is possible. This is the legacy I wish to leave behind.

All of this is possible because I have chosen to honor my God-given gifts. I am ordinary, just like you. In fact, I know you, I see you ... I am YOU. Every soul who graces this earth has unfathomable potential and purpose. Every single person has extraordinary God-given gifts that are true super powers. Your only job is to say "YES," to show up, to connect with your inner guidance, take inspired action, and STEP INTO YOUR LIFE'S MISSION.

I promise, I am the same as you. I am raising two young children, balancing my husband, and my dream, and still trying to keep up with carpool. But I have connected with my purpose and, take it from me, once you know it, you cannot un-know it. I committed to showing up and subsequently built three successful businesses during nap times. I share this with you to be clear that there is always a way, miracles are around, and when you tap into the power of your life's mission, anything is possible.

I am grateful that one day I stopped and reflected. I am grateful that I took inspired action. I am grateful for my broken heart that showed me the way. I am grateful every single day that I said "YES" to my life's assignment. And I am so, so very grateful for nap time.

ABOUT KATE BUTLER

Kate Butler is a #1 Best Selling and international award winning author, speaker, and mindset strategist. Kate has appeared on HBO's new season of Sesame Street®, has been featured in Jack Canfield's newest book *Living The Success Principles*™, and has watched her children's books being performed live by the Garden State Discovery Museum™. She is also the author of *More Than Mud, More Than Magic*, and the *Ignite My Inner Magic Guidebook*. Kate is the founder and creator of Women Who Ignite, a movement to inspire and empower women to step into their light. Kate's #1 Best Selling books have remained on the Best Seller list for over 100 weeks straight. They have also been awarded the Mom's Choice Award for Excellence® and the Readers Favorite® International Book Award.

Kate is a graduate of Towson University, where she studied Mass Communication and Interpersonal Communication Studies. She studied abroad in Ireland during her third year and gained a global perspective which enriches her work even today. Kate is also a Certified Professional Success Coach (CPSC) and she now certifies others through her *Ignitor Coach Certification Program*™.

Kate is also the Founder of *Kate Butler Coaching*, where she helps thousands of clients to find their purpose and create sustainable income while doing what they love. She accomplishes this through live workshops and events, luxury retreats, group coaching programs, one-on-one coaching, and online program offerings. To learn more about how you can connect and work with Kate, please visit her website at www.katebutlercoaching.com, where you can find her programs, books, inspirational products and receive a free "Ignite Your Life Starter Kit". Enjoy the unfolding...

Facebook: Kate Butler Books, Instagram & Twitter: @katebutlerbooks

THE POWER OF WORDS

Melissa Camilleri

They say that what you gravitate toward as a child gives some insight into what you'll be passionate about as an adult.

For me, this has proven to be true.

I remember being five or six, soon after I started kindergarten, coming home from school, and lining up all of my dolls and stuffed animals in front of my chalkboard easel so that I could play teacher. If I wasn't playing school, I was reading books, writing stories, or playing word games. I've always loved words.

And so it wasn't a big surprise to my parents when I told them I was enrolling in the teaching credential program to become a high school English teacher.

In 2011, I was in my eighth year as a teacher. I had the great fortune of working with at-risk students in a program called AVID which stands for Advancement Via Individual Determination. Through the college-prep elective, my roles were teacher, counselor, advocate, and sometimes parent to students who had all the potential to succeed but lacked either the academic, social, or emotional support to do so. The majority of my students came from backgrounds of poverty, neglect, abuse, addiction, and low expectations. In AVID, though,

67

we were a family, and most of these students would eventually go on to break these negative familial cycles and change the trajectories of their lives through education.

Learning about and teaching AVID became my calling. I loved it because of the relationships I was able to form with my students. It was the only program in the high school where students entered my class as freshmen and stayed with me through graduation.

We built a pretty solid school family together.

And so, in the Fall of 2011, one of the seniors, Toni, who I had taught for the past four years, asked me if I could make her a cocktail ring to match her Homecoming dress.

I'd been making cocktail rings with Swarovski crystals for a couple of years as a way to decompress after school. I did it as a fun, creative outlet, making new color combinations to wear with my outfits to school.

"Of course !" I said to Toni. "I'd be honored!"

That night I made her the ring and delivered it to her the next day in class. I included a little note with it, a short card that said, "I'm so proud of the woman you've become. I hope you have a fun time at the dance. Thank you for shining your light and being such a great example to others."

"OH EM GEE, Miss. Thank you! I love it!"

She slipped it on her finger and wore it around school the rest of the day.

By the end of the week, I had 22 orders on my desk from other girls who wanted me to make them rings to match their Homecoming dresses. And so I went home each night that week, after chaperoning duties, and was up until the wee hours making the rings and then writing cards to give to these girls from class. My husband thought I was crazy and that I was working way too hard. He was also a teacher at the same school, and after we stumbled into the door, exhausted from extra long days at work, I made my way up to our office to make the rings for the girls.

Homecoming came and went and the following Monday I asked the girls how the dance was. A few gathered before class around my desk.

"It was so fun!"

"We had a blast."

"You should have seen Kaitlyn! She was getting down the whole night!"

As they were recounting the weekend, I noticed something interesting. One of the girls had the card I'd written her in the front plastic cover of her binder.

"You put that note in there?" I asked, kind of surprised to take up such a significant portion of the prime real estate that is a high school girls' binder.

"Are you kidding?" she said. "This is literally the nicest thing anyone has ever said to me."

***

A couple weeks later, these same girls were filling out their college applications. This process was very momentous as it was something we'd been working toward during our time together in AVID. The same girl with the note in her binder came to my desk with big tears in her eyes.

"I've done everything right, and I still think it's not going to be enough," she leaned in and whispered.

"What do you mean, sweetheart?"

"I have no clue how I'm going to pay for all this. I know that education is my ticket out of here, but I don't know how it is going to be possible for me."

And what was heartbreaking was that she was right. Money was a significant barrier for her and her family.

Her words weighed on my heart so heavily that night. I got quiet and prayed. And though it may sound silly, I had a flash of insight: I could sell those rings that the girls loved with an opportunity for people to personalize the packages with kind words. I could sell them to the families at the neighboring high school that had money. They could give them to their daughters for special gifts at prom or graduation. With the money I made, I could form a scholarship program for my students.

I knew I needed to give this project a name and I was really stuck, until one night, I was reading an article in a magazine and saw the word "compliment."

That's it, I thought. The jewelry will be the gift. The compliment will come in the box. We all need validation and affirmation and someone to shine a light on the parts of us that we're proud of. Compliment.

In that moment, Compliment—the jewelry brand that fundraised scholarships for girls—was born.

But I was a teacher—a former English major for heaven's sake. I was no business mogul. It was my husband who filed the paperwork with the city to get a business license and registered our names as sole proprietors. Never in a million years did I anticipate this flash of insight would turn into a legitimate business, let alone a successful one. But sometimes God has other plans for our lives—better than anything we could have imagined.

***

Six months later, on an ordinary Monday night, my husband and I had just finished dinner. He was in the family room watching a tennis match on ESPN and I was finishing up with the last of the dishes. I joined him on the couch.

"Hey," he said, without turning down the volume of the match on TV. This was a detail I'd later find uncomfortable and strange, given the gravity of the conversation we were about to have.

"I need to tell you something."

"Um, ok?" I said, tentatively awaiting some sort of news. *Did he get pulled over for a speeding ticket? Did he have a tense conversation with his parents?*

"Well, um, I don't think we should really be married anymore."

Just like that. That quick. That calm.

There was no fight. Just a declarative that I didn't see coming.

"Excuse me? I don't think I understand."

"Yeah, you heard me. I don't think we should be married anymore. And I don't really want to talk about it."

"Well, um, I do," I said. In the moment, I think I wasn't even in shock yet. I couldn't even comprehend what he meant. I thought he was just saying stuff to get a rise from me. In the ten years we'd been together, he'd definitely thrown me for a few loops, but we always got through them. Sure, he had an explosive temper, but we always made up. And we weren't even fighting tonight.

"What the hell do you mean? Are you seeing someone? What's the problem? Can we talk this out? I'll make an appointment with a counselor tomorrow."

"I'm sorry, but my mind is made up. This is real. I think you're going to need to find an apartment because I put our house up for sale."

"What?! You're joking."

I started to sob. Heaving sobs, because I knew he wasn't joking.

"And don't worry, you can keep the stupid business. I just want half of the $400 in the business account. I need two hundred bucks to bleach my teeth."

***

Ok. This was not how my life was supposed to go. I am good, smart, a rule-follower, and a high-achiever ... I have done everything right.

Like good girls tend to do, as soon as I left home I started checking the life milestones off the list, and in record time.

Go to school. Check.

Graduate. Check.

Get a great, fulfilling job as a teacher, where I could make a difference in the world. Check.

Get married to a cute guy I knew in high school. Check.

Encourage him to also teach, and then eventually get a job at the same school as you. Check.

Become *that* couple who works together at the same small town high school where they were once students. Check. Check. Check.

We bought a nice house, went on nice vacations, and on the outside, everything was perfect.

But behind the scenes, no one really knew the depth of what was going on.

If I'm honest with myself, I can now see, four years after that fateful Monday night, that our relationship was troubled from the beginning. And if I'm really, *really* honest, I was married to someone who was emotionally abusive in our last several years together.

He screamed and yelled and called me horrible names. He chased me through the house and got violently angry for things like putting the wrong brand of sunflower seeds in the dinner salad, throwing the whole bowl across the kitchen.

At the time, I did not see the irony that I had started this little business called Compliment, and kind words were exactly what I had been starved of all those years. I definitely didn't see what an enormous miracle was about to unfold in front of me.

***

The last half of 2012 was, hands-down, the deepest valley of my life. In July 2012, I moved from my beautiful home to an apartment across town. A month later, my aunt fell off a horse, hit her head, and passed away. That week, I started teaching at a new school, away from my ex. In September, my grandfather was diagnosed and then died from cancer all within a few short weeks. And three days after Thanksgiving, my godfather, seemingly fit and healthy, passed away from a sudden aortic aneurysm. I was steamrolled by a divorce, a move, a job change, and three deaths within the span of 120 days. I went to work, was home by 3, changed into my pajamas, and watched the Food Network until I fell asleep each night on the couch. For three months I didn't once sleep in my bed. I couldn't. The blue glow of the TV and the quiet banter of the *Chopped* judges kept me company while I slept. Wash, rinse, repeat. Week in and week out, I was a walking zombie.

"I can't keep going," I sobbed to my counselor who had been helping me through the divorce. "This is too much for me." I explained how I couldn't possibly be there for my students when I had less than nothing in my tank.

"Take a break," she said.

"How? I've been working since I was 14. How can I take a break?"

She led me through the process of requesting a leave of absence from teaching, for stress. I somehow made it through the last few days of class prior to Christmas break and finally gave myself permission to take the next semester to grieve, mourn, heal, and then get my life in order.

I knew that if I didn't wake up each day with a concerted effort to find joy, the weight of this grief would keep me down. But I wanted to live. So I tried to find things that made me happy.

On the first day of my hiatus, I woke up at 5:30 in the morning, like I'd always done, and wrote in a journal. I strolled down the tree-lined streets of my new neighborhood into the art store and purchased a new set of watercolor paints, paper, and brushes.

I went home and painted in my tiny kitchen nook and listened to silly '80s love songs on the radio. I sang. I cried. I read. I napped.

A few days later, I realized that trying to figure out how to make Compliment work was kind of a fun puzzle.

So I spent the next couple of days researching stuff online and building a new website.

A couple of days later, my first order came through. Someone ordered a pair of earrings with a compliment request to send to her friend: "I am so grateful for you."

I pulled out my stamps and stamp pad, carefully hand-stamped the compliment card, and placed it inside the box.

Soon more orders started rolling in. In the very early months of 2013, this business literally healed me. I got to be the conduit between one person sending love to another. I had unintentionally surrounded myself with kind words. Every surface of my tiny apartment was covered with pieces of handmade jewelry in progress or stamped out compliments from one person to another.

I learned, quickly, that creation is the antithesis of death. I don't know why that concept had never clicked for me.

Telling others just how much they were loved helped me to undo all the years of unkind words that had been hurled at me and stored in my subconscious. Making something from nothing, and passing it along to bring joy to others, helped me to believe in life again.

I was starting to see that finding the word "compliment" in that magazine was no accident or lucky coincidence after all. It was an intention in the making, a divine miracle pointing to where my life was headed.

Within six months, I was forced to decide whether or not I'd go back to the classroom. It wasn't an easy choice. Teaching was in my heart and had totally shaped my identity. I was a teacher through and through, and yet something deep inside me stirred and said that I needed to give Compliment more time to grow. I didn't have an extraordinary plan of how it would all work. I didn't have a certain amount of dollars saved up before I made the leap.

I just knew that the fear of staying stagnant, or worse—going back to the familiar because it was safe—was far greater than the fear of the unknown. I owed it to myself and the new journey I was embarking upon to give it a little longer and see what I could do with this business.

***

It's been three years since that decision and Compliment has now grown into a six figure business.

Oh, and in that time, I started dating again and fell in love with my actual soul mate. Nick has the kindest heart and shares my vision to spread the mission of Compliment. We recently got married in a garden courtyard beneath hundreds of twinkling lights. We live in a little house with a sprawling lawn on a street that lazily winds through giant sycamores.

And this may very well sound like the happily ever after I've always hoped for—a happy ending to a once sad story. While it's no lie that I'm happier than I've ever been, it's not because I've built my business to be profitable and I am able to pay my bills, nor is it only because I've finally found the person I'm meant to be with forever. Of course, those things play a large part. But more than those things, my contentment with the journey rather than the attainment of something I'd wished for is what brings me the most happiness.

Owning a business (especially retail) isn't all smooth sailing once you hit a revenue goal. And just because the business is profitable, doesn't mean that I don't worry about how to make things continue to move forward. Each day, Nick and I work on our marriage to make sure it gets the attention it needs as well. This often means that I must put away my computer (it's easy to get sucked in when you love what you do!) and stopping work at a normal hour so that we can keep our time together sacred.

Weathering so many devastations in such a short amount of time taught me something invaluable. I'd heard it a million times before— "life's a journey, not a destination" —but I don't know if it really sunk in until I felt like I was directionless. Or maybe more accurately, the direction I had so carefully planned to walk turned out to be very, very sad and not the road I'd thought it was.

I had to learn to be proactive with my contentment and not rely on the circumstances around me to be "just so" in order for me to feel satisfied.

I had to trust that God had a bigger plan for my life and that everything was unfolding in divine order. One of my favorite mantras during the more challenging times was: *my business is growing at a pace that is perfect for my life and my development. I have all I need. I repeated this one over and over until I started to believe it.* There was also: *God does not close one door without opening a better one. My soul mate is looking for me.* And then I just started living unafraid. Because the ultimate truth is that when the thing you fear the most happens and you're caught in an absolute whirlwind of devastation, there's nothing left to fear.

You can take risks.

Because your only two options in that moment are to be brave, or roll over and die.

I chose courage.

ABOUT MELISSA CAMILLERI

Melissa Camilleri is a writer, educator, mentor, and business owner. Her company Compliment, Inc., a place to find "gifts that uplift," is founded on the premise that "we rise by lifting others®". Since 2012, Compliment has given tens of thousands of dollars to young women with a dream of rising beyond their circumstances through education.

You can find her spreading this positivity every other week on the Pay Attention podcast, which she co-hosts with her biz-bestie, Nikki Stern. The girls focus on one thing we should all pay a little more attention to, helping us all focus on the good things of life.

The kind words that accompany Compliment gifts have become a social media sensation. Ever the teacher at heart, Melissa now teaches the 21-Day Instacourse. This course helps fellow business owners spread their messages to a larger audience and get the word out about their mission.

Melissa continues to serve as a consultant in the AVID program, specializing in the support of long term English Language Learners, and coaching other educators through professional development workshops.

She lives and loves in Sacramento, California with her husband Nick.

You can find Compliment online at www.shopcompliment.com
On Instagram @shopcompliment
You can find the Pay Attention Podcast on iTunes or
@payattentionpodcast on Instagram.

PAIN HAS PURPOSE

Michelle Simkiss Dunk

Everyone has a story, and I'm no different. I, like so many people, believed that there was an author outside of myself who had already written my life's memoir for me. I existed by reacting to every event and chapter as it unfolded. The truth is I lived most of my life this way pretty happily—no harm and no foul. There was joy, but certainly not a lot of passion or meaning. There were also aches and pains, but I had never experienced any real tragedy or felt the need to call on courage in a big way. That all changed in my late twenties when a difficult and dark event took place. In order for me to make sense of it all and begin to heal, I knew that I could not stay the same. The immense fear and anxiety of this incident caused me to desperately search for hope and peace. I needed the revelation that I was indeed a co-author and creator with God in my personal autobiography. You see, transformational stories can only be written by HIM through YOU. They are the messy scribbles, reformulated thoughts, and soul lessons written, rewritten, and read over and over until you take full responsibility for your life—EVERY LITTLE BLESSED BIT OF IT. This, I would discover, is how to find your personal power ... what I call Your Inner Spark!

If I am being honest, I would say that as a child I always knew that there was something unique about me. I was extremely perceptive to energy and the feelings of others. I could easily translate the energy that I picked up from someone into feelings in my own body. This was difficult if I was around anyone who was suffering in any way. I was determined to take away the pain that I saw in the world, even carry it myself, so no one else would have to. I felt very connected to what I would call the "knowing" part of me. This gift of intuition brought me comfort as I tried to navigate through the incisive worrying and desire to fix everyone and everything, especially myself. I was constantly told "not to be so sensitive," and I took this message to heart. I beat myself up for having this trait and attempted to shut it down. My Mom delighted in my sensitivities and gifts that everyone else seemed to judge. She encouraged me to be visible with them. Sadly, I listened to outside pressure and essentially turned off a part of myself that I would spend years searching for again.

Growing up, I was very attached to my Mom. She was the most loving person I have ever met. She sincerely was a sacred force that made me feel safe and adored. I was her shadow, constantly wanting to be near her, and feel her authentic tenderness and affection. Her devoted, effervescent personality poured into our family with such power. She was the glue that held us all together. I relied on her beautiful, warm energy and love to feel whole. My Mom instilled strong family values in my sisters and me. We were her world and she was ours. I wanted to love as deeply as she did. With my innate sensitivity, this was something that came naturally to me. I grew up with the desire to spread love to people who needed it the most. I wanted them to feel the way my Mom made me feel. In 1997, I met a man deserving of the greatest love I possessed, and I gave my whole heart to him. Three years later I said yes to his proposal, and on November 10, 2001 we were married.

I was so in love with Jimmy and felt blessed beyond my dreams in the life we were building together. We lived in a beautiful new home that was within a two mile radius of my parents and both of my sisters and their families. It brought me such joy and stability to be able to see my family every single day. I knew how lucky I was to have this strong foundation, yet I couldn't shake the feeling that something was lurking just outside of my safe life. I tried to convince myself that I was picking up on the energy of other things happening in the outside world, but I could sense that it was much more personal. For a few weeks, every time I got into my car I looked into the passenger seat and instinctually felt an emptiness. I ignored this feeling, until the feeling chased me down.

I was spending the weekend at the beach with my girlfriends. It was the most gorgeous day, not a cloud in the sky. I remember the peaceful feeling I had while gazing out into the ocean. There were sparkles dancing off the water from the intense sunlight. Our beach chairs formed a circle as we sat there eagerly chatting with each other. I had no idea that I was about to receive a phone call that would change my life forever. When I first answered the phone I could hear Jimmy, but couldn't make out what he was saying. I had bad reception down by the water, and the call kept dropping. I knew it must have been important, because he relentlessly kept calling back. I walked up to the Boardwalk to reach him. When he answered he told me that there had been an accident. My middle sister, her husband, and their three boys were driving my Mom to a party when they were hit by another vehicle. He wouldn't give me any details but asked me to have my friend drive me to the hospital immediately. I started to go through scenarios in my head on the two hour ride up. Every one of my thoughts ended well, because everything had to be ok. My family was my life. I was only partially aware that my heart was beating too fast, and my breathing was labored. The other part of me was focused on willing everything to be fine. It was the beginning of a long, intense, internal fight for the power to change things that were out of my hands. The drive to see them was endless torture. I never cried, I just prayed.

When we walked through the hospital doors, the front desk clerk told me to follow them. We walked down a long hallway through doors that didn't seem like anyone outside of the staff should be allowed to use. I was suddenly terrified. I was shaking and I couldn't tell if it was because I was still in my beach cover up, or the sheer fear that was running through my body. As we turned the corner I started seeing members of my family and my brother-in-law's family. I wanted to run to them, but I could no longer feel my sandy feet and my legs were like bricks. Everything about the environment felt fast-paced and chaotic; only I felt like I was moving in slow motion. I couldn't process what was happening around me ... I could hear my nephew screaming and calling for his mom behind closed doors. I made my way to Jimmy and finally broke down in tears.

Jimmy went on to tell me everything that I had feared most. My sister was driving and my Mom was in the passenger seat when a truck, going well over the speed limit, ran a red light and crashed directly into my sister's mini-van. The truck hit the passenger side and my Mom and my brother-in-law took the brunt of the blow. The van violently rolled a few times and landed on its side where my sister was pinned to the asphalt pavement. To say it was a miracle that they were all alive was an understatement. I pleaded with God to let everyone be ok and come home to us.

Everyone eventually was, except for my Mom. I do not know how we survived the roller coaster ride that we were on during that time. I have never felt so helpless, desperate, and out of control in my life. It was my biggest nightmare to see someone I loved suffer in ways that are unimaginable. I had fear gripping my heart every second of every day as if it was mocking me and confirming that I was not in control of anything. One night, I was sitting with my Mom in her hospital room while my Dad went to find the doctors. My Mom was having trouble breathing. I was trying to talk to her to keep her mind off of it. In the middle of a random conversation, she looked at me and said, "If I die, I know it will be ok, because my girls know how much I love them." I have replayed this conversation in my head over and over during the last 14 years. I wish I had said something loving, meaningful, and encouraging back, something that would have changed destiny. I KNEW what she was telling me. She was sitting up, leaning forward, and looking me directly in the eyes. This was so difficult for her to do with the state she was in, and all of the tubes that were connected to what seemed like every part of her body. She wanted me to be sure of her love before she left us. It was clear that neither of us had any fight left. I replied, "It would never be ok, Mom." At that moment, I really did believe that I would never be ok without her. That night she took a turn for the worse. I never saw her awake again.

Grief is a lifelong journey. We all experience it differently. In the beginning, I continually dropped to rock bottom, and then realized that there was another layer even lower with more despair and hopelessness. It was pain that had no appropriate description and made me question everything I thought I knew. Grief is lying on the bed for 48 hours straight while my husband silently handed me boxes of tissues, knowing that my body had lost the will to move or care. Grief is when my Dad told me that he thought he may be having a heart attack and couldn't form complete sentences, when actually it was the exhaustion and heartache from losing his wife and soul mate of 35 years causing these symptoms. Grief was being angry at God for not answering my prayers the way I wanted them answered, and then in the next breath begging HIM to have mercy and erase all of the images that I had etched in my brain of the trauma and afflicted body of the woman I loved most in life. Grief was missing someone I needed so much and coming to terms with never seeing her again in this lifetime. But, grief was also missing who I really was. It was becoming a lost soul walking the wrong way on my path. It was the feeling of separation in every way imaginable. I've come to realize now that I not only pulled away from my daily life and people I loved, but I was separate from the larger part of myself for many years after. My Inner Spark was calling me back, and I just could not remember how to listen to it. I could only hear the chatter of pain, fear, and loneliness in my mind.

On the opposite end of grief is who you really are in your greatest power, in pure bliss and supreme love. I've come to understand that we are always either moving in the direction of this love or away from it. Grief was moving me away from it. I hold the belief that there are really only two emotions: Fear and Love. We experience these two emotions through many different positive and negative feelings. They are all just signals of which direction we are moving in. Grief was a symptom of my fear. Losing my Mom in such an unexpected, tragic way left me skeptical about life and love. I was afraid of being without my mom—I felt broken without her. I was afraid of what I saw and experienced in the hospital. I was certainly living in fear of ever losing anyone else again. However, I now see that I was mostly in fear because I was alone without my higher self, the part of me that held faith. Losing my mom shattered my trust for life. I didn't know it then, but grief would actually be my journey to rediscovering who I really was, and remembering how to be guided to love again. Grief was my Mom's last gift to me, as if she was holding up the light towards the life of joy and meaning that I didn't know was possible.

I wish I could say that I connected with this guidance and moved from fear to love with ease. However, the journey back to myself consisted of a lot of life lessons and deep healing. I had to learn how to develop an awareness of the presence inside of me. When I was engrossed with fear, I was so far from love that I couldn't make out the whispers of my Inner Spark. Anxiety took up residence in the space where my truth should have been living. Looking back, it was so obvious how the laws of the attraction worked from the things that happened during this time of fear and anxiety. My initial fear and worry invited more and more things to worry about into my existence. There was pain that manifested in my body, a bout of depression, panic attacks, lost identity, affected relationships, and I endured many health issues because I was a walking fear magnet. My obsession with trying to protect myself from ever experiencing the pain I had when I lost my mom just created more pain in my life. At the time, I could not see that all of the fear that I focused on just magnified and grew.

Thankfully, I slowly began to comprehend that the amount of fear I possessed was equal in proportion to the amount of love that was available to me. I had to shift my thoughts in the direction of my desire for love, not the lack of it. I got to the point in my life that I knew without a doubt that I did not want to live in fear anymore. Obtaining a loving, peaceful life became my infinite burning desire. I was determined to go after it. The greatest motivation that I had was the fact that I became a mother to two beautiful little girls whom I loved and adored with every ounce of my being. A year and a half after I lost my Mom, my oldest, Madelyn, was born, and two years later Cassidy completed our family. They gave me a connection back to my own mother that I was missing so much. Watching them live in wonder, and seeing that they were so trusting in life, helped me remember what I had been training myself to forget. They knew that they had value and were worthy just because they were here.

They had purpose and took pride in every little thing they did. They paid attention to the things that made them feel good and refused to interact with the things that did not give them pleasure. They showed love so easily and so abundantly that it took my breath away. It was evident that they were here to teach *me*, not the other way around.

I was aware of a strong calling that I had great work to do. I thought becoming a mother was tied in with this intuitive pull. Therefore, my husband and I decided that I would stay home after I had my oldest. I loved everything about it. There was never a more fulfilling, fun, and meaningful job for me. However, it was extremely challenging because my anxious thoughts were not under control yet. They were constantly feeding me messages that I wasn't good enough or deserving of the gorgeous life that I had. I was still addicted to the negative thinking that I developed after I lost my Mom. I was always waiting for the other shoe to drop. However, I was prepared to smile through any worry or pain and not let people know I was suffering. I had become really good at this, as I felt my time for sadness had "expired." No one knew the agony I endured on the inside. I felt so unworthy of the gifts I had because I could not align with the happiness and joy that was right in front of my nose. I portrayed a perfect picture because I could not let anyone know the deep hurt I carried around.

I threw myself into trying to overachieve in my role as Mommy in every way possible. I hoped that this would somehow give me the sense of acceptance and approval that I had when my Mom was alive. I made sure that I dressed and looked my best, I squeezed in gym time at 5 am, and participated in grueling hour-or-longer runs to stay fit. I tried to keep up with the Joneses with home decorating and hired all of the must-have people. I took my girls to baby gyms, music classes, "Mommy and Me" dance classes, and playgroups. I cooked organic, non-GMO, vegetarian, healthy meals. I entertained and threw over-the-top celebrations and birthday parties. I coached soccer. I was room mom. I volunteered at everything I could and joined every committee or group that I could fit in. I looked for praise from the outside world to try to fill the void and the anxiety I had on the inside. No matter how much I did, I still never felt capable or accepted. Don't misunderstand me, giving of myself was something I truly wanted to do and it uplifted me. And now that I'm on the other side of fear I somehow do even more of those things. Yet, back then, I was doing these things for all of the wrong reasons. I hoped that filling my schedule up would give me a sense of purpose and I could find the happiness and peace I was searching for. I didn't know that happiness was a choice and I had the ability to choose it in every moment. I wasn't aware that I could then pour this authentic joy into anything I wanted. I was hoping these roles would give me an identity that would bring this elation. I knew I was a good Mom, I knew I was a good wife, I knew I was a good friend and citizen, but I had no idea who I was or what I wanted out of life! I hid this so well for so long from everyone.

Eventually, I became exhausted from chasing what I didn't know was already inside of me. I could not go on being so dishonest with myself and everyone around me. On a cold winter night, I was staring out of the window at the snow coming down. Jimmy was at work, and my girls were both on the floor playing quietly and contentedly with their toys. Anxious thoughts triggered the last panic attack I ever had. I was alarmed at the way my chest was pounding; I broke out in a cold sweat and felt extremely dizzy. A thought flashed across my mind: *I do not want to live like this*. It was at that very moment that I finally saw my anxiety for what it really was. Thoughts. Thoughts that did not serve me. Thoughts that I had habitually to scare me into staying the same. Thoughts that reinforced my distrust in life. Thoughts that became my friend, because they kept me connected to the pain and suffering that proved I was never going to be ok without my Mom like I had promised her.

Thoughts can be changed, and I set out to do exactly that and to find out who I really was. While my husband and my girls gave me the motivation to find this alignment, I still had to do all of the work to rediscover my true self. Wishing for it surely wasn't enough. I became a seeker of knowledge. I read every book about metaphysics, self-help, and healing that I could get my hands on. I was especially drawn to the teachings of Abraham Hicks who focused on an individual's natural born guidance system. This concept resonated deeply with me. I went to therapy, I tried a variety of energy work, I journaled, saw a kinesiologist, made joy and gratitude lists, I prayed like never before, and began to consistently meditate. My Dad had meditated for most of my life and taught me how to do it. It was such a frustrating task to commit to at first. Nevertheless, it would turn out to be the most life-changing habit that I developed. I once heard that praying is talking to God, and meditating is listening to him. This was so true for me. For the first time in my life I became quiet enough to hear His message. When I would slip into the space between my thoughts for just a second, I would observe that there was a higher power inside of me. I wanted to unite with it more. When I began to get quiet enough to hear the whispers of my Inner Spark, I recognized it as the same voice that I had shut out all of those years ago. It had always been inside of me, trying to lead me, even when I wasn't identifying with it. My life began to change dramatically. Everywhere I looked were blessings!

I felt more alive than I ever had in my life, and there were no conditions on my happiness. I was truly living and not just existing. I could think clearer; I had a vision of what I wanted; I was connected to my Inner Spark, and as a result, everything around me improved fiercely. I expected things to go well for me, and they did!

I retrained my mind to think positively and it felt soothing, natural, and exuberant. I began to remove anything that felt toxic from my life and surrounded myself with likeminded people that inspired me. I started overflowing with joy and gratitude like I had never before experienced. I laughed more, loved more, and appreciated every single thing in my life. I couldn't wait to wake up every morning, for suddenly everything was a miracle in my eyes.

When you have this type of awakening, you resolve to accept nothing less than living in the direction of love. This doesn't mean that there aren't hardships or discomfort; it just means that you react to uncomfortable things differently. I had discovered God's Grace by getting in touch with my Inner Spark. It was the peace of knowing that if any loss or fear occurred again, I would still be ok. It was from my greatest pain that I made the biggest, most impactful leap towards peace, fulfillment, and love. These painful breakthroughs were part of my guidance escorting me back to what I really wanted. I could clearly see that everything was always working out for my higher good—when I got out of my own way. By paying attention to my Inner Spark I was able to allow myself to embrace ALL emotions as signals of where I was on my journey. This awareness moved me quickly out of fear or discomfort and back to peace and love. During my healing, I rediscovered my ability to read and sense energy and it gave purpose for those dark periods I sustained. I let go of fear and crossed over to the side of love. I unearthed the fact that love was my natural state of being and I could live in that state no matter what was happening in my life. I knew that this was the way I was born to live; the way we were all born to live!

I was reconnected with that deep maternal love that my Mom taught me, and a fire was lit inside of me to share what I learned with everyone. At first I would just tell bits and pieces to friends who needed advice. Soon, it was apparent that I had a gift for identifying blocks that were holding people back from stepping into their own personal power. I could relate to their confusion and was able to clear a path for them on their journey. Every single person I nurtured would say, "You missed your calling." I believed them in the beginning, I thought I "missed" it too. Eventually, I was holding weekly retreats and hosting women in my home to teach these lessons and help others discover their own Inner Spark that is guiding them every step of the way. I was teaching women meditation and Emotional Freedom Technique (EFT). As I saw their lives transformed, mine did too. I picked up on the vibe that I was being called to spread this message to even more people. I realized that it's never too late to take action on your dreams and life's purpose.

My personal drive was for my girls to understand that they were born with this Inner Spark, too. I wanted to make sure they didn't lose communication with it. I wanted them to accept and love themselves exactly as they were, the way they did as babies. In 2014, I created a Non-Profit Corporation called In beTWEEN Girls. This organization is my legacy to my two daughters. The program empowers TWEEN girls by teaching them self-love, self-worth, and confidence. By developing these skills, the girls learn to love and accept themselves. I match them with compatible Teen Mentors and they learn about their unique Inner Spark that is lighting their path for them. The events in my life not only led me to this mission but made me extremely passionate about teaching these values. Through the inspirational community events that we host throughout the year, we raise proceeds that are put in educational funds for the Teenaged Mentors to use when they graduate from our program. These scholarships are in my Mom's name, Gerry Simkiss, as she was the reason why all of this emerged from my heart and soul.

As successful and satisfying as In beTWEEN Girls was (and still is), I knew I still had some unfinished business present in my heart.

Coaches and mentors that I surrounded myself with told me I was still playing too small. They encouraged me to follow my calling. Presently, along with running and expanding my Non-Profit, I'm now committed to educating and coaching adults in the areas of personal development and achieving their personal and professional success goals. It gives me tremendous pleasure to teach from my energetic core and speak to those that need guidance in an extremely relatable, deeply loving way. I am open about stumbling all over my path in every direction that I could find, so that my clients feel I understand where they may be standing at the moment.

The girl who thought she wasn't enough, wasn't strong, would always have fear and anxiety, and would never be ok without her Mom was certainly wrong! Instead I am a loving healer and have the beautiful honor of being a channel for the message that I fought so hard to learn. Today, I hope to touch as many lives as I can with this platform. I can say with confidence that this is only the beginning of what I am meant to do.

As it so often is, my suffering was my greatest teacher. My pain now has purpose. I want to take these teachings and enlighten others so that they do not have to suffer the way I did. The knowledge, compassion, strength, and peace that I found from those dark times were worth the struggle. However, the fact that I lived in that struggle for so long was my choice. It took great insight, work, and a deep change of perspective. I hope to help others make a different choice. Making use of your natural born navigation and loving where you are in life every step of the way is the key to remembering your joy. Being able to see difficult times as teaching moments creates the path of least resistance to all of your dreams.

As I close this chapter, I begin to scribble about what I want in my next book of desires. I put my trust in my co-author, as I know with Him all things are possible. They are for you, too. When you connect with this knowledge, you will eventually recognize that the story of LOVE is all there is, and all there ever was.

ABOUT MICHELLE SIMKISS DUNK

Michelle Dunk is a Visionary Entrepreneur, Speaker, Author and Coach. She is President and Founder of a unique mentoring and scholarship program called In beTWEEN Girls. This non-profit 501c3 corporation is dedicated to empowering the lives of TWEEN and teen girls by teaching them self-worth, confidence, invaluable life skills, and how to connect with their own Inner Spark.

Michelle is also the CEO of Visionary Mentoring Group, which has a mission to bring personal and professional visions to life. Her role as a motivator and mentor for women began several years ago when Michelle hosted a weekly woman's group in her home teaching meditation, EFT tapping, and empowerment. She is passionate about inspiring like-minded women in their own personal journeys. Today, she is a certified Transformation and Success Coach. She taps into the deep maternal, nurturing love, and warm energy that she inherited from her Mom to hold the space for those seeking to find clarity and accelerated results with their goals. Her signature process takes her clients from pain to purpose to achieve peace, passion and prosperity.

Michelle holds a degree in Sociology from Rowan University and a concentration in International Studies. She is most at peace in nature, particularly the beach, and enjoys traveling. Michelle treasures spending time with her family and friends and can typically be found with her husband Jimmy, cheering on their daughters, Madelyn and Cassidy, on the soccer fields, basketball courts, dance recitals, and various life endeavors.

For more information or to connect with Michelle visit: www.visionarymentoringgroup.com or www.inbetweengirls.org.

LEAD WITH NO

Anjela Ford

" *You remind me of someone."*
Mmm, delicious recognition, noticing.
She SEES me!

H-A-L-T
Who?! What?!
Who do I remind you of?
What are you talking about?
*You and I have **never** met before*
… or have we?!

Hmph, if only you knew the real me
The me that is startled awake nightly
By anxiety
Tossing, and turning—fretting myself awake from my fears
Again.

*I **hate** feeling this*
EVERY night.

If only you knew
The real me
Not this fake
People pleasing
Self-sacrificing
FAKE

If only you knew ...
You wouldn't be so awed and impressed.

Do YOU have an opinion?
Can you remember the last time you did?

How do you answer these questions?
Can you answer them?
    Truthfully and honestly?
    Without hesitating?

What's your gut response?
And what is your truth?
Not the same I bet.
Come along with me and I'll share my path back to *rediscovering*
my own opinion.

It is May 2014.

Billie Kat is 19 months old. Jalen is almost four years old. Jane
and I are coming up on nine months of marriage and nearly eight
years as a couple.

Feeling overwhelmed is the norm. Feeling overwhelmed is *my*
norm. I am constantly busy, and yet getting nothing (important)
done. I am always in movement but very rarely present. Too many

choices keep me from making any choices. I stall. I procrastinate. I live in a state of constant anxiety …

I wonder, quite often, "How did I get here?"

Now, I can give you many, many reasons—or excuses.

CHILDHOOD TRAUMA

I can look back at the oft scared, emotionally numb little girl who never knew when the next argument would erupt or why. Not in her body, or really of her body. And no, this doesn't mean I was having some kind of spiritual experience. I was having a survival experience. I was trying to survive the yelling and my stepfather's drug-fueled, constant threats to steal my little brother so we'd never see him again. The physical numbness from hiding in my flesh, but not of my flesh, so that I could numb out from the sexual abuse. Still that trauma heals. But no, this is not it.

Maybe feeling overwhelmed is still a side effect of surviving Encephalitis. This is one of my greatest storytelling gifts—I can so easily take you back to that day. That day driving west on Highway 113 headed home to Woodland from my job as a Teen Educator at WEAVE (Women Escaping A Violent Environment) in Sacramento. I was filled with pride for my accomplishments and longingly wishing for the moment I would enter my apartment at 260 West Court Street. And then, while driving, I remember feeling startled because I couldn't remember where I was or what I was doing. Yes, whilst driving! The pedals below my feet were strangely unfamiliar, frighteningly foreign. I didn't know what to do. I didn't remember *how* to drive. Thank the Goddess this lasted mere seconds.

But, the memory haunts me to this day. And even more haunting were the 18 months of life-consuming recovery and lost memories between May and October of 2001. I felt like a foreigner in my own country. I had absolutely *zero* recollection of the trauma of 9/11 in the US of A. Nothing. My only memories were of what was told to me, and even those are cloudy. My birthday on October 24th of the same year … well, let's just say thank goodness for pictures. Though I still don't recognize the woman gazing back at me in those pictures.

But, no, not even my Encephalitis accounted for my continued state of being overwhelmed.

And so it continued.

February 14, 2015.
Taking care of me—it's getting easier to put myself first. And it feels better and better each time.

Last night, Mom arrived for a weekend visit from Vancouver (British Columbia, Canada eh!) to visit us here down in Vancouver, WA. The self-care gift I gave myself on the day of her arrival was that I allowed myself to go to bed early. Jane was left to entertain everyone, including Mom, while I fell asleep in the kids' room, cuddled with Jalen and a snoring Billie in her crib. And my sleep was magnificent—almost 10 hours of rest!

Today the self-care is becoming more habit. Now, I sit enjoying the quiet candlelight with a purring Luna, with the only other sounds being intermittent snoring and the hum of the heating and air filter.

These are the moments of juiciness. I LOVE my life right now. So, how in the heck did I get here?!

I made *so many* selfish choices. Yes, you read that right—SELFish.

As Mamas, we are reminded daily to put our needs low on the list of priority. Let's be real, we are *taught* to be self-sacrificing "she-roes." Put everyone else first. Keep going, no matter your depletion. Family first, kids first, marriage first. Heck, some of these phrases are plastered on bumper stickers and at rallies. Presidential nominees broaden their scope of support by ranting, "Family first! Kids first!"

Now, I don't deny the positive effects of putting family and children above all else. But also please consider the depletion of spirit that is a direct negative consequence of Mama's needs not being on the priority list at all.

As parents, and *especially* as Mamas, we are not only encouraged, but forced to believe in the martyrdom of motherhood. Well, I say toss it! Put YOU first. Be willing to disappoint your family, your tribe. And be ready to embrace the freedom of spirit. To paraphrase Lisa Nichols, who continues to inspire me, remember to give from your abundance. Be willing to let yourself be filled, and give from that overflow. Be willing to say NO more often, so that when you do say YES to helping others, you are giving without sacrificing you.

But, let me caution you—embracing the opportunity to disappoint others is not easy. Folks will have feelings, especially those closest to you. The ones you fear to disappoint can hurt the most in their reactions. Our responsibility and our new opportunity is to become teachers to our tribe.

For so long, we've taught them that we are ever-available.

Oh, it's ok, I have time.
No, don't worry about me.
No, really it's not last minute, I can do it.
Really, I don't mind. I would tell you no if I couldn't do it …

Now, it's time to pause and say NO first.

Say no to making yourself last on the list—on their list. But even more importantly, say NO to being last on your own list. Dare you put yourself first and ahead of everything and everyone else?! I can tell you from the other side, the view is magnificent. Being on the side of prioritizing me and taking care of me first has been one of the most heartening and heart-filling choices I have *ever* made. And it's a choice I must continue to make again and again, every single day. And while it's becoming a more familiar choice, it's rarely the easy, comfortable choice.

But, the quiet moments begin with a pause. These moments are divine sweetness that I am not willing to sacrifice. Ever. Again.

The present.

Let me share with you a brief glimpse into this sweetness and how it manifests—how I choose to manifest more of me.

The most unfamiliar and yet most necessary movement is pausing. When I allow myself these quiet moments, I find more to reflect on and notice.

I've been noticing my pattern of pausing. When the overwhelm strikes, my mind begins racing. I can't make a choice. All options seem viable. And at the same time nothing seems right. These are the moments I pause. Or on the flip-side, when overwhelm strikes and my inclination is to freeze, feeling no discernment powers over what choice is best. Often this comes after some new breakthrough or awareness of my pattern of avoidance. Ironically, the overwhelm mostly appears in direct reaction to some great success. I recognize an opportunity that I manifested and which brought me success, especially financial abundance. And bam! The door of opportunity is slammed shut as I succumb to the familiar mind-game of "This can't last. How did I do this? I don't deserve this. Better appreciate it while it's here." And then ALL continued movement forward stops. Completely. And so creates further overwhelm.

But now I redirect this intention for pause. I used to negatively associate this pausing with failure and giving up. Now, I see it as integration and reflection. For so long I've burdened myself with the belief that changes must occur quickly and without hesitation.

And for me the inspiration leads to a dramatic shift to whatever is the most positive for growth. I'm persistent for a brief time, and then I pause. Sometimes I pause for quite a while—often because of being overwhelmed and fearing all of the feelings that are now set free from this new, deeper attention to presence. And it freaks me out! The voices of overwhelm tempt me to label this pausing as yet "just another failure." And I'm tempted further to just give up (again!) and admit defeat.

But now there is a new shift in me to just allow the pauses. A shift to stop fighting and listen to my inner calling for rest, to allow myself to pause. And instead of looking ahead to all I still have to do, succumbing to overwhelm, I turn my gaze back and acknowledge how far I've come. I challenge myself to let go and ask myself just one question: What needs to be released to allow this new growth space to expand?

Now when I feel overwhelmed, I've started to look around for some physical clutter to release, and boy is there a lot of potential for that! Sometimes this gaze leads to being more overwhelmed. So I return to my breath to calm myself. I breathe in the overwhelming feelings and exhale with a loud sound to give physical release and "voice" to my feeling of overwhelm.

Sometimes even that doesn't work, and so I allow myself to speak out the fears and rant a bit. I've even timed myself sometimes so that I don't get out of hand. The privacy of my car while I drive is a great place for this!

And if that is still not enough, I get up and move my body, outside in nature if possible, or at least near an open window. I allow my gaze to fall upon some view of nature and sit still to notice all of the tiny details. I observe the sounds, movement, and texture, when possible, and I ground myself in the present. And then I allow myself to reflect on my challenge: the thought, the fear, the thinking.

And then I examine it anew. If after five minutes of this new relaxed attention, I'm still stuck and can't let it go, I allow myself to stop and come back to it later—maybe even set an alarm to remind myself to reconsider the situation.

A great inspiration is to reach out to a friend who is farther along on the journey that I currently struggle along. I ask for help and I allow myself to receive their support. And I remember that I am not alone. I acknowledge how far I've come and that I'm still willing to go forward.

I'm committed to myself and my freedom. And so it is.

The abundant future unfolding, looking ahead and forever forward.

Again, the questions we started with …

Do YOU have an opinion?
Can you remember the last time you allowed yourself to have an opinion?

Now, how WILL you answer these questions?

I am here to remind you …
You CAN answer them.
    Truthfully and honestly.
    Without hesitating.

Pause and recognize your gut response.
Allow yourself a moment to reflect.

And then dig deeper and remember,
You've always known, for it's always been within you.
Your truth.

For so long, your instinctual response
and your truth
have been too often opposite.
Not the same. Ever.

But now you have a new choice.
And in every moment you *can* make a new choice.

For myself, the deeper and deeper I dig into my own truth, the more I come back to the root of pain: unworthiness, or more clearly, lack of self-worth. For so long, I have depended on the approval of others for my own decision making. Now I continue to train myself to embrace complete self-worth at all times and in all situations. But this is not a common theme reflected back to me in the media or my everyday experiences in the world. And so, when I feel the temptation to retreat and sacrifice my own needs to please others, I dare myself to **STOP** and reconsider the consequences of being last on my list of priorities.

Why are we tempted to self-sacrifice? Well, look at the outcome: appreciation, devotion, and other's (conditional) approval.

The better question is ... what do you lose?
The answer is simple, but true. You lose you.

I dare you to consider the reality that lies on the other side of your gut response to self-sacrifice. It is a reality of wholeness. More so, it is a reality of truth—the truth of your innate infinite self-worth. **Without condition, you are ALWAYS worthy of everything your heart can dare dream to imagine.**

I leave you with these questions. When will you be worth the sacrifice? When will you embrace the vulnerability of responding more oft with no, in order to say yes to you? Are you willing to embrace the vulnerability of disapproval from others? Are you willing to embrace this vulnerability for the opportunity to blossom into the woman you have always been? I dare you to imagine.

When I am tempted to forget, I remember this poem inspired within from my own inherent truth.

"Along the Warrioress Path"

Their fear is not my reality.
Not yet, they warn.
Wait til it's safer …
When you have more planned
When you have more money saved
When you have more …
*Wait until you're **not** worried,*
When you are really ready.
*I used to cower under **their** fear,*
To back away from MY path,
To be willing to wait.

But no more.
I can't wait for them.
I realize my path is my own.

I look to those further ahead
As my guides of hope.
And I take all of you
On similar paths
Along with me.

We CAN do this.
We ARE doing this.
Just keep moving.

I am inspired by
This resilient,
Brave Woman
I'm meeting
In the mirror.

Won't you join us?

ABOUT ANJELA FORD

Anjela is the blissful mama and Owner/CEO of Anjelabundance. Anjela believes the world is a better place when mamas are well-rested, nourished, calm, and infinitely more. She uses her years of facilitation and teaching to lead overwhelmed mamas on their own path back to the woman in their mirror.

Anjela's background in crisis intervention and management amplify her leadership skills, as evidenced by the numerous awards and accolades bestowed upon her. When the words just won't come, Anjela relies on her heart-language, American Sign Language, to help her connect to and convey her own healing truth. Yet above it all, Anjela's biggest teachers are her own children, Billie Kat and Jalen, and their assistant and Anjela's wife, Jane.

Anjela invites you to join her online at www.anjelabundance.com, Facebook, YouTube, Pinterest, and Twitter. She offers direct support via live classes, downloadable meditations, group coaching, one-on-one private consultations, and direct Mothering Mentorship. Anjela also offers dynamic keynote presentations on a variety of subjects including Overwhelmed Mama Relief, Teen Dating Violence Awareness and Prevention, and Vicarious Trauma Relief for Domestic Violence and Sexual Assault Service Providers.

Anjela invites you to reach out today.

I am inspired by
This resilient
Brave Woman
I'm meeting
In the mirror.

Won't you join us?

PERMISSION TO SHINE BRIGHT

Belinda Ginter

This is a short story about unearthing your true gifts—about allowing your true purpose to shine through you, while you're at service to millions of people worldwide that need to hear your message. This is a story about pursuing your path so far out of your comfort zone that the only option is to use your God-given talents to increase your abundance, which allows you to be of service to even more people who NEED your message. This means getting out of your way and allowing people to pay you for something that comes as naturally to you as breathing!

Most of us, from a young age, have been told to keep our differences to ourselves. People around us model this behavior and authority figures say outright that we should stifle these differences. They are not something to talk positively about, let alone embrace and be proud of. We are told never to outshine our neighbors, friends, colleagues, and siblings for fear of being disliked or potentially making others feel less worthy. As we age, it is reinforced that we should never outperform (economically or socially) our spouses or our parents, because it may be seen as being ungrateful or as snubbing their efforts. Between spouses, financial and emotional

107

successes may hurt and diminish relationships.

The message we receive is not to be unique; blend in with society. Don't recreate the wheel; don't take the path less taken. These "risks" are only meant for people who have put in their time and retired, the financially well-off, or for young people to "get it out of their system" before they get to the business of being just like everyone else. You WILL be "successful" if you just follow the masses, do what they do, think like they do, act like they do and eventually have the same careers as they do. Just smile, work hard to prove yourself, and maybe you will be just like them someday. Keep your true self and your unique gifts hidden, because what would they think of you if they ever found out your deepest desires and ambitions?

In particular circumstances, we're told it's okay for us to feel like we have a gift to share with the world. But we must never rely on those gifts to feed our families and secure our futures. Our gifts must remain a hobby, and we must be grateful to have an outlet while contributing to society and making safe and reliable choices. We can be a hobby painter, photographer, sculptor, or author, but it's only ever going to be a hobby. No one will ever pay well for our gifts (artists don't get sick time and benefits, don't you know?) Somewhere, deep down in our subconscious, we start to believe all that we are told. We hear this from those who love us and only want the best for us, therefore it must be true. Even if we suspect that we're destined for greater things, ignoring their advice might hurt their feelings. So we conform and begin to think that only some can make their life purpose (their gift to the world) their full-time "job". But we are quick to rationalize and create narratives about those people being born into money, or maybe someone supported them, or simply (and the most likely option according to our subconscious) they are just more talented than we are.

Once we establish that story, we let ourselves off the hook for not pursuing our gifts, because it's not the socially acceptable way to act. This creates negative beliefs around our gifts which solidify our narrative and prove (as we humans like to do) that what we believe is always right. We change our behavior to match our thoughts. How, you ask? We continuously attract people, experiences, and events into our lives that prove our narrative is right. We take jobs that are safe; we date the same type of people over and over again who remind us that we don't deserve to pursue our dreams. We work for domineering bosses who let us believe we only deserve to be exactly where we are. Sometimes our quest for proof isn't so subtle. Sometimes we have great jobs, great partners, and great kids. But we never strive further than the end of our driveway and we dim our light around spouses and parents. Maybe we just work really hard at keeping everything status quo. These are still binding negative beliefs that limit our real and unrestricted potential.

The situation I have described above plays out all over the world every single day, and it is what led me to work globally with my clients. As an international Emotional Kinesiologist, I help people release their toxic beliefs. These untrue but heavily validated stories are picked up through negative past family programming or narratives we concoct to explain our unrecognized and unfulfilled status in life. These stories are called Negative Belief Systems. Negative past family programming and negative beliefs keep us from sharing our gifts with the world. They keep us from shining so bright and visibly that the world as a whole is thankful they found us and fully accepts that we can help them through the service, message, and creation we provide.

The exchange we see most often in North America is that of goods, services, and time for money. We're told that we must work at jobs that already exist, led by people who have worked a long time to get "where they are today". We find it impossible to believe that we can become wealthy doing what we love and what comes naturally. This vision can be met by judgement and criticism. Pursuing our passion is seen as irresponsible, selfish, and down-right foolish. We're considered unsuitable partners and unable to provide for ourselves and others. The honesty and vulnerability in those life choices scares off a lot of us. It causes so much fear and insecurity that we shut down and keep these beautiful gifts to ourselves, or we undervalue them so much that we continue to play small, and the world never gets to fully see our gifts.

So, what are the consequences of entire nations of people not stepping into their power and claiming their life purposes or gifts? We have created a world of millions who feel depleted, depressed, and anxious. We substitute the feelings we could get from following our passion with coping mechanisms to get through our days. We rely on the help of caffeine, alcohol, illegal drugs, anti-depressants, anti-anxiety pills, prescription drugs, massive consumer debts, and full blown addictions to unhealthy food-like substances.

We are aching inside. The act of suppressing our authentic selves is literally rotting us from the inside out. All we need to do to release this agony is just let our true selves out—to break free from the stories others tell us and more importantly the ones we tell ourselves—and to live as big and boldly beyond what we even think is possible.

What lies in your wildest dreams is the ability to be 100% authentically you, to be accepted for you, and to have your gifts embraced by society (with the ultimate goal being to make a living from your innate gifts.) We all long to be truly happy and finally feel complete and full. What that looks like is beyond anything we can currently imagine.

As a mother, I am trying to be aware of this. I try to focus on the light in my children's spirit. I try to locate what my children's unique talents truly are. I watch carefully to see what activities they find interesting. What do they do that makes their eyes sparkle a little more than usual? What do they do so naturally and brilliantly that it comes as quickly and organically as the air they breathe? What are they talking about when they smile from ear to ear?

All of these are clues to what their true self desires and point out their God-given gifts which may become their life's purpose. I want my children to grow up knowing that not only is it okay to have their gifts fund their lifestyle, but it is also expected and nurtured. I want them to live the life that continually fills them up. Eventually, when they have families of their own, they can pass on this level of acceptance. If we offer this scenario to ourselves, then we know better and we do better for our children. If we could change societal views, and if more of us grew up with acceptance, then I feel there might be fewer lost souls wandering the earth, searching for someone or something else to complete them because they are convinced they could never be complete within their selves.

I was turning 40 when I finally felt the need and gave myself permission to shine the light on my God-given talents and make an incredible income doing it.

At the time I was working a corporate job, and I loved certain aspects of it, but I was only using 3% of my full potential. I was explicitly told not to shine as brightly as I was capable of doing. I was told that I didn't want to be perceived as "better" than others, and I certainly did not want to step on anyone's toes or make others uncomfortable in their designated roles. I was also told that there was no growth potential for the future. I felt suffocated. (This is, quite honestly, the fastest way to lose a rockstar employee.) My dreams were crushed.

I was commuting for hours a day to and from my corporate job. If there was a storm or a bad traffic accident, it could take me up to three and a half hours to get to work—ONE WAY! At work I was eligible for a 1% - 3% performance-based raise per year. Of course, there was no special increase for Ultimate Rock Stars, so even when I was overachieving I capped out and was not compensated accordingly! Many of us face this reality and we are not only told to accept it, we are told to strive to be placed in such situations. These conditions allow others to determine our worth based on an equation that keeps us feeling marginalized, frustrated, and under-appreciated. For five years, I functioned at my 3% potential. But once I was pregnant with my second child, I finally woke up to the hard truth that I was working hard and not smart.

After my second child, I lasted a year in the corporate world. But if I'm honest with myself, from the minute my maternity leave ended I was already planning a way to leave. I knew I needed to follow my life's purpose and learn how to work smarter, not harder. The first thing I did was write a letter of resignation; however, I did not date it. By writing the letter, I emotionally, spiritually, and physically made a commitment to myself. I had committed to figuring out what made me happy. I needed to discover what made my eyes sparkle and to notice when I smiled the biggest and brightest. This letter gave me freedom from the 9 - 5 toxicity I was experiencing. It immediately reduced the level of negative emotions that arose while working in such a limiting position. I still cared about my job and the people around me, but I could disassociate when the work drama came up. I knew I had a better plan, and I wasn't as concerned with playing small. Hey, I was leaving soon anyway! I was going to pursue my dreams and figure out how I could be useful to the universe. With this mindset, I was unbothered by things that would normally upset me and send me spinning for days or even months. My spirit was already free, and I knew it wouldn't be long before this freedom manifested physically. It was like all of the work chaos and drama was floating past me, and I was fluid like water, allowing the experiences to run off of my back. I started to *breathe* again.

Eventually, I was able to lead my clients through the same process to find their own life's purpose. I taught people how to see their true, God-given gifts and helped them recognize what was already there and what they had become blind to. I taught and continue to teach thousands of clients that living fully is as simple as listening to what their inner child wants. We need to think back to the time before we were told our gifts were not enough. I help my clients recall what excited them as a child, adolescent, or even as a young adult. I coach them to draw out the stories and give that little girl or boy a voice.

I don't remember a time as a child that I didn't want to change the world! What I would have given for the opportunity to do just that. I have always been a deliverer of messages—a messenger of sorts. I had to learn and overcome many hurdles, the biggest being the act of surrendering to the fact that I didn't know anything yet. I needed to commit to focusing and becoming quiet enough for my creative self to show up and provide me with all the answers I desired. So that is what I did. I became silent and I listened. I learned to trust my strong sense of intuition, to listen to my gut, and to the God whisper within. I am telling you, it said loud and clear what the next step was for me. I can assure you that the voice within yourself will NEVER lead you astray. It is always on your side and looking out for your very best interests.

Once I was sure about the next step on my path, I told my husband that I had taken an emotional release technique course ten years prior, and somehow I knew that was part of my plan. I wished to take a refresher and to focus my efforts on this avenue to deliver my messages. My intuition reminded me how much I loved emotions and working with others. I loved helping them to really understand their feelings and the deep roots those emotions had. It reminded me that for as long as I could remember, I had a God-given gift and a passion for delivering these messages. As a message giver, I always innately knew the EXACT thing to say to someone in order to help them shift and change their lives for the positive. I even do it in my sleep. As a child, my mother's boyfriend told me that I would often wake him up in the middle of the night; I appeared to be sleepwalking and would deliver a message to him from his father who had passed years before. The message was very confidential, only something that he and his father would know, and it was always the exact thing he needed to hear to shift his life in a more positive direction. He considered each message a very special gift, as they were life-changing every time.

I've also been told that I visited friends, family, and childhood classmates in their dreams. Again, I delivered a powerful message about what they needed to do at that exact stage in their lives to shift things in a positive manner. I knew this was my special gift. Working with emotions was something most people ran away from. Not only was it what I ran towards, it also gave me the most joy and made me want to run towards it harder and faster. I took my amazing ability to deliver these imperative messages and combined them with the techniques I learned 10 years earlier during the emotional release program. I could really give clients the most amazing life shifting experiences.

I continued to develop my unique form of Emotional Kinesiology and began specializing in removing negative past family programming from my client's lives. I worked directly with people all over the world to release limiting narratives and used my strong intuition and keen sense of perception to deliver healing messages to my clients. This process would completely clarify their lives and allow them to come to the same conclusions that I did. We are the masters of determining our worth. When we use what makes us happy to support our lives and the lives of those we love, we cannot be led astray. Once we remove what has been continuously programmed into us about our worth and value in this world, we can so clearly see how we should contribute and give back. Each of us is created to bring something to this world. Who are we to stand in the way of that truth?

I now live the life I once dreamed of and find myself dreaming bigger every day. What I thought was impossible a few years ago, I now see as a stepping stone to bigger, bolder ways to serve and heal our world and those that seek out my services. I have eliminated my commute and created a community of lovely, supportive, worldwide companions and clients who wish to heal themselves so that they too can begin to share their dreams and goals. The ripple effect of healing that started with me standing up to my fullest potential is possible for us all.

I currently work fifteen hours a week and make five times what I did in my corporate position. I have tons of physical, emotional, and time freedom. I can be infinitely creative and have fostered an ability to tend to my needs to continue this lifestyle. Perhaps the most exciting thing is that my business is 100% mobile, so I can work from anyplace in the world and follow any future drives and aspirations I desire. Every day, I work on fostering my connection with my gift, and like an athlete, I appreciate that I'm the vehicle and it is important for me to give myself every opportunity to tend to myself. I couldn't put myself first until I took the reins of my life and became my biggest and greatest champion. I got out of my way and repaired any flawed stories I had created about what was possible for my life. I protect that fiercely.

I now share my gifts with the world. The people that benefit from my gifts recognize the investment in their well-being and pay extremely well for my time. I feel blessed every day to have had the courage to break the mould, to dream bigger, and to question everything that didn't serve me. I am constantly reevaluating what I need to continue to be my best, and I tweak and adjust accordingly. I have become wealthy while shining bright and sharing my gifts with thousands of clients worldwide. This is possible for anyone, and I am fortunate enough to have the gifts to teach others how to achieve the same. Determine your worth and be confident in your value!

ABOUT BELINDA GINTER

Belinda Ginter is an Emotional Kinesiologist, Author and empowerment speaker. She has a thriving private practice with thousands of clients worldwide. Belinda is passionate about educating and empowering women to love themselves by fully reclaiming and sustaining their personal power. She does this by reminding each and every one of them that they were born to be UNSTOPPABLE! She doesn't just share her knowledge: she creates an experience. Her unique interactive presentations will have you hanging on the edge of your seat! They are not to be missed. Not only will you walk away with tons of take-aways, you'll also experience her abilities first hand.

Belinda uses her intuition and a unique talent for removing negative past family programming to facilitate BIG personal and professional shifts in her clients' lives. Belinda likes to say: "We are all a product of each year of our lives. We have attached meaning and stories to each of our experiences. The interpretation of these experiences can contribute to our own internal negative beliefs. Our souls can be a product of our environments; we tend to take on negative past family programing and store it at a deep DNA cellular level."

Using Emotional Kinesiology, Belinda can locate and remove negative beliefs and negative past family programming that may be blocking you to leave you feeling happier, healthier, wealthier and open to all sorts of MAGIC.

Belinda is a mother to two amazing children, Natel and Gavin, and wife to an amazing, loving and supportive husband, Derek. She can be contacted at www.belindaginter.com.

AWAKEN YOUR CREATIVE SPIRIT AND SHINE

Jennifer Granger

Creation Day

Oh little creator on your creation day.
The spirits conspired and decided on your purpose.
The light was so bright at your first breath.
In that second you became the intention of the Universe.
It is in those first days and years that you create your destiny.
Are you the creation that your life intends?
Is this day as it was written in the stars decades ago?
Be present in the light that always shines through you.

by Jen Granger, December 30, 2015

I will forever remember the day and the life changing question I asked myself. It's the kind of question that you carry in your gut. It's the question buried so deeply. It's left unanswered over the years, mostly because you're afraid of the answer, or you're not sure how to handle the answer. But then, one day, it breaks free and the voice cries out for an answer. It screams at you with a voice you can no longer ignore. Because, this time, it's your truest voice asking,

119

"Am I living this day as I intended to live this day?"

This was the question that I was afraid to answer. I knew I had been ignoring the question for over ten years as I was living in the flurry of my life. However, on February 8, 2014, I finally chose to answer it—with complete honesty—"*Am I living this day as I intended to live this day? No, not really.*" That answer, that truth, set my soul free that day, even though I was feeling completely overwhelmed by the next question, "So now what do I do about it?"

For the first time though, because of the events and the safe space I found myself in that day, I felt a glimmer of hope that it would be okay. A good friend had invited me to come along to a women's retreat that day. It was the first time I had ever dedicated an entire day to unplugging from the world and turning inward to rediscover myself and my soul. Free from the mobile phone and family obligations (aka "mommy demands"). It was just me and a small tribe of women who were sharing a path and protected space for the day. We peeled away all the roles where we served others and all the stories we told ourselves. We showed up and stepped into our truth, no matter the outcome. We shed tears of many emotions as we journeyed through the authentic story of our lives. It was in this messy and honest truth that I was finally able to answer the question. Giving pause to speak honestly to myself is why my life is forever changed. When I left the retreat, I wasn't sure how long it would take me to fully explore all I discovered and start using the tools I learned that day, but I could at least trust one thing again. I could trust myself to explore my new awareness.In the weeks and months that followed, I felt alive again on my self-development journey. I was bringing clarity to goals in all aspects of my life like personal joy, spirituality, health, career, entrepreneurship, and family. I was incorporating a new practice of meditation even though I had so much mind chatter. When I finally connected to my truth, I was reminded of my lifelong dream to be a writer. This is the one goal that ignited my soul and I could visualize and affirm my dream effortlessly, just as I did in my childhood. If I could live my life as a writer every day, that would mean I would be living as my truest self and sharing that gift. It meant I would be creating everyday, rather than only writing the occasional poem during life changing events or for a family member's funeral. It also meant I would need to explore what it truly meant to become more creative in my day-to-day living. If I ever wished to truly "live a life as I intended," I knew that everyday would need to become a "hell yes" to the question, and I would also need to free my creative soul. The same creative soul that wrote this poem over 25 years ago would be free to write with a passion for living.

The Pulling
There is something pulling inside
A feeling that won't subside
It is a piece of the unknown
But the pulling won't leave me alone
Telling me which road to take
Then again it might be a mistake
    You won't know until you try
    You won't know until you fly
    You won't know until you cry
You can do anything you want, or so they say
Is "anything" pulling or taking me away?
All I want is to hold on till tomorrow
Praying that there will be no sorrow
The pulling never takes me back
It would only show me what I lack
    You won't know until you try
    You won't know until you fly

You won't know until you cry
I'm blinded by the present
The pulling may be something pleasant
Of course there is always time
It's treated like a sacred shrine
Will the pulling take me to a special place?
Will it take away my empty space?
You won't know until you try
You won't know until you fly
You won't know until you cry
You won't know until you die …

by Jen Granger, 1987

The day I read through all the pages of my poetry, stories, and writings from my youth was one of the hardest days in my self-development journey. It hit me like a ton of bricks. What happened? How could I have abandoned my creative spirit? I recall with detail the nights as a young teenager when I would drift off to sleep thinking about what life could be as a creative writer. So what is it that held me back from actually believing I was a writer? The answer scared me and, quite honestly, pissed me off. "Myself." I had allowed my doubts to cloud my dream. I recalled those doubts clearly as if they were yesterday … I wasn't trained as a writer … I didn't read enough or know all the classics, so how could I be a writer? … I'm not like other published writers, so that could never happen to me … it's not a "real" job that will support me … since it's just a hobby, I'm probably not any good … how will I survive on an income from writing? So, then those questions led to more thoughts and questions. How dare I question where I was in my life? I had a lot of good things in my life. Maybe that dream wasn't meant to be. If I'm a good mom and my son is happy, maybe I don't need to realize my dreams. Maybe I should stop being selfish and just focus on making sure he reaches his dreams. I certainly had a lot to be joyful about in my life. I had a successful career with quite a few amazing colleagues and mentors I worked with along the way. I was living the American dream with my husband and young son. We enjoyed our special connections with our family. I was blessed with fun and amazing friendships. My husband and I worked really hard and had a savings we could rely on. We lived comfortably in our dream home. We "had it all," except, I didn't have it all. I was missing the one element to connect it all. I was missing my true self and the pure joy that comes from living my true passion in life. I needed to "be creative" again and, more specifically, to write.

That's when my creative spirit showed up in my journaling. Once I called into question the "status quo" of my life, she showed up with her tough love. She said, "Wake the fuck up! Shake that shit out of your life! Shed all of these doubts and frustrations until you can shed the source of them and work on your new belief structure. Until then, you need to know something, so repeat after me ..."

(excerpt from my journal)

I am the gift I am.

My path in life is my gift.

I need to change my thoughts, not my soul.

What am I energizing and giving power to?

Inventory my thoughts.

Be present in the path and stop letting my life just happen.

When I see how pure the light is, I can't help but be more thankful for all that I am blessed with.

Be aware of my thoughts.

Catch the bad thoughts and move them to another distant space.

Love myself unconditionally.

Forgive myself for being too perfect.

I was so grateful to my creative spirit that lived in my meditations and journaling because her raw and honest truth is what transformed my thoughts and brought me to the next phase of my journey. When you shine from your creative soul, that is when the magic happens and your creations spread pure light into the world. As I worked on myself and discovered new facets of my creativity, all aspects of my world began to expand and I was more than a writer. I was manifesting new opportunities for creativity and the expansion of my new awareness allowed me to step into a new creative living mindset. It was time to live through my creative spirit instead of "making some time" to be creative.

When you are living your life with intention, you make daily choices that make sense on an intuitive level. You finally trust and listen to your inner guide. There was a point at which my life shifted because of my intentional living. I don't want you to think I'm living perfectly. In fact, it's quite the opposite. Sometimes it's messy and I repeat lessons until they are finally learned. But the awareness comes through the entire journey. And the shift comes when I take inspired action toward my dreams. And sometimes, it happens when I am completely unaware of the impact of my actions.

I attended another retreat in June 2015 that I know was the catalyst for my major shift. During that retreat is when I journaled after a very powerful guided meditation. The meditation resulted in answering the question, "What are you here to do?" The guided meditation ultimately led me to visualize a gift for myself inside of a box. What came to me was a crystal—it was flooded with healing love, and my Mom-Mom presented it to me. She had died several years before this day, but I was always deeply connected to her. She was always a believer in all my talents and gave so much love. So, after this meditation, I found a comfy spot in the corner near a window that overlooked a historic building in Wilmington, DE. The messages literally screamed at me from the building across the street. Inscribed between columns were words like "painting, architecture, sculpture, history and poetry." From the view of that building, I received a message to explore all av-  enues of creativity in order to grow in my writing. There was also a street sign literally crossing the intersection in front of the building: Market Street. In the total view from this quiet space with a window to my insights, was I being asked by the universe to explore what I was willing to exchange for my creative power? What was going to be the balance between the essence of my creativity and the commercial marketplace where my creations could be exchanged? It's a question that all creative souls struggle with as they know the marketplace can place constraints or demands on their creation.

I ended my journal passage with an affirmation that was the key point in my shift. In fact, I wrote "THE SHIFT. Create more in different ways," under it.

I am so happy and grateful that I
amplify creativity
to shine a love light and fill hearts
with joy.

In the days following this retreat, I had the most powerful med- itations in the evening on two consecutive nights. I was resting comfortably on my screened porch. It was my happy place to relax most evenings in the summer. I share these journal entries with you so that you may also explore your own creative living intentions.

Evening Meditation, June 24th
From the darkness, sparks the light of my intention tonight.
Each flame expands and creates the quiet presence of gratitude.
Marvel at the joy from all the light and dancing shadows.
Be still to pause for a peace filled presence with love.
Love each connected moment as they expand time and my heart.
Surrender to the moment and suspend your thoughts.
Simply grateful for the space that is created for my spirit.
Completely aligned to my peace, my silence, my heart.
It is in the evening that the flame shines my light.
And breath after breath I spread my light.

Evening Meditation, June 25th
There is the moment before the silence that speaks to me.
In that moment, I hear the language of the Universe.
Hear the pouring rain that slaps against the ground.
The rush of water down the spouts floods the puddles.
Broken only by the steady dripping of raindrops in puddles.
I breathe in the summer, damp rainy night.
Distant flashes of lightning in the corner of my eye.
Rumble of the thunder calls to me with a message.
Stop, listen to my message when you sit before the silent moment.
It speaks softly to me, but, oh, with more clarity than spoken words.
Relax, it says to me, and immerse yourself in my quiet cathedral.
Rain pounding.
Drips and drops are steady and beating.
Flashes of flickering light.
Rolling thunder.

Oh, what do I hear? It is the natural moment.
That moment before silence.

The awakening of a creative spirit is possible for anyone who is aligned to that lifestyle. The key is to live with intention as you journey through your awakening. The most surprising discovery of my creativity happened one evening not too long after these mediations. It was on July 2, 2015, to be exact. I had just finished meditating and a message of creating space came to me. I wrote this affirmation:

I am so happy and grateful that my journey of infinite
possibilities have led me to my one true life purpose
to live in my creative spirit.

Within an hour of writing this affirmation, I was outside snapping some photos of the sky directly above me. I had been over the many months capturing photos during meaningful moments of joy and contemplation. The late afternoon meditation on my porch didn't just end with an affirmation message—I was indeed gifted with a much stronger connection to my creative spirit. I was so grateful for that peaceful evening to enjoy the beauty of the clouds as I continued to capture photos. I still can vividly recall they were so white and puffy above me. The sun wasn't setting just yet, but it was definitely that magical light. And then, SNAP—there it was, the perfect photo. Just as I captured the perfect photo, I thought about this editing app I downloaded recently where I could combine text and images. So in that app, I created a meaningful statement to honor my experience, "Create the space for a journey of infinite possibilities" beautifully bonded with my photo. It looked pretty cool in a matter of minutes. And that is when I created the one single image that I will always view as the catalyst for my product creation called #jenmoments. I also did something I don't usually do: I clicked the "yes" button to print my creation, in addition to sharing the image on social media. I thought, what the heck? It seemed like no big deal until the day a shiny red bubble wrap envelope showed up in my mailbox. It was 10 days later, so I had forgotten all about my creation. I opened the

mailbox after another long uninspiring day at the office. WOW, what could this be? What did I order? It was so magical and way more exciting than the countless other shipments that arrive in a week.

I peeled back the top of the envelope. Oh wow, MY CARDS I ordered. I held them in my hands and I swear it was like the world stood still and I was in a swirling vortex of feelings. I flashed back to all those years I worked for Hallmark Cards at the very beginning of my career. Of course, it was another reminder that I was getting back to my aligned purpose in life. I flashed through all the struggles I experienced in my youth in really digging into my creativity. And I flashed through my most recent year, of all the work I had done on ME to truly awaken my creative spirit. Yes, I had done the hard work to really uncover the magic that was burning so bright inside of me—the light that smolders inside us all until we ignite. In that moment, I said it—"Wow, I could make my own cards." I could create and share soulful messages that allow people to truly connect to the moment they are in. Through my #jenmoments card creations, I could live as I intended to live that day and every day forward.

And that was the day everything shifted. That was the day that the Universe shared it's most treasured secret with me. I have EV-ERYTHING I will ever need inside of me. All I have to do is create the space for my creativity to expand.

My gift is my creative spirit and it manifests most purely through my writings and images or through journaling. As I was exploring my creativity over the past few years, I found a technique that I like to call "journaling with my light." I would use this technique to either open myself up to new creative ideas or if I was struggling with writing or creating. This had such profound results that I wanted to share this with the world, including you, as you read this chapter.

I start by setting an intention for the guidance I am seeking from the source of my light. You can substitute words for the source—God, the Universe, your inner guide (ING), your spirit guide, or your guardian angel are a few that I use interchangeably. Intentions could be something like:

I am open to receiving your message.
I am love and open to receive.
I am my light and willing to shine.
I allow my creative spirit to soar.
Then I ask a question like any of the following:

What will you have me share?
What creation will serve the highest good?
Who will you have me help?
What is my greatest gift?
What message should I explore or share?

Then I meditate quietly to create space for what will come through me. I typically repeat my intention and question like a whispered mantra as I meditate. It's all about creating the flow, so you can use what you are most connected to when you meditate. When my meditation is over I express gratitude. I then quietly start to scribble circles or waves on a page in my journal to disconnect my active brain from what I will write. I say the intention again along with the question. Then I allow my hand to just be free flowing and open to receive the messages I am to hear or read. Sometimes, I will follow along as I write down the messages. Other times, I kind of just observe them. When the journaling is over I release, breathe, and step away to reconnect to the world. Then, when it seems right, I read my entry. Trust me, your light will shine on those messages you read, and you will manifest something truly amazing. And, when you read them over again many months later you will see how the journaling enhances your manifesting to achieve your dreams. Here is a sample of my journaling during a session at the end of 2015. It was during this time that I was opening up to new creations and ideas for 2016, which ultimately led me to take part in *Women Who Ignite*.

Journaling with My Light

It's okay to be loved in such an amazing way.
The experience of that love is what the world needs.
You have magic in your soul and your thoughts need to become words.
That is the gift for all of eternity.
Be brave little one.
You are truthful and you work really hard at your dreams.
Who do you want to be when you live every day?
Live with passion and be the most amazing writer who brings life to ideas.
by Jen Granger, December 11, 2015

The past two years I have spent in self-discovery and living in my creative spirit have been the most exciting and rewarding period of my life. I don't diminish any of my other experiences or accomplishments by saying this. For one, I fully own the entire story of my life and I am so inspired to be a mentor for others who are seeking to awaken their creative spirit or who are just awakening to a new awareness and gift. My gift to the youth of today is to show them a way of living that supports their dreams. My gift to everyone, no matter their age or journey, is to know that they can always trust their inner gift. There is always time in life for the heart and soul to both ask the question AND seek the truth from the answer.

I leave you with this parting poem. My intention is to awaken the creative spirit. My mission is to show others how to do the same.

Lovelight Mission
*Light has no judgment, nor is
it forgiving.
Light shines from a source so pure.
Shine your light on all the lives
you touch.
Allow your love to flow freely.
Love light is your source.*

ABOUT JENNIFER GRANGER

Jen is a writer, entrepreneur, and creative living mentor.

Her creative spirit guided her in 2015 to craft simple and clear messages that melt into her personal photography, to offer a heart-centered intention to expand the moment. These creations are called #jenmoments and have been shared on social media and printed as a line of greeting cards to offer people an opportunity to share in their moment when they send and receive their card.

Most recently, Jen launched a brand new blog community at MySunriseSisters.com, that celebrates and supports the awakening of the creative spirit at any age of life. She offers guest bloggers the opportunity to engage with visitors through their soulful messages of help and encouragement in their own journey of awakening. Her creative living tools and experience along with her #jenmoments products are shared in her web community. Living with her husband and son in Severna Park, Maryland, Jen is dedicated to her creative living approach and spreading joy with family and friends.

CHANGE IS POSSIBLE FOR A NEW YOU

Colleen Hauk

One December evening I found myself alone in the office where I'd worked for over eight years. The majority of employees departed for home by five o'clock, but it was two hours past and I was the only one remaining. Interrupted by my calendar alert, I was reminded that instead of laboring over account plans I should've been celebrating with fellow committee members at an executive women's holiday party. I looked forward to spending time with these women, simply chatting and laughing over a glass of wine. Another one of the countless occurrences stripped from my life in the previous twelve months. And here I was, once again deprived and missing out on what I began calling "the working mom's f-word"—*fun*.

My body and mind lacked self-control and I was instantly weakened. Warm tears slid down my cheeks then quickly developed into harrowing sobs. Crying is not my MO yet I found myself crying more this year compared to any other. Oftentimes when I was home alone, I'd break down with that same cry, that ugly cry you never want anyone to see.

But there was something different this time in my office. The moment I dreaded and attempted to deny all year was finally upon me on this empty and lonely night. I realized my life was not how I ever imagined it would be. I was not only frustrated and exhausted, I was undeniably miserable!

From an outsider's perspective I had it all together, but it was simply a façade. I was absolutely drowning, and not from my tears, but from the weight of every responsibility in my life. These bricks of responsibility were chained to my body and no matter how painstakingly I searched, I couldn't find the key to unlock and release them. It seemed as if these bricks would be infinitely attached.

"I'm drowning!" was an expression I often verbalized but it never occurred to me I was actually sinking into an ocean of helplessness, loneliness, and suffering.

But that night in my dimly lit office, it's as if there was a radiating glow above the water's surface. Unsure of what that glow represented, but with an unexpected resurgence of energy, I swam with determination toward it. I discovered this glow was the light of hope. Breaking through the surface, gasping for air and with my hands held high, I proclaimed, "It's not too late! I *can* make a change and I *must* do it now!"

Do you ever feel like you're drowning? Does it seem as if you're caught in a vicious cycle every day? Are you unhappy and wish you had more balance in life?

That year I would've answered with a resounding, "Yes!" to each of these questions. I was there, just like you.

Born in Southern California, I was raised by two loving parents as an only child. My mom returned to a full-time nursing career soon after I was born. I'd briefly see her in the morning and then not again until shortly before dinnertime. After a long week of work, her weekends were consumed with grocery shopping, folding laundry, paying bills, and shuttling me to whichever activity I was participating

134

in at the time. Yet my mom appeared to be completely happy, living the life she'd dreamed of—a wife, a mom, and a career woman who was independent, successful, and thriving. This woman, my mom, was a strong, influential, role model for me and I wanted to be just like her. Well it seemed I was on my way to fulfilling that dream.

I married my loving husband, Matt, and immediately became a mom to his wonderful son, Jordan. Our family expanded with the addition of our two amazing children, Ethan and Reese. In my professional life, after an initial period as an elementary school teacher, I transitioned into the corporate arena. Over those first few years, trial and error were faced on every front—career, marriage, parenting, and friendships. But I navigated my way through and appeared to be progressing in the direction I desired.

After several years of working for my current company, I earned another promotion; one I had desired for quite some time. I was beyond thrilled! But I failed to evaluate the additional time requirements or impact this promotion would have on my family and me. I was reveling in the opportunity and didn't hesitate to accept the advancement in my career.

The first few months dumped me into that ocean of helplessness as I dove deeper in with my new responsibilities. While I absolutely loved the role, I simply didn't have enough time for everything. And because I refused to be a disappointment to my management, my team, my clients and myself, I quickly found that I was working nearly 60 hours most weeks. In the days before marriage and children, this schedule may have been acceptable. But I wasn't single. I had a home, a husband, and three children to support and care for.

It's no coincidence that during this time my husband awarded me the nickname "The Machine". It was of course meant as a compliment. He knew that no matter what obstacles I encountered, I was persistent and relentless on my path to success. And while my identity from the outside was "The Machine," I questioned how much longer I could operate at this pace. For every gain made in my professional world, it was at the sacrifice of other meaningful areas of my life.

Health

Prioritizing work over my own wellbeing caused me to miss nearly all of my medical and dental appointments. Prolonged work hours resulted in poor food choices and rare occasions to exercise. I gained weight and suffered a loss of energy. High stress levels produced knots between my shoulders which ultimately became concentrated lumps of tension, oftentimes paralyzing me. Sleep was sacrificed at an attempt to accomplish everything, and that meant sleeping as little as only four hours a night. I discovered that sleep deprivation truly does wreak havoc on your body and mind. I recall a colleague asking me a simple question which required a simple answer. But no matter how hard I tried, I couldn't recall the information needed to answer him. I was barely functioning, aimlessly wandering around in a fog, feeling almost as if I was intoxicated.

Happiness

At the end of a 12-hour work day, with enduring commutes home or out-of-state travel for several days, I was impatient and spiritless. My children's laughter could be heard through the front door when I returned home, yet upon my entrance, there was only silence. My husband later told me, "The moment you walked in, we were all on high alert."

It was heartbreaking to learn that my children's pure joy in life, expressed through their laughter, was abandoned because they were afraid of what type of mood their own mom was in! The evenings were consumed with screaming and arguments over taking showers, brushing teeth, and going to bed. And I avoided invitations from other families to enjoy cocktails and conversations. Pretending to be happy required too much effort. And I most certainly didn't want to hear how "perfect" everyone else's life was while I was merely trying to survive and avoid a mental breakdown.

Not only was I unhappy, I was angry and jealous, feelings I rarely experienced during my first 38 years of life. I despised the way I felt yet it seemed uncontrollable. I was angry at my management. How could they possibly think I could handle all of this workload? I was angry at those coworkers who didn't appear to have as much responsibility as me. And I was angry at my husband. He worked from home so he enjoyed more sleep and free time, while my time was spent readying for the office, packing lunches, commuting, and squeezing in other demands in lieu of sleep.

I was jealous of other women, especially those who didn't have the traditional out-of-the-home, full-time J-O-B. I missed out on most of the stay-at-home moms' outings because they took place during the day when I was working. Social media amplified these feelings. Check-ins and pictures of beach outings and day trips to Disneyland made my stomach sink. Why do they enjoy time with their family while I'm trapped in the office? How do they manage to see their child's school performance while I'm rushing through the airport and away from my family for the next few days?

Balance

Balance was the final sacrifice. One specific moment really hit home when my daughter asked me, "Mommy, why do you always tell us to hurry?" I shared with her that I hurried because I felt as if I didn't have enough time to accomplish my never ending to-do list. I could barely keep up with daily chores, much less try to enjoy any type of fulfilling activities. Every ounce of my energy was focused on work and so I was depleted with nothing to give to my family, my friends or myself. Snuggling with my children as they readied for sleep felt more like a chore, as I knew a project was waiting to be completed on my laptop downstairs. Forget about providing love to my poor husband. He quickly fell to the bottom of my list and we saw ourselves as roommates throughout the week. Yet I didn't verbalize my feelings to anyone other than him.

When you work in the type of environment that I do, with such high caliber talent, you begin to think everyone has their shit together. I was surrounded by other female executives that never appeared to waiver. They were each married with children, yet seemed content with working long hours and frequently traveling. I *never* heard anyone complain. I certainly wasn't going to speak up and sound like an idiot for not being able to figure it out!

I also felt selfish. *Selfish.* This is the word and feeling that thrust its way into my consciousness each time I felt unhappy. How much *more* did I deserve in life? Didn't I already have enough? Didn't I already have more than enough? I was married to a supportive husband, I had three wonderful children, and I had a respectable career. There were those close to me that were facing financial difficulties, health problems, failing marriages, and unemployment. How selfish could I possibly be?

I suffered on this wave of emotions for twelve months, engulfed in the sensation that I was unhealthy, unhappy, and unbalanced, all because I was working. Working what felt like all the time!

And there in my office that December evening, I was utterly desperate. I knew I needed to make a change but the only change I could foresee that would finally bring balance into my life was quitting my job. And it's not that I disliked work; I actually loved the company I worked for and the people I worked with. But during that time in my life, I was under the misguided impression that you either work *or* you stay home, in order to feel happy and balanced. The belief that it was possible to have both seemed illogical to me given my current emotional state.

138

I'm thrilled to share with you that I did *not* quit my corporate life! I determined a way to have both a full-time career *and* have balance. In fact, I've again been promoted with that same organization. I'm currently a Group Director engaging with individuals to achieve personal and team goals. In addition, I'm now the Founder of Balance Point Coaching which gives me the opportunity as a Certified Professional Success Coach, speaker, trainer, and author to follow my passion to inspire and support high performing women. I maintain a significant amount of balance in all areas of my life but most importantly, my family and I are now thriving and enjoying laughter together.

How did I manage to go from angry to happy? From depleted to healthy? From off-balance to on-balance?

I'm sharing a few of my awe-inspiring discoveries and simple practices I've implemented with the intention of empowering and nourishing you. Empowering you so you don't have to feel like you're drowning, depressed, or completely overwhelmed. Nourishing you so you can finally feel happy, healthy, and balanced.

My first discovery was all about "choice". Remember that I assumed my only choice was to have a full-time career *or* stay home with my family in order to feel balanced? Yet I began to see and, most importantly, believe that I had the power of choice beyond that single option. I embraced the reality that my future was determined by the choices I made. This was a game changer.

Choice is an extraordinary gift, yet we often forget, dismiss, or even deny it. In times when we're angry or irrational, we're quick to blame others for our current situation. It's easier to do this versus assessing ourselves and discovering we're the creator of our own circumstances. Taking responsibility requires introspect and could lead to guilt or resentment over choices we've made in the past. It requires effort that we may not be willing to invest our energy into.

It's quicker and simpler to place blame on others.

But I needed to accept personal responsibility for my feelings, responses, and outcomes. I could no longer place blame and be angry with management and my husband, or be jealous of stay-at-home moms. My choices ushered me into the current life I was living. And if my choices brought me there, then it would be my choices which would rescue me and help me to alter my future course so that I could live the life I wanted to live.

During this time, I was well aware of the type of life I did *not* want to live, but the next step was to determine the type of life I *did* want to live. What did my ideal life look and feel like? What was my vision?

In college I would've described my future in such simple terms: married with children and a full-time career. But I would've stated this with conviction because 20-year-old-me believed I had it all figured out. However, that vision was vague, lacking specifics and details to clearly describe what I wanted. And that was the issue right there. I graduated college and began walking down the road of life, letting the path itself steer me in a particular direction rather than purposefully choosing a direction. What I needed was a crystal clear picture of the type of life I wanted to live in order to create the roadmap to get there. I couldn't change the course if I didn't know where the course should be taking me.

So at the age of 38, I sat with a pen and journal and designed my future. I'll admit, I thought it was too late, that I was already beyond an age to make significant changes that would adjust what lies ahead. But did you know that Vera Wang didn't design her first dress until she was 40? And Julia Child didn't write her first cookbook until she was 50? And even Laura Ingalls Wilder didn't publish the first *Little House* book until she was 65? It's never too late!

A fundamental activity that provided unforeseen insight into my vision was the practice of meditation. You may be thinking, "Meditation is for dreamers, the 'way out there' type of people!" That's what I thought when it was first suggested by my coach. But I strongly believed if I desired a change in my life, I had to take a chance and be willing to try new things. *True change only occurs if we're willing to change our mindset and change our practices.* So I accepted her recommendation and began meditating.

There are several benefits to meditating, but I want to share one specific component that resulted in the most significant and immediate impact on my life. Each day, and I truly mean each day, for nearly two weeks I began my morning by sitting quietly on a comfortable chair with my phone timer set for ten minutes. After a few deep breaths to relax my body and mind, I asked myself one specific question, "What truly makes me happy?" As simple as this question and exercise may appear, the outcomes were mind blowing!

Peeling away one layer at a time, I recalled experiences that were seemingly insignificant but left me feeling absolutely elated. Each time I asked myself this powerful question, I experienced "Aha!" moments, another time in my life to which I hadn't given much thought in the past. I cannot stress the impact of this activity enough. Scheduling periods every day where I could simply allow myself time in a quiet space to think about my happiness was life-changing.

Without consciously deciding to, I became outwardly exhilarated simply because I was thrilled to discover what made me happy. But even more significant, because I now had my "happiness remedy", I set out to incorporate happy moments into my daily life.

I must mention that, before my mindset change and as a high performing woman, I complained about being too busy (as most high performing women do.) But in reality I wore it like a damn badge of honor, competing with others to prove I was busier than them. Nevertheless, I knew I wasn't going to stop being busy because

I also thrived on busy-ness. But there's a difference between being busy with the *wrong* things and being busy with the *right* things. The right things are those that generate happiness and joy.

I'm not suggesting that I limited myself only to activities which were always pleasant. It's impossible to enjoy each and every task. Let's be real, grocery shopping isn't a thrilling outing, but being with my daughter is. So why not create an enjoyable grocery shopping experience with my daughter, making it a mommy-daughter adventure? The goal was to focus on doing *more* of what made me happy and incorporate joyful elements into mundane efforts and requirements as often as possible.

Soon I was weaving this happiness remedy into my career. At work I focused my time and energy on coaching, training, and supporting others. I didn't forego the other aspects of my job, but I *focused* on those where I found the most joy and where I subsequently demonstrated great skill. Focusing my energy in these areas brought about even more awareness of my strengths, both to me and to others. This awareness is what influenced the additional promotion, the one that allowed me to incorporate my passion in an even greater capacity, including an opportunity to speak about balance on the main stage at my company's national sales meeting. And as I learned this happiness remedy, I translated that into my purpose in life which is what led to developing my own business. Here I was, actually taking on more, yet I was happier than ever.

And as I became pleasant and playful, my family responded in the same way. It's remarkable how my attitude influenced our home's energy and atmosphere, even more so than my husband's did. And when the family was content, we were all much more productive. The kids excelled in school and managed their fears and stress in healthy ways. There was a sense of cooperation and willingness to help one another resulting in a healthy and loving home. Instead of my daughter asking me to slow down and not to hurry, I was the one asking if she'd sit on the couch and snuggle with me while talking or enjoying a movie.

Additional changes needed to occur if I were to sustain this new sense of joy. What's the best way to sustain anything in life? By becoming focused on health, and that meant the total package—physical, mental, spiritual and emotional.

Based upon my past experiences, I was convinced I had a solid grasp on my physical health because I exercised and ate a low-calorie diet. However, as the responsibilities and stress increased in life, my physical health deteriorated. And not just from an outward appearance of weight gain, because I knew physical health was more complex. My physical health was a function of adequate sleep, nutrition, supplementation and exercise. When I set this combination at the appropriate levels, my energy accelerated like nothing I'd ever experienced before.

I knew that I only had one body and that it must be cared for, which is why I made sure my children had a strict bedtime, ate healthy foods, and participated in limited screen time. But I wasn't tending to my own body in this manner. I was overly occupied with taking care of everyone else so I wasn't taking care of myself. But if I didn't take notice of myself, I wouldn't be able to continue looking after my family in the future. It was crucial to achieve at least seven hours of sleep each night, exercise daily, eat whole, unprocessed foods, and drink enough water throughout the day to remain hydrated. In order to achieve this, I began planning out my week each Sunday morning. I'd set a bedtime each night determined by the time I needed to rise the next morning. I scheduled my daily exercise around my work and personal agenda items. And I planned healthy family meals based upon my travel schedule and the kids' extracurricular activities. Surprisingly I found that this planning routine took less than 30 minutes but afforded me more time during the week than I ever thought was possible.

For my spiritual health, I continued the practice of meditation. It wasn't necessarily every morning; at times it was only a few days a week and could take place in the afternoon or just before bedtime. This timing plus duration and type of meditation fluctuated from week to week. On some occasions it was only five minutes of quiet time, and on other occasions it was a fifteen minute guided meditation. However, I recognized a drastic decline in my energy, mood, and knowledge when I didn't meditate for more than a week. In my opinion, there was no wrong way to meditate; it was all about taking a few minutes each day to center myself.

With the other two areas of my health—mental and emotional—I embraced reading and listening. Once I had children, I had neglected to read (with the exception of reading aloud bedtime stories which, other than a handful of Dr. Seuss books, rarely stimulated my mental and emotional health). Quickly I found that motivating books, audiobooks, and podcasts filled my digital library. Listening to positive messages and new ways of thinking became part of my morning commute. Talk about inspiration to start the day! And if I had a particularly exhausting day, I'd plug in again on the evening commute home. I couldn't control every event during my day, such as an angry clients or unexpected traffic, but I could control how I responded to it. The decision to engage in a positive activity in lieu of responding with a negative attitude was an imperative choice to ensure that I remained happy into the evening so my family could be too.

Feeling happy and invigorated once again in my life, I was excited to embark upon new endeavors. But my promotion and starting my own business, while intriguing and aligning with my passions, would require more of the little time I had to begin with. I simply couldn't do it all. Because I believed I was strong and independent, it was difficult for me to relinquish control. I wanted to be Superwoman and proudly display that cape around my shoulders. I wouldn't admit that I needed help with everyday tasks for fear of being viewed as inadequate or because I didn't believe anyone else could do it as well as I. I needed to get over myself and let things go.

With that, my voice became stronger in asking for what I wanted. In order to have more time with my family, I requested to work from home on Fridays. I no longer waited for my husband to notice I was struggling around the house. Instead, I asked for help. Trust me, it's not that my husband didn't *want* to help; he simply did not see that I needed it. And when my husband didn't return freshly laundered items to the linen closet the "right way," I took a deep breath and realized nobody ever looks in my linen closet. Who cares if it's a mess? I became creative with our finances in order to hire a cleaning service that would also wash the bedding and towels. This eliminated a few loads of laundry that once preoccupied my weekends and now I could instead invest my time with the family.

I also began to prioritize what was most important in my life. The executive women's network I belonged to for nearly five years had offered several good learning and leadership opportunities. But with my limited time and aspiration to fulfill more of my purpose, I couldn't settle for *good*. So I left this network, prioritized my passions, and went out to explore *great* opportunities.

Prioritizing and delegating did not make me appear inadequate to others as I suspected it would. In fact, during the initial stages of my transformation, I confided in a trustworthy colleague.

One morning I stood in her office doorway, and I can't explain why I felt compelled to share, but my story unfolded. After rambling on for several minutes about my past tumultuous feelings, lack of sleep, anger with others, and previous thoughts that I couldn't continue living that way, I finally paused. She sat silently, staring at me with an unreadable expression. I couldn't decipher if she was going to bolt out of her office to tell everyone I had thought about quitting or if she couldn't believe how incompetent I sounded. This was one fear I harbored for years. To my astonishment, neither was true.

"I'm sorry if I'm staring at you and not saying anything, but it's as if I'm looking in a mirror. I feel the exact same way!"

Are you kidding me? Someone else in my office felt just like me! I couldn't believe it!

The more I began talking with other women, those I historically assumed had it all together, the more I uncovered that we felt the same way, and experienced the same challenges. We had a polished, positive, and peaceful exterior, but we were all struggling on the inside. I wasn't alone!

This act of sharing carried into other aspects of my life, too. Once I determined my passion and purpose, I slowly expressed it to those around me. You wouldn't believe what showed up once I did. Past colleagues and friends I hadn't seen for years suddenly appeared in my daily environment. Connections that I never knew existed were there and ready to help. Perhaps these people were in front of me all along but I didn't notice them. Once I determined what I really wanted, the rest started to fall into place.

Some of this may appear so simplistic that you're wondering if there's any merit to it. Believe me, I understand. And I've been fortunate enough to share several other techniques through my coaching, seminars, and speaking engagements. But I must emphasize the power of these activities because they were absolutely the first steps in changing my life, and they can be for you too.

- Realize you do have a choice.
- Accept personal responsibility.

- Redesign your future … it isn't too late!
- Uncover what truly makes you happy.
- Maintain a healthy lifestyle—physically, mentally, spiritually and emotionally.
- Let go and delegate more in order to focus on what makes you happy.
- Share your story—you never know what is waiting for you.

Before I wrap up, I must bring you back to the belief I held that I was being selfish. That belief dominated my subconscious for an unreasonable amount of time. And that belief was finally shattered!

I now know that it's acceptable to want more and having a desire for more is certainly not selfish. In fact, what *would* have been selfish of me would have been to discover my strengths and life's purpose but withhold them from others, keeping my findings all to myself and holding them in as guarded secrets.

This is why I'm on a mission. My mission is to share with other women what I've already learned. To provide women like you with the key to release the bricks of responsibility that I painstakingly searched for. This key can keep you from sinking to the bottom of the ocean I sank into and instead help you to swim gloriously toward the light of hope much quicker than I did. I'm on a mission to support you and other women to lead happy, healthy, and balanced lives.

Will you join me in this mission by not only sharing my story, but more importantly, sharing your story? I'd love to hear from you and until then, remember that you don't have to continue living this way, you do have a choice and change is possible for a new you!

ABOUT COLLEEN HAUK

Colleen Hauk is like many women of today—executive, wife, and mom. Founder of Balance Point Coaching, Colleen is a Certified Professional Success Coach, speaker, trainer, and author. She is following her passion to inspire and support high performing women to lead happy, healthy, and balanced lives.

With over 10 years of corporate sales experience, Colleen has worked with a variety of international organizations. She is currently a Group Director at Catalina, a personalized digital media company. Prior to her corporate career, she was an educator and master teacher. Colleen obtained her CPSC certification from Success Coach Institute. She's completed "High Performance Academy" and "Experts Academy" with Brendon Burchard, an online trainer who is hailed as one of the most successful by Oprah.com. In addition, Colleen completed "Breakthrough to Success" with Jack Canfield, America's #1 Success Coach and co-creator of the *Chicken Soup for the Soul Series*™.

She and her incredibly supportive and loving husband, Matt, live in Southern California, where they were both were born and raised. They enjoy life with their beautiful children, Jordan, Ethan, and Reese, camping in the desert, hosting fun-filled evenings with friends, and spending quality time with their nearby extended family.

Colleen's clients describe her as inspirational, passionate, dedicated, and enthusiastic about empowering women to discover how to live happy, healthy, and balanced lives.

Do you have a story to share or a question to ask? Colleen would love to hear from you! She can be contacted at colleen@colleenhauk. com or visit her website www.colleenhauk.com.

LEADING AS A LIFESTYLE

Shelly Hodges

You are a leader. Whether you know it or not you are a leader today, at this moment. Somewhere in your life with friends, family, co-workers, clients, spouses, or children—you are a leader. Regardless of whether you are an entrepreneur, stay at home mom/dad, executive, wife, employee, boss, or any other term you identify. You influence someone with your words and actions right now. You inspire them. You help them create ideas and dream. You reach out to someone else in their time of need. You help someone else become a better person. You may not recognize these small moments as leadership—but they are. Each time you take a positive action to help someone, you are leading. Leadership isn't always seen in the big grand acts, but, rather, the hundreds of smaller ones. It is seen in the everyday actions we take for granted that are acts of leadership. It is seen in moments that we help others see something possible beyond what exists today.

The definition of traditional leadership is the ability to lead other people. Typically, what comes to mind when thinking of a leader is someone in high authority, perhaps a CEO, government official, or head of an organization or one of history's great leaders—Lincoln,

Martin Luther King, or Gandhi. These are all great examples of leaders. However, in each case, leadership seems out of reach. Leadership is meant for someone that has achieved what society deems great success. It makes leadership appear to apply only to the few and not the many.

I define leadership differently. I see leadership present in every person. It occurs in everyday places when one person connects with another. We have all influenced another person in a positive way. We have helped someone have a better day. We are powerful in ways we do not even realize because we are helping even one other person. These moments reflect leadership. Leadership happens on a daily basis since our life is based on connecting with people.

Why is it hard to recognize leadership? We have been taught through media and conditioning that leadership is a big grand event or a high ranking title. We think we are not worthy since we have not yet created massive change. We have to change our mindsets to think of leadership as something each and every person is capable of. Great leaders recognize the good they can share with the world no matter what they do for a living. Leadership is not exclusive but inclusive to all. Everyone can be, and is, a leader. YOU are a leader. As you go through your daily life impacting others, you are showing leadership. Take a moment to think about this. Where in your life are you leading? Who are you already helping? Where in your life are you inspiring someone else, even one person, to be better? Everyone has at least one person they are showing leadership to through their actions.

If everyone is already a leader, the question then becomes what kind of leader do you want to be? I already know you are someone who wants to be more in life. You want to be the type of leader others aspire to be like. You don't want to be just any leader, but one that uses your gifts and skills to make the world a better place.

You want to be a leader that speaks truths from the heart to create greater abundance and success for those around you. A leader that leads from a place of higher purpose. The type of leader that leaves the world better. A leader that has great success but also feels fulfilled at the end of the day and can inspire others. You want to influence more than just a few people because what you have to say and share matters.

The first step is recognizing that you are a leader and then taking actions to step into leadership as a lifestyle. It is showing intention about the type of leader you want to be with others. It is sharing a message that creates positive change in someone else's life. My mission is to empower others to claim their leadership abilities and create abundant success in their lives. I help those who are looking to create leadership as a lifestyle to meet their professional goals. I do this through sharing proven tools to accelerate leadership and get promoted. I know how to do this because I have been there. In my life, I have had both the big titles and I have learned how to create leadership daily in my life. You too can expand your leadership through implementing a proven method of mindset, identifying how you can be of service, creating clear communication, prioritizing, and taking action. You have permission to be a leader and tap into what you already know. I will show you the steps to make it happen.

What I have come to know is that it does not matter your title, position, or place in life. If you have a message and vision to share, you are a leader. If you have the ability to inspire, to teach, to guide, and to lead others to a better place, you are a leader. Making leadership a part of your daily lifestyle will allow you to develop additional skills accelerating the path towards your goals. Other people will see the results when you have achieved great things through leadership—the titles, the grand events—but what they don't see are the smaller acts of daily leadership that lead up to the big impacts.

MY STORY

I started my professional life sitting in a small gray cube with a narrow doorway. A phone and computer sat in front of me with handwritten yellow sticky note reminders covering the walls. I dialed all day, looking at the walls around me dreaming of a bigger plan. I told my manager the first week I started that I was going to be a manager someday. I stayed focused during the day exceeding goals and continued my education at night taking courses towards a master's degree. When a new position posted, I was encouraged to apply. I stood in front of a mirror, looking myself straight in the eye, and practiced my interview and put on my best thrift store suit. It all paid off. In less than two years, my declaration became reality. I became a manager! I was thrilled to have met my goal, but it didn't stop there.

My leadership path continued to accelerate with a new role and title every couple of years—Senior Manager, Associate Director, and Director. My big break came when I was suddenly called to the president's office. My heart raced, my hands were sweaty on the wheel, and my head spun with theories as I drove to his office. I was asked to start up a new division with only the barest of information to go on. Several days later, I stood in front of a new team, asking them to take a leap of faith, knowing the general direction we were going but without a full plan of how to get there. I grew this new team from 50 to 300 in under a year, and together we created a plan for success. Through this opportunity, I became the youngest Vice President in my role, not even 30 years old yet. From there, I was promoted even further to lead another division of over 600 people. In time, I moved into strategy development and operations to create changes that would impact thousands of employees and customers.

I have been in professional leadership now for over a decade. I know what it is like to have the top floor office looking out over the city. I have invested in dozens of leadership courses and received the coveted MBA degree. I have spoken in front of thousands of people. I have been very successful, by most standards, professionally.

None of it made me a leader.

Positions and titles do not encompass my leadership path. My leadership story starts much earlier and takes place mostly out of the workplace. I had actually been preparing for years to be ready for that meeting in the president's office. My story starts back in 1979. That was the year my first brother was born. Suddenly, I was not alone in the world of little people. I had someone who would be watching me. By the time I was 11, I was the oldest of 5—three boys and two girls—living in a little three-bedroom house. Growing up in a large family, and being the oldest, you are naturally expected to set the example. We didn't have much but what we did have was family. My parents worked hard to give love and attention but with so many children it was inevitable that I would be asked to take on more responsibility. Each day, my mother, who stayed home, would get us ready to go out into the world, making us peanut butter and jelly sandwiches in brown paper bags while I helped watch my siblings. Nights were spent around our wooden dinner table working on homework. I would lean over to help a sibling with a complicated math problem or learn a new word. At that moment I did not think about it as leading, but looking back, that is what it was. At that moment, I had four younger siblings looking up to me.

As I got older, there were more situations where leadership was developing, although I didn't know it at the time. In high school I joined the marching band. We were out at six in the morning on the dew-covered grass field, practicing as a team, with more practice starting as soon as the end-of-school-day bell rang. I led other members through our routines, starting over dozens of times to get the show perfect. During the summers, my forward-thinking grandparents gifted me with the opportunity to attend a sleep-away summer camp to be a junior counselor. I had the experience of living in a wood cabin with 12 campers leading them through activities. I taught friendship bracelets making, sang silly songs, and hiked through the pine trees daily. Tight bonds were created while sharing stories around the light of a campfire. Leadership development continued in my early adult life through volunteering at several organizations. I raised money for cystic fibrosis, coached at a woman's center, and interned for a food bank. Leadership happened naturally when I gave myself to others through causes I believed in.

Although I started to have some experience in leading, I still made many mistakes along the way as I transitioned into traditional leadership roles in the workplace. In my first role leading a team, I had a 360 review completed. My team of 10 filled out a survey to give feedback around how I showed up each day to work. I was young and certain I was doing a great job. The review came back, and although there were some great items, it was apparent I was making mistakes. When someone spoke to me at my desk, I would continue on my computer ignoring them. A simple act of looking them in the eyes instead of continuing to look at my computer when they came to speak to me sent them a message that what they were saying was not important. I was not showing leadership since my focus was not on service to my team. From my mistakes, I learned new ways to lead and connect with others and I changed how I behaved. Each mistake was a stair step into learning how to have a tremendous impact leading.

I wasn't always confident about my ability to lead, either. In my early 30's, I began to get nervous about being a leader in all areas of my life. I began to think about starting a family of my own. I thought I could have a family or a successful professional life, but

I didn't think I had the ability to have both. I heard about a great opportunity, which I knew I was qualified for, but hesitated to take the lead. It would mean overseeing a team twice as large as I had previously—doubling from 300 to 600 team members. Late one night I sat in a hotel room on the edge of my bed debating for hours if I should or should not apply for the position. If I took this role, would that keep me from starting the family I wanted to have? Could I do both at the same time? Would I be able to lead this team? I took a leap of faith the next morning and went straight to the executive leader to indicate I wanted the role. He had no idea I was interested. By taking action, I ended up being selected for the position which led to even greater professional success over time. Several years later, I also started a family and now have a precious little boy. I was able to fulfill both of my goals! I learned I could be a leader and be successful in all areas of my life.

My leadership experiences were not always grand, paid, or in a traditional workplace. I made many mistakes and it took time to build up my confidence. The key for me was continuing to practice leadership through all areas of my life. The more I demonstrated leadership and made it a part of my entire life, the better I became and the greater success I had. The first time I had a traditional leadership title I was 26, but by that point I already had years of experience without a title.

WHAT CAN LEADERSHIP DO FOR YOU?

I know you are someone that wants to make a massive impact. I want you to have crazy, unbelievable, amazing success. I want you to have incredible relationships, a raise or promotion you are dreaming of, and grow your business if you are an entrepreneur. I also know that being a leader is a critical step towards making a bigger impact on the world and reaching your goals. It is the momentum that helps you to share your story and changes the course of history. This starts with one person at a time. Every great leader started with talking to one other person. Change doesn't start with large crowds. It starts with someone being brave enough to think differently and influence another person. What you have to say matters and through leadership you can share your gift with the world.

You just have to start with one other person. When you wake up in the morning to hug your children, you are leading the conversation about what the day will bring. As you talk to a spouse, you can lead the conversation with love or respect. You can call a friend and lead with listening and caring. If you walk into a meeting, you have the ability to lead it to an outcome that creates positive change. When connecting with a client, you can lead from a place of service to a service or product that changes their life. If you want to create greater abundance, you need to recognize you are the tool to get yourself there. By acting upon your leadership potential, anyone can expand their reach.

Leadership is not something for the few, but the many. It is not something in an ivory tower. It is present in your everyday life and can be the change that gets you to your goal. Like anything else in life, you get better at leadership with practice. Practice must occur in all areas of your life to be the most effective. It is present from the moment you wake up to the time you go to sleep. I know this because I live a lifestyle of leadership and continue to learn new ways to lead. Over time, I have learned ways to help others learn the leadership process so that I can teach others to create a leadership lifestyle to meet their goals.

Throughout the next few sections, I challenge you to take action by working through the following five steps to add more leadership to your life.

STEP 1: LEADERSHIP MINDSET

Leadership begins, first, with the mindset. Our minds are capable of amazing things if we fill them with positive, clear plans of who we want to be. Make the decision here and now that you are a leader. Just the act of thinking about the word "leader" will program your brain. I am a believer that the things you tell yourself on a daily basis create your reality. You must be a leader in all areas of your life and with all of those that are connected to you. Leadership doesn't just happen without clear intention.

An effective leader comes from a place of optimism so that they can create energy around what they want to accomplish. Programming your mind with positive leadership thoughts creates optimism. Optimism helps a leader to show others a positive and attainable view of the future. The greatest leaders see challenges as opportunities since they look at every issue through a lens of optimism. Optimistic leaders believe those around them come from a place of good intent and what they communicate will create positive change.

There are several ways you can add to your daily dialogue to program your mind to believe you are a leader and create optimism. You can condition your mind to think of leadership as you go about your daily life. Thinking of yourself as a leader is a choice. A choice that you get to make daily.

First, create an affirmation that you review and recite throughout the day. Affirmations are a way to program your mind to receive what you want. You can place the affirmation on a 3x5 card to keep on your bed, on a device like a phone you review daily, or even on your bathroom mirror to look at as you get ready.

Some examples of affirmations around leadership:
• I am so grateful to impact others through leadership.

- I am making a big difference in the world through my leadership.
- My leadership creates positive change to those I love around me.

Now take a few moments to define what type of leader you want to be and where. Answer these questions:
- Where do you want to be a leader in your life?
- Who do you want to impact?
- What message do you want to use?
- What is the best case scenario if you step up to be a leader?
- Who supports your leadership?

Lastly, create your leadership vision. This is a compelling statement of how you want to be seen as a leader. Ask yourself, what type of leader you want to be. I recommend that you pick three qualities that define the type of leader you would like to be and make them into a sentence. Finish the sentence, "I am a leader who ..." Here are some words that could be associated with leadership to get you started: inspiring, honest, integrity, committed, passionate, positive, approachable, communicator, sincerity, empowers others, creative, visionary, decisive, confident, and adaptable.

Keep your leadership affirmations, declaration of the type of leader you want to be, and your leadership vision written in a place you can review daily.

STEP 2: LEADERSHIP SERVICE

The biggest mistakes that I have made as a leader were when my choices were all about me. When my message or actions were not from a place of service to others. If you want to lead others, you are asking them to think differently or change how they perceive a situation. Leadership includes thinking of how you can serve others before yourself in a given moment. Coming from a place of service develops trust. People will follow your message if it comes from a place of positive intent and service. You can do this by sharing the why, taking a moment to think of how the other person is receiving the message, and how it will serve the higher good.

For example, you want to lead your spouse towards something that you believe would benefit your whole family. For example, to have dinner together. One method would be to tell them what you want to be done, in this case to have dinner as a family. This could work, but is more likely to be effective if you share from a place of service to the other individual. You must think first why it would be important to the other person rather than why it is important to you. A more effective way to would be to share what a difference they make in your life and the kids when they join in the family dinner, ask what would make it more enjoyable to be there, and that family dinners serves the greater good helping kids have consistent rituals in their lives.

In a professional setting, when you can tell an employee or peers to do a task, it may get done due to your position. However, it doesn't inspire or give them optimism unless you share from a place of service. Share why it is important. Ask them for feedback on how to complete the task, and how it will make an impact with peers or customers. The task suddenly has more meaning. Sharing the impact it will make helps to lead others with vision and inspiration.

This same concept applies to customers. If you want to lead a potential customer or client to a product or service that will benefit them, you must share from a place with their best interest in mind. It should be about them and not the sale. You create a partnership by providing another person with something that could greatly benefit them and create connection on why it will serve a higher purpose. As a result, it is likely that you will create a loyal, repeat customer.

The time is now to think about where you can be of service. You get back more than you give when you are a leader with an intention of service.

I want you to look at all areas of your life for the ways you can be a leader and serve others every day.

• A great starting place is to think of how you can be a leader in your family. A hug, a small token of appreciation, or a card are all great ways to start.

• In your home, who needs a listening ear at this time?

• What does your family need at this moment to create joy?

• What can you give back today when you come home?

Walk through a typical day with me to see where and with whom you can be a leader. Answer these questions:

• When you wake up who do you see?

• Who sits next to you eating breakfast or lunch?

• Where do you go after you eat?

• What activities do you have in the morning, in the afternoon?

• Who do you eat dinner with at night?

• What do you do in the evening?

By this point, you should see several places where you can be a leader in your life.

Anytime you are interacting with another person the moment can be a leadership turning point.

For areas outside of the home, think about professional and personal organizations that call to your heart.

Write down where you feel you serve and lead outside of the home.

• Volunteer with a local non-profit

• Church groups

- Local community organizations
- Club chapters for a cause you are passionate about

In your professional life, regardless of how you define where you work, think through ways you can be a leader:
- Are there projects that need additional leadership?
- Is there another employee who could learn from your experience?
- Is there a customer or client that would benefit from learning something new from you?

STEP 3: LEADERSHIP COMMUNICATION

You have now created a leadership mindset and clarified how you can be of service. How will you now give the message that you want to be received? Great leaders create simple, memorable messages. In this age of quick responses on cell phones, relentless emails, and constant commitments, there is limited time to get communication across. Most people receive over 100 emails and day and some hundreds of emails. It is estimated that you have 3-5 seconds to get something across online and 3-5 minutes if you are communicating face-to-face. If you are not clear and intentional about your leadership message, it will be missed.

To be effective, you must be clear with what you want to communicate. Your communication is only as good as the message that was received by the other person. The old saying "keep it simple" applies here. How do you keep your message simple? I use the "bumper sticker" method. If you cannot put your main idea on a bumper sticker, it is likely too complicated.

The first step is to see what you are currently communicating and listen to feedback. Ask those closest to you, such as your children, spouse, siblings, and friends what they believe is most important to you. Repeat this same activity with several people you trust in your professional life. Write down the feedback—it is a gift!

Once you know what you have been communicating, you can adjust it to align with what you want your new leadership message to be. Think about something you want to communicate now.

- What is your leadership "bumper sticker" around this topic?
- What is the number one point you want others to walk away knowing?
- What are the messages that you want them to understand and feel?
- Why is it important for them to listen to you? Think about how you can add the emotional connection with a story.
- What is the big idea behind the idea—not the "what", but the "why" behind the idea. People want to feel a part of something bigger than themselves. Give them the reason why your messages create an emotional connection to a higher purpose.

When you are about to connect with someone, taking even a moment to think through how you want to communicate and set the intention can make a difference in how your message is received. The bigger the idea or amount of people you are hoping to impact, the more important it is to prepare.

STEP 4: LEADERSHIP PRIORITIZATION

Every person has the same 24 hours in a day but some seem to be superhuman getting things done in that time. What makes those people different is how they use the time they have. The most successful leaders have a method of determining what is most important in life and focusing on what gets them the greatest results. The common phrase, "to have it all," doesn't work for me. What most people are asking for is to have the time to do what they feel is most important in life that creates the abundant success they seek. To do that, they need to find, and eliminate, what is not important.

First, let's look at what you may already do:
- Do you have a system for what you need to do today? A "to do" list?
- If you have a list, is it prioritized?
- Do you know the top five areas you want to impact in the next day?

If you don't have any of these things, you are not alone. It is common for one to go through the day without having methods to ensure that the most important goal oriented items are completed. Time gets away from us when we do not pay close attention to how we spend our time. If you want to create leadership as a lifestyle you need to determine how to prioritize where you can lead to have the biggest impact.

If you don't have a method yet, this is your time to create a way to prioritize. If you already have one, this is a call to action to use your method so that you can make sure your priorities align with what you want to accomplish. To be most effective, your system needs to follow several steps:

1. Create a list of everything you believe you need to do.
2. Review the list, placing a high, medium, or low priority next to each.
   a. "High" items are those that have a big impact. Items in this category can include people you want to spend time with or projects that create positive change in other's lives.
   b. "Medium" items are those that demand your time but may

not directly or quickly make an impact. These items need to get done, but if they don't it will not be critical to your success.

c. "Low" items are those that truly do not make a big impact. If they didn't get done today or in the next week it would not impact how you want to lead your life. Be brutal in this area. If you hesitate when deciding whether something is medium or low, it is probably low. These items are preventing you from growing.

3. Re-create your list to choose only those top five areas that will make the most impact.

4. Update your list each night. You will start the next day focused on what is most important to you. Do this activity each evening and see how your life becomes prioritized! You will find the time to use your leadership skills to create abundant success in your life.

To take this to the next level, track what you do for three days to really see where your time goes. How often are you spending time on your high priority items? Write down every activity you did and how long you did it. I guarantee that this will be hard to do at times. You will find places where you are not staying on high priorities which is normal. One must learn to make the shift to have more time in areas that make the greatest impact. Use this information to adjust your time to focus on the areas of your life that propel you towards your goals. By doing this, you will be able to find the time in your day to be a leader.

STEP 5: LEADERSHIP ACTION

You have created a mindset, found where you can be of service, created your message, and prioritized areas to make an impact as a leader. These steps are only part of the planning process and do not create results until you step into action. The best leaders spend time planning but do not stay in the development stage. They step up and get started implementing. Doing is always better than thinking. Even if you make mistakes along the way you can correct your course and take new actions. The actions in our everyday lives turn us into great leaders. Adding leadership moments into each one of your days in every connection you make creates the energy and momentum over time to reach your goals. The more you do it, the better you will get at it. Just get started!

Look back at your notes at the areas where you want to be of service. I recommend choosing no more than three areas, preferably less. It is ok to start where you are and create small wins!

For each area of service:
• Write down three ways you can accomplish each one.
• Define when you will do each.
• Add these items to your prioritized list. Set up an alarm on your calendar or phone to remind you of this leadership goal.

CREATING LEADERSHIP AS A LIFESTYLE

You now have a powerful toolkit of ways you can create more leadership within your life. Know that you always have the power within you to change someone else's life at this very moment. Leadership is like a muscle. You already have it within you but it can become stronger the more often you use it. You have full permission to live big and step into your leadership power now. Leadership can be expressed when you lend others a listening ear, place a phone call that was unexpected, and share an idea from a place of positive intent. You can be a leader with family, someone you just met, a customer, or co-worker. You are already a leader and can start right at this moment to expand your greatness. You can help those you touch, personally or professionally, achieve things they never thought possible. You can be the change in the world, one connection at a time.

ABOUT SHELLY HODGES

Shelly Hodges has a reputation as an inspirational leader impacting thousands through her charismatic style. She is known for creating actionable solutions leading to exceptional performance results. With over 15 years of professional experience leading staff up to 600, she knows what it takes to develop leadership skills. She serves people who want to learn how to up level their career through leadership. She has attended dozens of leadership development courses including at the prestigious Center for Creative Leadership. She received a Bachelor's degree with an emphasis in non-profit leadership, a Masters of Business Administration, and is a certified life coach. She resides in Phoenix with her husband Brian and young son. In her free time she is an avid hiker, loves to travel to beach locations, and volunteers. She can be reached at shellyhodges.com to learn more about her programs.

REROUTED: THRIVING IN SPITE OF LIFE'S CHALLENGES

Teresa Huggins

As I looked in the mirror, I noticed the odd rash appearing again on the right side of my face. I was curious what caused it: too many strawberries, spinach, or fresh pineapple? It had been there a few times over a month, and I put aside its significance since it would go away without much thought and a dose of Benadryl. I was eating foods prepared at restaurants, sleeping on hotel beds that might use different detergent, and joyfully busy facilitating inspirational programs. Yet, this cold day in January, something stirred inside of me that slowed me down long enough to notice. Later in the day during a yoga class, I quietly asked my body, "What is the gift in this inconvenient rash?" I heard, "Something wants to leave your body!" I thought the message was reminding me of my desires to create my day in a more balanced way. My goal was to focus on what served me in addition to what served others. This was my default pattern and often I changed my schedule to meet the needs of others. The message lingered. A few days later, I really noticed … something. It looked like a shooter marble underneath my skin in another part of my body. This prompted a phone call for an annual doctor's appointment. That appointment was followed by another,

169

with a radiologist, who confirmed that something was "worrisome".

At this moment, I realized that it was a wonderful opportunity to empower myself to navigate my medical journey the way I navigate life. I haven't always been an optimistic, relaxed person, yet by learning strategies through my personal and professional work, I decided I would approach this journey in a way that most may not. When I heard the word "worrisome" and saw the radiologist's face, I felt his uncertainty and lack of hope. In this moment, I realized that many who navigate a diagnosis are greatly influenced by the responses of the "experts". Driving home, I couldn't help thinking, "You have got to be kidding me, I don't have time for this!" Two days later, I was at a surgeon's office, hearing news that certainly didn't apply to me! "What do you mean I might have something going on in my body? I feel great! I have no pain!"

A nurse described a procedure called a "biopsy" and a wave of shock spread throughout my body. I felt my mind disconnect from the words being spoken and my body wanted to run out of the room at the thought of a needle penetrating my body. In this moment, I made a choice! Take a deep breath, connect with your spiritual gifts, find joy in the journey, and be present. There was a dance between what my spirit knew was helpful and my racing heart and uncertain mind. An avalanche of positive self-talk flooded my mind. I took a deep breath and declared internally, "I am on a journey of WELLNESS." I would learn how to navigate with faith and find joyful moments along the way. I would empower others who received unexpected news and I would create a movement to transform the traditional conversation of disease! A flood of positive affirmations and feelings of greater purpose swelled within me while a compassionate woman explained what would happen next. Though, feeling the increase in my heart rate, "checking out" would have been a more pleasant idea to me.

As the doctor described the biopsy procedure, the words "pain", "discomfort", and "swelling" didn't feel reassuring, so I spoke aloud what I was saying silently to myself. "I will trust you and close my eyes and imagine going to a beach." We chuckled, yet I was serious when I said I was going to a beach! My mind imagined the pain, yet as a way to diminish what I was experiencing, visualization and long steady breaths transformed the pain into sensation, allowing my heartbeat to slow down and my thoughts to calm.

As a needle was inserted into my body and cells were removed to see if there was malignancy, warm sunshine graced my body and the feeling of sand beneath my feet created peace within. "We're done!" And with those words, my life was rerouted! Even if the biopsy reflected benign cells, "what ifs" entered my mind. How did this happen to me so quickly? Where did it come from? What is out of balance? This was too much to take in, too fast. "We will know the results in a few days …"

I kept myself busy. I acted like a visit to the doctor did not just happen and focused on the outcome I desired. I kept saying to myself, "Plan your life as if the test results will be benign. Keep busy, clean your bookshelves, walk the dog." For the next few days, I kept it to myself. My husband was away on a trip and I didn't want him to worry until I knew something more. I kept the news to myself as I wasn't ready to handle how others would respond. I made a conscious choice to believe all was well, yet doubt percolated from within. Questions entered my mind. What do you want to achieve this year? What do you want to create? Which book will you finish first? All the incomplete projects became a priority with a sense of urgency.

The phone call came. I took a deep breath and answered the phone. The nurse said, "You have CANCER and you need surgery." The surgeon would review the test results and probably recommend a lumpectomy and six weeks of radiation. I went into professional mode as if I was interviewing a future client and planning a seminar for their company. Then, I asked the hard questions. "How does radiation work? Do you go once a week?" "No it is five days a week for six weeks!" I was shocked. I instantly thought of my travel schedule, my planned events, my busy-ness.

Pause. Life stops for a moment. There is a detour. You have been rerouted, yet your inner GPS knows the way!

In the stillness of my mind, I sorted through the dance of doubt and faith, uncertainty and trust, shock and peace. I stayed calm through most of the journey, leaning on my faith and my spiritual belief that this news would enhance my life, even though I had no idea how!

In the months that followed, throughout doctor's appointments, genetic screenings, blood work, surgery, recovery, a second opinion in another state, and treatment plans, I made a choice to honor my feelings and understand the options while leaning on my beliefs and surrounding myself with people who would support my journey, my way. I created an "Empowered Wellness Team" and shared what support looked like for me. This included physical, psychological, energetic, and spiritual healing.

Many people offered their own form of support, and with gratitude I received the ideas while honoring my own choices. My husband listened to me, my son who was away at college called me more often to check in with me, and my daughter sent me a teddy bear and journal to comfort me and encouraged me to get a second opinion in Boston where she lived. Friends walked with me, listened to me, and laughed with me. They shared their cooking talents, prepackaged smoothie ingredients to make healthy choices easy, and sent inspirational cards and notes. I was touched by the unique ways people reached out, but I also honored people who were uncomfortable acknowledging the diagnosis I was given.

I made conscious choices to redesign my life. I imagined that every cell in my body was completely healed, and I focused on language that affirmed wellness, embraced dreams, and lived with the fullest expression of myself. It was important for me to align with people who could hold the intention of my complete healing. I wanted people to believe I could heal and I wanted them to think of me as one who was on a wellness path, not a sickness journey. With each comment others made, I understood they were reflecting their own experience with disease, and I made choices based on this understanding. Sometimes that meant spending time with myself quietly or speaking up when a suggestion didn't serve me, thus transforming language of self, family, friends, and the medical community. I began transforming my relationship with the medical field. Instead of being frustrated by some people's negativity, I chose to bless them, understanding that they were coming from their perspective. Hearing how nerve wracking it would be for the next five years, until a doctor declared me cancer free, I chose to declare "my body is completely healed" from the moment I heard the diagnosis. I imagined my cells being filled with healing light and love daily.

I was direct with my questions to the medical professionals and held gratitude in my heart for their expertise. "I understand that there were cells that wanted to leave my body and you removed them with great care, and I believe I am completely healed," I said. "Now radiation will allow my body to transform any cells that might have been released during the surgery, yet there is no evidence I have any cancer in my body, is that correct?"

The nurse practitioner replied, "You know, you need to take this seriously. People die from this disease." With confidence, I said, "I am not afraid to die. I am grateful for every day and celebrate moments within the day that add to my joys. I am choosing a wellness journey and will create images that help me thrive in this journey." Later, the doctor entered and I was still unsettled with having to do six weeks of treatment (which later turned into eight weeks.) She said, "You just need to put your life on hold!" But then she apologized and said, "I am not sure what I would do if someone told me that!" Inside I pondered, thinking I was on a mission to transform healing practices.

Medical professionals have great power and I am grateful for their knowledge, dedication, and expertise, yet how many people walk away from an appointment with words of fear, uncertainty, and doubt surrounding the cells craving for healing? Could I be part of the solution to add healing language to the medical profession? Could I use my skills to empower others as I empower myself? I began paying closer attention to the lessons and the insights that were emerging.

How many times in life do we plan ahead, only to have our life's vision interrupted, delayed, detoured, or modified? Every day, we move through life with our agendas and to-do list as if life should follow our intentions, regardless of what shows up. Yet we know there will be unpredictable moments in everyone's life.

What do you do when you receive unexpected news? Do you invite the fullest range of emotions to dance within your spirit? Do you honor the "uncomfortable" within the safety that each day is a new day to connect with your resilient spirit? This diagnosis stopped me in my path. When handling other's responses to my disease, I could feel the energy of fear, doubt, and judgment. I could feel the desire to help me cope without knowledge of what to do. I could also feel the love, compassion, and dedication others had for me. It was time to pause, go inside, connect with myself and renew my spirit.

Journaling helped. Meditations calmed. Visiting friends and families brought normalcy. Being in the present moment began to become my new normal. My relationship with the disease became a curiosity. My life was out of balance and this diagnosis was an opportunity to redesign my life. "This is temporary" was a mantra spoken quietly throughout the day. The ability to live my life as I had in the past was temporarily taken away from me. I had to reconcile with the realization that I might not have the energy to do multi-day trainings, or I might need to take a nap midday. Since I didn't know, I created a story that strengthened me, and when I was frustrated I paused and created an understanding of what I was noticing.

What is your relationship to the word cancer? For many, the word cancer conjures fear. When helping others on their wellness journey, I had wondered why someone would receive a diagnosis that appeared to be out of sync with their life habits. I supported family and friends, offered strategies and guided imageries, gave loving support, and presented a compassionate presence while focusing on their healing. Yet could I embrace my beliefs in my own journey of uncertainty?

Aware that our language influences our sense of well-being, I began to transform any messages that felt uncomfortable. I perceived, "You will be a survivor," as a message filled with fear, suggesting I wouldn't survive or I needed to think I could. Of course, I would survive. I had cells in my body that didn't belong there, a talented surgeon removed them, and now there was a treatment plan that, while I wasn't certain I needed, I created a space within my body to receive healing and welcomed any cells that did not serve my highest good to be transformed. My body wanted to heal peacefully, joyfully, and fully. My spirit soared with images of lightness, freedom, new choices, and love.

I felt lingering frustration based on the fact that there were so many things on the internet and in books about healing practices, but there wasn't a medical industry protocol that acknowledged the power of one's ability to create healing. It was important to be aligned with my belief system: positive thoughts, healthy nutrition, music with uplifting lyrics, daily exercise, life choices, and encouraging support systems. What if we acknowledged that healing is MORE than a surgery, a pill, a chemical, or radiation? What if we strengthened the healer within and added that to other medical protocols? What if we expanded our definition of healing?

I had a choice: The path of Transformative Healing.

PUT YOUR LIFE ON HOLD

As I drove home from the surgeon's office, the words "you just need to put your life on hold for a while" vibrated within. I knew her intention was to help me, yet why would I put my life on hold? Why wouldn't I integrate this temporary medical condition into my life? Eventually, an openness within came forth, and I viscerally felt what was possible and made a commitment to joy in the journey. My body began to feel more relaxed and tension seemed to evaporate. I discovered what was underneath the surface, since the tumor came from underneath the surface, and was able to find inner peace in a turbulent journey.

I made a choice to live with focused intention on navigating an uncertain path in life. I put my life on hold in my way!

LIVE JOYFULLY

Regardless of what news we experience in life, we do have a choice. I made a choice to find a joy in the challenges. I invited my mind to slow down and engage more fully in the present moment from something as simple as a walk with my dog Roxy. It was not a time to plan the next business seminar in my mind, but to notice how the forest changed with the seasons. I openly connected with all of my feelings: the frustration, the anger, and the uncertainty along with the joy and love of believing I was on a healing path.

INSPIRED ACTIONS

I made a choice to find medical professionals who aligned with my way of being. Customer service matters to me. A genuine smile brightens my day. Someone asking how my weekend was let me know they cared. Making direct eye contact with me let me know they weren't just going through the questions. As I became more aware of what I desired for my care, it resulted in changing doctor's offices. I wanted to be in a place of healing where others also believed it was possible. Sometimes I would get an idea to make a phone call or reach out to someone, and taking inspired actions resulted in a journey where I found what served me best.

FOCUS ON SOLUTIONS

By focusing on solutions, the answers came quicker. When I focused on the way an office employee spoke to me, it added stress, so instead I focused on "what do I want and how can I create it?" I wrote a plan with descriptive words that I was to find the best practitioners for me. Each person has different desires, so it is important to align with what matters to you.

EMPOWER OTHERS

I could have kept this diagnosis to myself. I could have kept the insights I gained to myself. Yet, what brought hope to me was when I found ways to share with others. That took courage and being ready for responses that might not support me. Yet I realized that my journey could enhance another's life. I shared with someone, "What works best for me is when people speak *with* me, not *about* me." So many people don't know what to say or do, so they talk about the person with the diagnosis instead of asking directly. It felt awkward to hear what others were thinking based on assumptions. I realized if I began sharing my experience it would help others in the future.

OPEN TO SPIRITUAL WISDOM

I do believe in messages from God and the angels, so I created more time to listen, to reflect, and to receive guidance. I imagined their presence in my life and I felt the fear uplifted and the symptoms shifting. Whatever you believe, lean on it. Embrace that you are fully protected, and when you connect to something you believe in, trust the feelings you receive from this connection.

NAVIGATE THE UNCERTAINTY WITH FAITH

I believe our brains are unable to hold two opposing emotions simultaneously, so when I felt uncertain, I embraced faith. What if I believed this treatment worked? What if I believed I was being guided for the greater good? What if I surrendered my fear and embraced my faith? When I felt most vulnerable, I found greatest comfort in knowing that I was one with my beliefs. I felt held in the presence of peace by all who were supporting me with their prayers and intentions. I imagined my mind being filled with calming thoughts.

HEART-CENTERED ANSWERS

It is important to have research and answers based on clinical trials, yet I also know we should listen to our hearts. Our hearts know what doctor to see, if a treatment plan will work, or what needs to be shifted in our life to live more balanced and healthy. I found myself frustrated when I heard, "We don't study that," or, "It works as a complimentary treatment to radiation and chemotherapy." What if we did study the power of one's thoughts and actions to create wellness within? What if we did teach others how to connect with the inner wisdom of their hearts to bring forth healing? Would the cure for cancer then be discovered?

OPTIMISM STRENGTHENS HEALING

There were moments during my days when I was discouraged. I didn't want to feel like I did inside my body. I wanted to sleep through the night without swirling thoughts. I wanted to expand my influence when I needed to rest to get through the day. I wanted to pretend this wasn't happening to me. It was especially in these moments that I looked within for optimism. It began with being real about the emotions I was feeling, ones that weren't my normal response. Then, I engaged in some form of reflection or action to shift me into the now. I wrote gratitude notes for those who supported me. I spent more time in nature, I planned dinners with friends, I noticed the sparkling stars in the sky. I became more present, and as a result I found an energy of resilient optimism that expanded the more I honored my entire journey.

LOVE EACH DAY
Whatever was happening each day, I found love. I honored my body in the fullest expression, grateful that my arms and legs worked, that my senses were alert and my mind was clear. I rekindled the dreams inside my heart and embraced them, which meant saying "no" to others by saying "yes" to myself. Before I slept at night, I did a rehearsal of what went well, what was a gift within the pain,

and found myself shifting my awareness of what life was all about. Present moment awareness has now become my companion.

DECIDE WHAT SERVICES YOU

It was important to pay attention to how I felt in the journey. It had to work for me, and sometimes that meant traveling further for an appointment. The energy of any person that was in contact with me mattered. It was important to be listened to and to have it acknowledged that I may not follow "normal protocol". It was my body and my life, and I was the one who decided yes or no.

Cancer is a word that has powerful energy. I wanted to transform the energy of the word cancer for me to accept there were abnormal cells in my body. With nervous energy, people begin to share, but my recommendation to everyone is don't share the challenges of others. Instead, be present and openly listen to where the person currently is in their journey. Allow them to share without being judged and believe they can be healed, fully and completely!

I asked myself, "What will my relationship to the word cancer be?"

Choose Joy
Awaken Spirit
Navigate with Faith
Compassion Within
Empower Others
Redesign Life

Breathing deeply, I felt a shift within. Can I navigate life's unexpected phone calls, uncertainties, and disruptions with a renewed sense of hope and grace? Can I welcome the feeling of challenge, embrace it, and transmute it into something that benefits us and others? This was the game I began to play.

The reality is that there will always be things that throw us off balance. We think we can plan our lives, and then when there is unexpected news, we flounder. My invitation to you is to act as if your dreams will become your reality while navigating the waters of life. Create practices that help you stay aligned with your life's joys, regardless of challenging moments.

How do you begin your day? Do you wake up quickly and start with the to-do list? Or do you pause and connect to the light within that wants to shine for others? Our relationship with the minutes in our day influences how our body responds when experiencing a challenge. What if we reframed our perspective of unexpected challenges and viewed them, instead, as life's opportunities to grow? When we become aware of the influence of our words, and our mind and body's response to a moment in time, we are more likely to find the alignment that we seek.

We are given opportunities to expand our thoughts resulting in new beliefs. We can open to a new awareness that allows us to see a new path, renewed sense of hope, and an ignition within to live our purpose more fully. When you choose a life path filled with healing on many levels, some may not understand you, and it is important to be comfortable with your own choices. Some may not know how to support you and their silence may appear as disinterest, yet honoring where each person is in their development is best.

What dream lies within you that isn't expressed or created? What idea lies within the pages of a journal? Are you comfortable with letting it be, or if you woke up one day with a doctor sharing a diagnosis with you, what would come to the surface for you? Pause. Notice. Become aware. Take action. Is there one simple action you can take today towards the fulfillment of your dreams?

As my journey of life became rerouted, the scenery was familiar, since I had supported others through their diagnosis, yet it felt surreal when it was happening to me. How *did* this happen to me? What is important now? My reflection led to a discovery that I had been hiding some gifts, squashing the bigger vision, and I had put my dreams on the shelf, hidden within pages in a computer. I realized we, as empowered women, are meant to support one another and hold one another's visions with faith while expanding the power of moving from challenge to creation! When we each travel life with an understanding that we will be rerouted, we understand that we will need to recalculate and redesign our lives. Instead of responding to the unexpected with fear and trepidation, we can have daily practices that keep us aligned with our soul's path, and we can navigate life with joy, regardless of what happens. By staying true to your own beliefs, while listening to options, we become aligned to our own healing powers and the journey becomes one of empowered wellness.

Now, I am on a new path, grateful for the future, trusting there will be many more moments to embrace, and realizing I have a choice—we all have choices! I can live as I was living, or I can redesign how I spend my days. I can add myself to the formula of life, being more conscious of embracing moments to generate joy, being intentional with experiences in life, and giving myself permission to live a life aligned with what serves me while serving others too. Learning to say "yes to yourself" while saying yes to others rebalances our spirits. When we nurture ourselves, we strengthen others, especially our children. While life offers many possibilities, it is in listening to the whisper of our hearts and the alignment of our bodies that we are guided to craft a life worth living and embracing wellness as our daily gift.

What's next in the journey of life? Looking ahead to the travels of life, believing that I am completely healed, my heart fills with gratitude for all who served me in my empowered wellness journey—family and friends who supported me, doctors who integrated intelligence and compassion to design the best healing plan, and people who shared their healing abilities. The power is within you to activate the healer within. Invite your mind to guide you to the healing practitioners that align with your inner beliefs, embrace the challenges as an opportunity to redesign your life, and trust your heart to guide you.

My awareness that each of us has healing powers that, when embraced, can enhance our life has strengthened peace within me. One of my favorite moments in my empowered wellness journey was when one of my doctors, who shared weekly what my side effects would be, was surprised by my final results when I focused my mind focused on a different result.

She said, "I have never seen results like this! Your skin looks great!" She was referring to how my body received the radiation, my healing rays, without severe burning.

I smiled and replied, "It was my intention!"

What intention is in your heart today? Trust it and embrace life!

ABOUT TERESA HUGGINS

If you could do anything, what would you do? Teresa made a choice to leave a secure career to design a path aligned with her vision. By taking a leap of faith, she jumped into a new version of herself and expanded what is possible. Her first book, *Pausing Long Enough to Notice*, reminds people to live in the present moment and awake to the answers in every day experiences. Her stories are featured in the internationally best-selling book *Chicken Soup for the Soul*™ and in books in Australia and the USA.

As an inspirational speaker and a dynamic trainer, Teresa helps her international audiences feel empowered to live with more joy by transforming what was and opening to what can be. In her personal and business coaching, she guides people to transform their limiting beliefs, to discover solution-focused approaches to life, and to live aligned with their truths. As a RIM Facilitator, Teresa helps clients unlock the blocks and free one's soul to become the best version of their selves. As a Master Trainer for the Jack Canfield Company, Teresa engages international audiences with interactive processes that enhance awareness and bring clarity to their lives.

She is here to support you, your employees, and your organizations to create a wellness approach to challenges and to engage in conversations where the power of language can transform self or an organization by increasing productivity, efficiency and joy. She also offers leadership and renewal programs for teens, college students, and adults with expertise on creating programs for women to speak their truth and design a life of balance and wellness.

Teresa can be reached at (315) 525-3296, teresa@teresadhuggins. com or www.teresadhuggins.com.

YOU ARE WHOLE. YOU ARE BRAVE.
A STORY OF SPIRIT & DETERMINATION

Dr. Faith Leuschen

The strength of a woman resides in her heart,
With courage and faith it never departs.
- Dr. Faith

I t was a hot, beautiful, sunny California day as I drove to the store to buy cases of crayons for an orphanage in Bali. Gwen Stefani's "Hollaback Girl" was on the radio and I was rocking it! My energy was high and life was perfect. I had just signed contracts to have my backyard completely remodeled and was adding a pool, jacuzzi and outside fireplace. My contractor, John, was remodeling the downstairs bathroom and installing a door to the yard so guests would have direct access to the pool. John also ran an import/export business in Bali, and we discussed building villas there together. I was all in. I had tickets to fly in a couple of days and check out the property. It was an amazing day and I was so excited about all of the new changes in my life!

There was just one more thing to do: get the crayons.

It was around noon on August 2, 2005. I had made plenty of

time to run my errand before going to work later that day. The light was as green as grass when I approached the intersection. Everything looked clear, but then I thought, "Oh, shit! What is *she* doing?!" (It turns out the "she" was actually an 84-year-old man.) Suddenly, an old, faded, red tanker of a Buick was driving directly into my lane. There was a sports car to my left and a family in an SUV on my right. I made my decision: I had to hold my position and drive straight into danger with my foot on the brake. Otherwise, I would have taken out a small car or a family. I just couldn't do that.

I watched as the huge car barreled toward me at full speed from the opposite side of the road. The other driver had failed to stop at the red left turn arrow. I slammed on the brakes. Braced for impact. But it was too late. We collided at almost full speed and I was blown back by the airbags. Everything went white—I felt like I was spinning. Things were in slow motion, time stopped, and I immediately thought, "Where's my purse, so they can identify the body?" All of the things I had seen as a former EMT 1A, working on ambulances and picking people up off the concrete, ran through my head. I knew exactly what could happen in these accidents.

I glanced to see my purse spilled out on the floor and immediately blacked out.

I woke up on the scorching asphalt. My back and legs were burning, and I could feel that my nylon sweat pants were melted into my skin. The pain was awful. I was lying in the middle of the intersection and a short distance away was my SUV, crushed and leaking fluid. I couldn't breathe well. My chest struggled to expand and take in oxygen. The man who was driving the sports car had pulled me out of my car. He held my hand and said everything was going to be okay.

"Did you have a baby or a child in the car?" he asked.

While I was passed out, he had seen the empty carseat in the back of the car. Once he determined I was alive, he searched for a child, then stabilized me as much as he could and got me away from the SUV.

"No," I said with one painful breath.

"That's a relief," he replied.

He said he would give the officer his information so I could have it. Then I blacked out.

Next thing I knew, I felt an incredibly sharp, deep pain in my right thigh. "What the hell?!" I thought. I looked up to the doctors and nurses leaning over me. "Aaaah, I can't breathe well, and my chest pain is unbearable. And what is wrong with my left arm?! Damn, my eyes and face hurt too!" They still had me strapped to a board and I was now in a C-collar. "Get me out of this thing!" I shouted. Nothing could be more uncomfortable. My legs still felt burnt; I realized they had cut my pants off.

I asked them if they had my purse and they said yes. Then I blacked out again. I remember later when I got my purse back, I opened it up and there was a card with the name and phone number of the man who had pulled me out of my car. He was my angel that day.

The next couple of hours in the hospital were filled with x-rays, ultrasounds, IVs, and waiting. I found out I wasn't bleeding internally—a small victory among the wreckage of my body. I kept telling the nurses and the doctor, "My chest pain is so bad. And what is wrong with my arm?! It has to be broken." They denied I had any fractures and increased my pain meds. I passed out.

I awoke to scapular and rib pain that had set in. That's when they found out I was a chiropractor (because I said scapula.) They wised up and began speaking to me in 'doctor language'. I insisted my elbow must be broken, because my pains were a 10—on a scale of 1 to 10—in my chest and elbow. The doctor reassured me that he saw no fracture. The nurse told me they had contacted my emergency contacts on my phone, including my nanny, Shelley, who was taking care of my three-year-old daughter, Sierra.

They cleared me to leave but I could stay if I wanted. I opted not to. Spending the night in that room and having my sleep interrupted, as is so common in a hospital, was the *last* thing I wanted to deal with. It may have been a bad idea, but I was feisty, pissed, in pain, and aggravated. Shelley picked me up and got me comfortable, or as comfortable as I could be with all of my injuries. Six hours later, the hospital called and said I had to come back because my elbow was broken. Of course!

REALITY SETTING IN

I was a single mom, business owner, chiropractor, and a fitness fanatic. I enjoyed mobility immensely. But I was realizing, "Oh my gosh, I can't work and everyone depends on me: my employees, the attorneys for reports, my massage therapists for consistent work, my daughter, and myself. I expect more from myself." The harsh reality that I had just taken out a $150,000 loan out on my house to remodel didn't help me feel any better. Luckily, I had a great chiropractor in my office who took on my patients, but I would be behind in the computer work and paperwork that had already piled up.

Then, the noise of construction began day in and day out. Jack hammering, trucks, tractors, workers. I lay in bed for weeks and weeks listening to the chaos of sound coming from my backyard. An endless parade of tractors were coming in. One knocked down a brick wall between my neighbors' house and mine to get access to my backyard. Another uprooted the yard to start digging the pool. The noise was unbearably loud everyday. All I could think of was the money flying out of the window, and me lying in bed making none! "WHY ME GOD? I ONLY DO GOOD," I thought. The pressure and the pain escalated.

On the positive side, Shelley took great care of Sierra and me. She was brilliant at it and so helpful and kind. Her compassion and forethought were truly as deep as the human spirit can get. She was anchored. My only regret was that she didn't come on the weekends!

As the depth of the damage set in and I realized how much rehabilitation I needed, I lamented the fact that the ER was really only there for basic life support. They never did a full body evaluation. I could barely walk because my right foot, right ankle, and both hips were injured in the accident. I couldn't breathe well because of a chest contusion, and my broken elbow pained me often. Initially, I didn't know just how many injuries I had, but the list began to grow as the pain settled into every area of my body.

During the weeks and weeks of doctors appointments, I discovered that the extent of my injuries would be lifelong. I knew it already deep down. I had suffered five disc protrusions total: three in my neck and two in my lower back. Add to the list face contusions, chest contusions, a heart contusion, sprained muscles in my eyes (which kept me, for all intents and purposes, blind for 3 weeks) and pain in my nose, ribs, and nerves. It all made for a crazy cocktail of overwhelming issues.

The insurance adjustors wouldn't stop calling. They wanted to know the details. The other person's insurance company called too, so I told them about my injuries. Both companies wanted to see me. They set appointments and came over on separate days. I told them I couldn't walk down my stairs, and I would have the nanny leave the front door unlocked so they could come up to me. I listened as they climbed the stairs on each visit. Both of their reactions were the same: shock and apologies. It seemed they couldn't bear to look at me and kept apologizing, telling me it was okay that I couldn't open my eyes. I kept trying to; I think it's human nature to want to see the person in front of you, plus I was taught to be polite and hold eye contact while talking. Finally, it was too excruciating. My eyes had gotten worse and I could barely open them. I really couldn't see my face, nor did I care to. My voice had been fine on the phone, clear and unaltered, so when the adjustors had first spoken to me, they figured I wasn't in such bad shape. But as they stood in my room, pouring over the details with me, the reality became apparent. I was indeed very broken.

I called one of my favorite attorneys and told them my story. They sent a representative to my house to interview me and check out my condition. I hired them

(with some lingering fear of the money issue) because I wanted the peace of mind of having someone experienced handle my case. They connected me with the best doctors for my injuries.

And that's when my life turned into a nightmare of appointments.

I had a load of doctors on board, starting with a cardiologist for my chest and heart contusions, an orthopedic surgeon who discovered the disc protrusions, and a neurologist who diagnosed me with a severe concussion. He classified all of my body injuries as sprain strains. He wanted to prescribe five medications that he sold right there in the office: a pain reliever, a muscle relaxer, an anti-inflammatory, an anti-depressant, and a stomach medication to treat the problems all of the other medicines would cause. "Thanks, but no thanks," I thought. "Give me some pain meds, but why prescribe an anti-depressant for a naturally happy person? My injuries are just physical!" I said. The doctor replied, "Oh, you are going to get depressed."

DIG DEEP

After days in bed, and construction going eight to ten hours a day, the first thing I wanted to do was get to my practice and see how the numbers were. My livelihood depended on it, and I *was* falling into depression and some panic. The patient numbers were on a decline. I was still in debilitating pain but I had to keep going. I told myself, " I AM WHOLE. I AM BRAVE."

There's no crying in baseball, right?

I went to work randomly without notifying my employees. They were astounded, but I was happy to be back in my office.

I turned on my computer and began to type. The letters came out all jumbled. My brain and my fingers weren't coordinating. Something was terribly wrong! I frantically pulled up the screen which listed our total profits. Nothing was computing; I couldn't understand the screen. I then tried the easiest of mathematical equations and couldn't do it. I was in overdrive, going into fight or flight, and feeling like my life was crashing down around me. But I breathed, maintained control, and made myself calm inside.

I called my attorney and told him my discovery. He went over a list of symptoms and sent me to a neuropsychologist to determine if I had a traumatic brain injury. They ran tests on my brain for eight hours. It was grueling and fatiguing. I was in tears, thinking, "Oh my God, how am I going to do this? Dig deep, Faith. Just dig deep. Dig deep, Faith. Just dig deep." I repeated it over and over like a mantra. "It's all so exhausting. What am I going to do?" I thought. They diagnosed me with a traumatic brain injury, and they didn't know how long it would take to heal. Apparently, my brain was skipping out on things I wasn't even aware of.

I went home completely exhausted, at a loss, and held my little girl while lying on the floor. She couldn't sit on my lap because I was in too much pain. I couldn't pick her up because I was in too much pain. I was too exhausted. We went to sleep. In the morning, I couldn't make breakfast, so I taught her how to get out the milk, pull over a chair to climb onto the counter, and get a bowl from the cabinet. I taught her how to step down safely, but I knew she would be doing this on her own in the future and there was a risk of her falling. I taught her how to open the milk and cereal to make herself breakfast. When she spilled some, I didn't care. I needed her to be independent at three years old.

Weeks passed. I continued seeing doctors and getting a mixture of medical, chiropractic, acupuncture and herbal treatment. My inner spirit was driving me to get back to my patients and see if I was capable of practicing chiropractic. I couldn't just lie down and heal. That wasn't in my genetic makeup.

One day, I went to the acupuncturist and during treatment he asked me, "What must be in your karma to have this happen to you?" I looked at him in disbelief. "What?" I asked. He repeated himself. My anger welled up. "First of all, I don't believe this is karma. I believe that 'shit happens'. I believe I was driving and an 84-year-old man, who should have not been driving, made a huge mistake and I was the aftermath of that mistake. That is it. No karma, just a circumstance. By the way, his wife was in the passenger seat and suffered a broken sternum. Is that her karma? I don't think so."

I was on edge, and my reactions to things which I could normally handle were suddenly severe. I laid low for awhile.

After about two weeks, I called my staff and asked how things were doing. I told them to call the patients who hadn't been in and I would return Monday with my schedule full.

Monday came and Shelley arrived at my house to watch Sierra. I was hurting but ready for work. I arrived and went right into my routine. Much to my surprise, my skill at adjusting was all there. I hadn't lost my memory or touch when it came to speed, specificity, coordination, or finesse. Everything went fine, until I had to wrap up the session. When I was talking to patients, I couldn't remember the smallest words for conversation. No one said anything, they just politely corrected me and provided the words that I was missing. I was excited, I felt accomplished, and knew I could do it!

We closed the office for the night and I began the drive home. Just a couple of minutes in, my mind and body slipped into chronic fatigue and a feeling of being lost emotionally. When I got home I let Shelley go for the night. Shelley was great about having Sierra already bathed and in her pajamas. I laid on the floor and fell asleep with Sierra snuggled up against my stomach and chest. She didn't move and we slept. Later in the night, I woke up with the worst pain from sleeping on the floor. I woke Sierra up and said, "Come on baby, we need to go upstairs and go to bed." Every night after that, when I came home at 7:30 pm, we went to sleep together in my bed so that I wouldn't have to tackle the stairs to watch over her.

Day in and day out, that was our life. To make matters worse, there was another looming problem. My heart was getting worse and worse and causing additional fatigue. The heart contusion may have healed, but I had arrhythmias that were throwing me off and I had to take my pulse often. Many times, I would feel a couple strong beats and then nothing; that wasn't good. I was experiencing bigeminy and trigeminy on a regular basis.

I set my patient schedule so that I was only treating patients for five hours each day. I performed like a master, except for messing up small words. If someone asked me how I was, I always replied with a powerful positive word: "I'm fantastic!"; "I'm phenomenal!"; "I feel GREAT! How are you?" I lived on the adrenaline that pumped through my body while helping others. I never showed the pain I was in and pretended all day long. I mastered my emotions. I mastered the critical self-talk where it didn't *need* to exist. I would rise to the occasion during work, and then crash and burn after I walked out of the office at night.

193

FINDING FAITH

Like clock work, the chronic fatigue and pain would set in each day. My cardiologist referred me to a cardiac electrophysiologist. The electrophysiologist explained that there was modern technology which would burn cells that are electrically malfunctioning. The procedure was called a cardiac ablation, and I would have to take ten days off of work. They would put me under anesthesia and go up a vein in my right leg using a catheter with an electrode at the tip until they reached the area of the heart muscle where the damage was located. Then, with radio frequencies, they would burn the damaged cells so that they stopped conducting irregularly. He convinced me that, because they would literally be guided to the damaged cells, it would be a very precise process, thus ensuring safety and efficacy. I booked the procedure weeks out; all of my patients were taken care of by another chiropractor and I took myself off the schedule at the practice. While I was still treating, I informed my patients that I would be out for ten days to have the cardiac ablation. I asked them to pray for me and get their churches involved. I must have had 2,000 people praying for me! I felt good and ready to have the surgery.

The day of the procedure, I felt strong and was happy to go under anesthesia because I knew I would feel no pain. I trusted the doctor completely and knew he was using the latest in technology.

But, sometimes there's a downfall to being a doctor and having another doctor working on you—some of them do weird things. The electrophysiologist woke me up in the middle of the procedure and said, " Faith, I got them." I looked up and could see a screen for a moment, then suddenly the doctor said, "We didn't get it." They put me back under anesthesia quickly.

I woke up on a gurney and was being wheeled down a hallway, past my family who all had sad faces.

I looked up at the nurse and said, "What happened?"

"Faith, the surgery failed," she replied.

Apparently, when the doctor got me into the operating room, he didn't check to see if the fancy ablation machine was working. They had already put me under anesthesia, so the doctor made his own call—that he would do the procedure without the high tech unit to map it out for him. He failed.

That night a Jamaican nurse came into my room. She was so delightful and cheerful, and she asked me what was wrong. I explained that my surgery had failed and that I was missing ten days at work for nothing, and that I had about 2,000 people praying for me. She spoke to me about the blessings of God and how he answers prayers. My reply: "I no longer believe in God." She said, "Oh, don't say that, truly." And she began to preach again. "Please stop," I said, "to me there is no God. How could there be, with all of these people praying, and me believing 100% that it would turn out good? And yet it did not happen. A cardiac electrophysiologist decided to play God and it failed. Please leave."

Later, when I went to sleep, I had the most dreadful, awful, demonic experience inside that room. There were demons and ghosts around me. Suddenly, a chainsaw was coming through the wall to the right of me. The person holding it was my dad, who had passed years ago. I was scared beyond reason and prayed that they would go away in the name of the LORD! Then they vanished. I had to lie in that bed until the next nurse came in to check on me. I didn't say a word. I just turned over and cried. I was done. I was losing the battle and I didn't have anything left.

Later that day, my Jamaican nurse came back. I said to her, "I believe. I believe because I don't ever want to go to the other side again. There is only Hell to pay in darkness, and we all must step into the light when things seem to get dark."

I must have cried more that day than any day of my life, honestly. I felt sad in my house; I was mad at the doctor; and I was upset because construction was still going on, so I started micromanaging that. I returned to work and came home in debilitating pain. At that point, Sierra lost a productive, happy mother. Whenever I played with her it had to be on the floor. I couldn't pick her up because I was so exhausted and my existing pain was evolving into nerve pain, ice pick headaches that lasted for weeks, depression, anxiety, neck pain, lower back pain, foot pain, leg pain, numbness in my hands and feet, and severe muscle tightness. I had to save my strength for lifting, pulling, and adjusting patients. All my energy was put towards survival. I thought, "This is it, this is as good as it gets." And that was okay to me at the time …

… until it turned into full-blown fibromyalgia and a sleep disorder where I was waking once every four minutes.

SOARING FURTHER

Despite all of that, something spectacular happened at that time. It was exactly a year and a half after the accident when I regained my ability to do mathematics, my vocabulary returned, and I was able to type quickly on a computer with very few mistakes. What a victory! I felt so free and finally on the road to healing. Admittedly, it was a bizarre turn of events and a simultaneous surge of connections.

Though things were improving, I still had to pretend that I was fine at work. The chronic fatigue was disruptive. I would get up in the morning just to greet Shelley and have her take Sierra to school. Once I was alone in the house, all I could do was suffer and sleep. I would wake up in the afternoon sweating and hot, then take a quick shower, blow dry my hair, do my makeup, get dressed for work, and make it there by 2 pm to treat patients. I felt much better at work than I did at home. Things had to change.

I decided to bring on two more chiropractors to help with the workload. They wanted to start their own practice within my office. At the time, I had five massage therapists, three receptionists who would work the front desk, a chiropractic assistant, and some interns here and there. I worked very little because I was getting sicker and sicker. Months passed and one day I looked at my bank statement. My merchant account wasn't going up. It was depleting. I knew there was a thief in the office.

I hired a female private investigator who had a background in computers and who could play the role of a receptionist at work. She watched the activity that was going on when I was not there. Apparently, the two new doctors had their own credit card machines and they were swiping my patients' cards so the payments went into their own accounts. I had the investigator pull their files and more than half of their "new" patients were actually patients who were referred from my current patients, from my marquee, or from my marketing. I was livid. It didn't end prettily. I fired both doctors, but made one of them stay and treat patients until they found another space. I didn't want any patients to know what had happened, and I wanted to set a new status quo. That week, I not only fired the two doctors, but five other employees as well, because I needed to have *total trust* in my office. I couldn't go into my practice thinking there was anyone there who didn't have my back. I didn't want to waste any energy on people like that.

I put out an ad for a new receptionist, interviewed some great candidates, and hired two right off the bat. That same day, the mail came in with an advertisement for a practice management seminar. I had always thrown away these ads; since I began my practice, I was so good at what I did (in my mind) that I didn't need the help. Now, things had changed. So I signed up and the two new employees came with me. They were great. The seminar was intriguing and we learned a lot that we could implement to improve the business.

During the seminar, a slide came up on the screen that said, "If any of you are suffering from headaches, neck pain, back pain, depression, anxiety, sharp/shooting pain, numbness and tingling, all-over body pain, chronic fatigue, brain fog, irritability, forgetfulness, IBS, etc., please come to the back of the room to be tested."

I looked at my two new employees and said, "You know what? I have 25 out of 30 of those symptoms." They were astonished! I was always so happy at work; I never complained and I always said I was fantastic!

That day changed my life forever. It unlocked the mystery of my symptoms and gave me answers. It changed my life so that I could work relatively pain-free. I could be a mother again and play with my daughter in an interactive way. I went on to grow my business into a larger space and added a Neurologic Relief Center. I studied in-depth neurology, thought patterns, and new techniques to help patients. I became a Master Trainer of the Neurologic Relief Center Technique and patients flew across the nation to see me. I sought out expos that helped disabled people, the "incurables", and put together a team of interns to help me run a booth where we tested hundreds upon hundreds of people. I found out that we could successfully help not just people with Fibromyalgia, but also patients with a plethora of other issues: severe chronic pain, reflex sympathetic dystrophy, PTSD, some traumatic brain injuries, post-stroke symptoms, multiple sclerosis, phantom pain, certain cases of Autism, and so much more.

The experience was priceless and so rewarding. It led me to understand that I needed to shift my efforts in order to better serve people. My spirit kept "knocking," dropping little hints here and there to remind me not to wear out my own body, to go global, because practicing on an individual scale no longer served my purpose.

I treated my patients for nine years after my accident, and I loved every minute of it, but my spirit cried out for more. I still had pain in my neck and back. My left arm would "go dead" often. I developed thoracic outlet syndrome, but I kept going. The facial numbness and ice pick headaches were coming back. I loved my practice and my patients, but it was time for a change. My spirit continued nudging me to get out. MRIs revealed that my disc protrusion had gone from five to eight disc protrusions—four in my neck and four in my low back. I was okay though. *Nothing* could touch me after living through such trials.

So, I listened to my spirit, closed my practice and said goodbye. I felt whole. I felt brave. I knew I would go on to do even bigger and better things, where I could soar even further.

The strength of a woman resides in her heart,
With courage and faith she never departs.

Step out in courage, there is nothing to fear.
And you will find that delight,
You will always endear.

We have to make up these things.
And be persistent with this.
Because if you don't,
You'll never know
What you have missed.

My message to you: Let your light shine brightly and keep moving forward with your dreams. That is one of the most powerful things that you can do for yourself and the ones you love. Your spirit and determination are the number one tools you can use to turn your life around or to reach further in your goals and dreams. You, and only you, can reach deep enough to decide to make a change, then surround yourself with the right people to help you make it happen!

God Bless,
Dr. Faith E. Leuschen

ABOUT DR. FAITH LEUSCHEN

Dr. Faith uniquely takes people from their life complications (physical, mental or financial) into liberation and a new concept of living fully in every category. She coaches in the purest form with authentic, straightforward, thought-provoking, life lifting strategies with a doctor's perspective when needed and the spirit moving through her. Her clients get the best of both worlds, with no stones unturned.

Her motto: "This life is meant to be lived, and the highest manifestations are ours to discover!"

It's a wonderful life when you're aligned with the right people.

You can reach out to Dr. Faith at:
www.thefaitheffectglobal.com
www.worldwideimpactcoaching.com
www.totalbodybalancedr.com

FREEZE TIME MOMENTS

Jeanine Mihalak

My Mom made me promise that I would always take care of myself and live a *healthy life*. I have spent a lot of time reflecting and thinking on that promise and about what has brought the passion of wellness into my life. My journey to health and wellness began when I was twelve years old, and my Mom was diagnosed with breast cancer. I think she felt like it was her fault she was diagnosed, that she could have caught it sooner, been healthier, or prevented it somehow. The moment she was diagnosed, time froze and my entire life changed forever. Up until that time, I was a normal tween with a wonderful family living a "normal" life—as normal a life as you can have in middle school, going through puberty and all kinds of changes.

After my Mom was diagnosed, she went through surgery, endured the pain, and began chemotherapy; it wasn't until she lost her hair that the invincibility of my Mother vanished. I remember the moment she came out of surgery she looked at my Dad and said, "It hurts." I felt scared and vulnerable. How could this happen? What do I do to help her? All she would tell me was to "be strong for her." So I was, and while most other kids my age were bonding with their mothers as they embraced the hormonal changes in their body, I was helping my Mom change her bandages and getting pain medications and crackers to calm her nausea from the chemotherapy. It was during these times that I became different. I became older than my actual numerical age. I began to release the innocence of childhood and take on the stress, worry, and responsibility of a young adult. At twelve years of age I became responsible, and I had to navigate the difficulties of adolescence without the normalcy of a healthy mom to help me. I felt alone and abandoned, forced to maneuver the changes in my body and my life alone because I didn't want to worry, upset, or cause my Mom any more stress. A few months after Mom's surgery, I got my period for the very first time. I didn't even tell her. I knew how much she was struggling and I thought, "Well, I know what to do." That was the beginning of being independent, being a go-getter, and being someone who just gets things done—because I can. I developed strength, confidence, and the ability to behave much older than I was.

Of course, my Mom was strong and tried to conceal so much of her pain and fear in order to protect us. She was truly the best at keeping a positive attitude. There was a time when she was obviously struggling with recovery, chemotherapy, and all the changes her body was going through. She had every right to be miserable. I came home from school one day, and she sat down with me, took the time to ask about my day, helped me with homework, and told me she loved me. I knew she wasn't feeling up to it. I knew she would rather be in bed. But she was so strong and positive, and she never once complained about what she was feeling. Instead, she focused completely on us. She even made us dinner, although she was too nauseous to eat. She continued with the routine and worked so hard to convince us, through her actions, that everything was and would be okay. She always had a smile on her face and a warm hug to give us. She always told us how she was going to be around for a long time and not to worry.

I admired my Mom's choice to focus on the positive because it invited me to BELIEVE that everything would magically be okay. Although she had cancer and was going through horrible pain, losing her hair, and felt sick a lot, she always said, "Everything is going to be fine, I am not going anywhere." Of course I believed her, and as an adolescent I began to quiet my mind and the emotions of fear and sadness. I believed everything would magically be "happily ever after." Even though all the signs and my intuition told me that something wasn't right, I believed in the power of positive thinking. My 12-year-old-intuition told me that something was not okay, but I chose to believe that my Mom wasn't as sick as she seemed. I realize now that I wasn't in denial—like many would think I was. Instead, I chose to cherish those moments because it allowed me to maximize my time with her and enjoy the moments that I now treasure as some of my fondest and most sacred memories.

That experience has given me the gift of appreciation, or what I call the *Freeze Time Moments* in my life. I have learned to appreciate the beauty in the sunshine of each day, the laughter of my children, and the peaceful elegance of a beautiful spring day. I believe in treasuring the gift of today, because it is truly the only day we are promised. When we live to find the joy in every moment we truly can live a life of pure happiness.

My mom had a six-year long battle with cancer. She was strong, vibrant, loving, and positive in every way at every moment. I don't know if I ever heard a negative thing come out of her mouth about her disease or anything for that matter. She was the epitome of strength, courage, and persistence. She inspires me to this day to see the sunshine in every cloud and a rainbow in every rainstorm. She is the only person I have ever known who always saw the bright side of things. So, of course, I learned to be the same. I adopted the "happily ever after"mindset. I believed that all people should be kind, do the right thing, and love one another. I learned to be strong and hid from most of my friends, teachers, and coaches what was happening in my life.

I began to push people away because I didn't want them to know that Mom was sick. I needed to be strong for her. To me, that sometimes meant pretending her disease didn't exist; other times it meant giving up going out with friends so I could stay home in case she needed me. I felt pulled in two directions: I needed to have courage to grow up and become strong and positive like her, but inside I had fear. I had anger because I just wanted my life to be "normal". We all fight fears within our mind; our ego tells us to have fear, to be angry. But when you quiet your mind, your soul guides you to where you are truly meant to be. Of course there were times I wanted to be a normal tween and teen. I wanted to magically wave a wand and make the cancer go away. I know now that it was my intuition and inner voice speaking to me. That voice that tells you something isn't quite right. That voice that makes your hairs stand up. That voice that now, as a mother, I call my "mommy instinct." I didn't have a magic wand then, and I still don't, but what I have learned is to listen to that inner voice and let it guide me.

My mom fought her battle with cancer hard, with love, positivity and passion. She even came to my high school graduation. She couldn't walk at the time. In fact, she should have been in a wheel chair, but she struggled with crutches onto the football field and watched me graduate. She made a choice to put her pain aside and to be PRESENT IN THE MOMENT to see her youngest child graduate high school. I didn't know it at the time, but she was diagnosed terminal just days before my June graduation. I reflect on that moment often and now realize what an amazing *Freeze Time*

Moment that was. It was a true testament that, regardless of what happens in your life, it's WHAT you do and HOW you handle it that matters. Wow, I still admire her actions that day. How did she put all her physical, mental, and emotional pain aside and smile and watch me graduate? I am so grateful my Mom was there that day. I remember the very last picture I took with her: me in a white cap and gown and my Mom in a red dress. She was seated because it was so difficult for her to walk. She looked pale and not herself, but she still had a smile on her face. She looked so ill, yet in her eyes all I saw was the love and pride she had for me in that moment.

Now that I am a mom, I know how she did it. She made the decision that she was going to be there no matter what, and she did it. Regardless of the obstacles and the physical and emotional difficulties, she made a choice and let nothing get in her way of what she wanted to do. This was when I learned another major life lesson: *Don't let anything or anyone stand in the way of your dreams and passion!*

Six months later she died. I remember that cold December day so vividly, and sometimes I still hear the phone ringing in my dorm room and my dad telling me she had passed. I knew it was coming, yet I felt denial and shock. I watched the snow as it fell outside my dorm room window. It blanketed the trees with such peace and beauty, yet I KNEW my road ahead was anything but peaceful. I cried on the floor as my roommate held me and I remembered that I had promised my Mom that I would be strong. I would take care of myself and my dad. I played one of the last conversations I had with her back to myself. She made me promise I would always stay *healthy* and also made me promise I would take care of my father. At 18 years old, I had no idea what the true meaning of that meant, nor did I know that it would set me on a path for my soul's true journey.

As Daddy's little girl, I took my promise to heart. I certainly didn't realize at the time how it would guide me to a passion for wellness and to inspire others to do the same. I graduated college with a degree in both elementary and special education and began teaching. While teaching, I even got a master's degree in counseling. I wanted to help others. All the while, I thought I was *healthy*. Being an athlete my whole life, I equated being healthy with exercising. I exercised a lot. I ran, I did kickboxing, aerobics, swimming—you name it, I did it. I was in great shape on the outside. I *looked* healthy. But just because you look healthy on the outside does not mean you are healthy on the inside. I had no idea that inside, my body was lacking essential nutrients.

In my late 20s, I married my amazing husband Tony. I knew I had done something right. He was and still is my best friend and biggest supporter, and he shared my passion for health and fitness. He loved to work out too, and we spent much of our time together at the gym, running together and being *healthy* through fitness. After a couple of years, we decided we wanted to have children. I made the choice to resign from my job as a teacher and counselor and be home with my children, enjoying each MOMENT. I thought that because I didn't have a mom, that I needed to be the best mom. I thought that meant being home with my children. I was missing my Mom terribly at this time. I was feeling down and depressed and wishing she was there to help me through the difficulties of having three small children. My oldest daughter began to ask questions about where Grandmom was, and I told her a made-up story of angels in heaven through the clouds and the sky. She asked me where Grandmom was and I told her she was an angel and that angel lived up in the clouds. Each day she would ask which cloud Grandmom was in, and we would find it together and talk about it. One day, when it was sunny with blue skies, she became confused and asked where the angels were. I told her they were sleeping but sent the sunshine to warm her face. This story has now become something we have added to and shared with all three of my children. I find that I have not only created a connection for my children with their grandmother, who they never physically knew, but I created a connection with her for myself. To this day, every time I look up to the sky, I feel her with me, guiding me, loving me, and inspiring me. This story helped me to heal and I look forward to sharing this story with others to help them do the same.

I continued to pour myself into my children and I thought that would help me be fulfilled, happy, and peaceful. I was *healthy* through fitness and I had gorgeous children. I had a happy and perfect life, right? Well yes AND no. Although happy and grateful for my life, in the process of being a mom, changing diapers, nursing, preschool responsibilities, and running a carpool, I had lost myself. I wasn't feeling healthy anymore. I was EXHAUSTED.

I was getting sick all the time and at the end of the day, I was asking, "Who am I?" The only answer I had was, "I am a mom." Although that was a big part of my identity, I needed to find me. *I also realized that I was breaking that promise to my mom to stay healthy.* I was feeling horrible and excessive exercise wasn't enough. I might have looked good on the outside, but I wasn't very healthy on the inside. All along, I thought that staying healthy meant exercising like crazy and eating well. So why was I constantly physically sick? I wasn't fulfilled completely as a mom. In fact, I didn't feel fulfilled at all. I felt LOST. Most days it was a luxury to shower, and as a mom everyday felt like Ground Hog's Day: get up, get the kids off to school, run the carpool, help with the kids' homework, make dinner, support the kids' activities and sports, then bedtime.. I began to get sick a lot: sinus infections, strep throat, exhaustion, stomach issues, migraines, etc. My inner voice screamed that something wasn't right. Could it be that my physical health was suffering because I wasn't fueling my body with essential nutrients, vitamins and minerals that I needed? I needed to find myself again, feel good, and get back on track with the promise to my Mom. I thought that I could start by getting my physical health in check. Actually, I just wanted to get through the day without a nap, stay up past 8:30 pm, and get off the vicious cycle of antibiotics and yo-yo dieting. I thought if I did that, then everything would be great. I would be *healthy* and *happy*.

I physically hit rock bottom when I was diagnosed with an auto-immune condition called chronic fatigue syndrome. When I asked doctors what to do to get better and feel better, they told me there was nothing I could do. In that instance, my inner voice told me differently. There is always SOMETHING. In that MOMENT I found the courage to ask a friend about her nutritional regimens and habits. She told me a story of how her health was transformed from making some simple changes to her regimen. I was *super* skeptical because I had tried many natural remedies. I learned about this groundbreaking 60 year old nutritional company and the difference in their product quality, purity, and performance. I was blown away by their beyond-organic standards, their attention to science, detail, and their commitment to quality and guarantee. I gave it a try, and my health remarkably improved. At the same time, my father's health was failing, so I introduced him to the same nutritional company and he saw similar positive results. I began to understand that, along with fueling the outside of my body with exercise, I needed to fuel the inside of my body with solid nutrition and the supplementation that it was desperately lacking. This passion to fuel my own body and help my father led me to become a nutritional and health coach. I committed myself to helping others do the same.

So now I thought I had it all. I was healthy inside through nutrition and healthy outside through exercise and fitness. Though I was feeding my body with the best nutrition and had a solid exercise regimen that physically had me looking and feeling wonderful, I still felt like I wasn't totally complete. There was a piece of the healthy puzzle missing. In order to enhance my own wellness, I realized the final component to healthy was to fuel my soul.

In my journey to fuel my soul, I found myself pushed to the edge to do new things—things that made me uncomfortable and scared. I took a leap of faith, went to a women's retreat, and hired a life coach. I had spent over eight years pouring myself into my family and others and being *strong*. It was time to work on completing me and finding peace. I spent time and money fueling my soul, shifting my mindset, learning to meditate, praying, and saying affirmations to help me have faith and BELIEVE in myself. I learned that in order to truly inspire and help others, I needed to first do it with myself. While working with a coach, I found myself coming back to practicing yoga.

Yoga was something I had loved years ago but stopped doing because, as a mom, I put everything else before myself. Again, I had no idea that the choice to start taking yoga would actually begin to create harmony, peace, and inspiration in my soul. Yoga isn't about the "workout." Yoga helps you slow down and *feel*. It helps you to be as you are: what yogis refer to as *yatta butta*. It doesn't matter what the person next to you is doing. All that matters is you and your mat. It allows you to go within and quiet your mind so that your soul can speak to you and guide you to your true purpose. It allows you to truly enjoy the moments you are in. It allows you to be you and to discover yourself all at the same time.

Yoga reveals what yoga is meant to heal—to love yourself just as you are. That you are ENOUGH. Many moms, wives, friends, and sisters have these struggles too. We all need to live a life feeling inspired and with the ability to inspire others. If we all can love ourselves completely and accept ourselves for who we are, then our relationships with others will be richer and more meaningful. Yoga allowed me to peel back the layers to find out who I am and who I am NOT, to figure out what being *ENOUGH* means. It was the final *piece* that truly fed my soul and allowed me to live a healthy and happy life. I realized that my mind was so powerful! Thoughts were constantly streaming through it. If I filled it up with positive thoughts, my life would start to change. Yoga was transforming me because being enough meant just being *ME*—authentically and completely *ME*. I learned how important it was to allow those who were meant to fill me up to join in and participate in my life.

I began to hear my kids fighting and screaming as the joy of hearing them being siblings. I began to stop and literally enjoy *Freeze Time Moments.*

I took a huge leap of faith and became a certified yoga instructor. I thought, "If yoga can help inspire and heal me, then it can help others as well. I have a deep inner *knowing* that I am meant to inspire and help make the world a more healthy and positive place. I am truly meant to inspire others to lead a complete life of wellness and find the pieces that complete their puzzle. My journey through life and through tragedy has led me to find wellness through fitness, nutrition, and feeding and fueling my soul through yoga and coaching."

I look back now at that promise I made to my Mom over 20 years ago and how my purpose has changed through the years. My understanding of *healthy* has changed because I evolved and was open to change with it. I had no idea back then that fulfilling a promise to my Mom to stay "healthy" would lead me on the path to my purpose. Over the years, I had every reason not to put the work in to become who I am today. I could have lived in grief and in sadness. I could have lived in a comfortable place and felt sorry for myself, for not having my Mom through the many moments in my life when I needed her most. I will be honest, sometimes I still do. I wouldn't be human if I didn't. But, I don't want to live in grief and be a victim of the circumstances of my life.

We all have battles that we fight. We all have moments in our life that change us. I chose to fight to become whole again for myself and for my family. I chose to inspire others so that they can be whole again, too. I could have made excuses. Instead, I made choices that scared me but allowed me to grow and thrive instead of just survive. I could have stayed comfortable, but I chose to continue to find the edge and challenge myself to be better.

I have found the pieces of the puzzle to live a life of wellness, fitness, nutrition, and fueling the soul. I have learned that wellness is about fueling your external body with fitness, fueling your inner body with the best nutrition, and fueling your soul every single day. Doing this has transformed my life. It has lessened my anxiety, it has deepened my friendships, and it has strengthened my marriage. I have learned that *I can write the story* because I choose how I will look at every situation I encounter. I choose to find family balance and life balance. I choose to share my story to inspire others to make healthier choices for their lives.

If you believe within your soul that what you are doing is good, your mindset will carry that and it will fuel your life. I have decided to share my story because I hope it inspires you and helps you deal with your personal pain. I want you to know that you are not alone. We all have *MOMENTS* in our lives that change us, guide us, and ultimately bring us to our life's purpose. My life's purpose is to inspire other families to live a life of harmony and balance enjoying their *Freeze Time Moments* while living to their best potential. Nourishing their body from the inside out, to create a peaceful mind and to find what inspires and fuels their soul and bring it for the world to see. I truly believe we all create and work from a space that we are our best selves and together change the world to a more positive place collecting and enjoying our *moments* and making the world a more inspiring place. We rise by lifting others and inspiring others. We all can find peace and inspire the world to be a healthier, happier, more positive place. We all can fulfill our purpose in life.

What you do and the success you experience starts with a positive mindset. Ask yourself these questions: What do you want to do? What are the desires deep in your heart? What are your passions? How do you want to be legendary? How do you want to remembered? Allow your soul to find peace while discovering the pieces of your puzzle in life. Just remember, every mistake is giving you the power to learn a lesson, to grow, and to transform your life. Give new meaning to your life and be the author of YOUR story.

ABOUT JEANINE MIHALAK

Jeanine Mihalak, M. Ed. is the founder of Inspired Wellness 4 Life, a concierge style wellness resource where she provides personalized yoga, nutritional counseling, coaching, and personalized fitness/nutritional programs.

Inspired Wellness 4 Life is a resource Jeanine crafted to share with others a healthier and happier lifestyle of total wellness of a healthy body, positive mind, and peaceful spirit.

Previously, Jeanine was a Special Education and Elementary teacher, and certified school counselor, where she facilitated a healthy mind, body, and soul for students of all ages. Now, she incorporates her teachings and lifestyle concierge services by working one on one with individuals, families, and businesses to inspire simpler and healthier ways of life.

Jeanine has been on an inspired journey for some time after finding that wellness and nutrition are key to living a wholesome life. A certified yoga instructor, fitness instructor, personal trainer, and inspirational speaker, Jeanine's mission is to help everyone, one person at a time, live a happier, cleaner, healthier lifestyle ... because we all deserve to Be Healthy and Laugh More!

Jeanine resides in Marlton, New Jersey with her husband and business partner, Tony. They have three children, Jessica, Matthew and Ella. As a mother and wife, Jeanine takes pride in creating a life that allows her family and others to live the life most people dream of. It is her passion and privilege to coach others to help them achieve their dreams as well.

Learn more about Jeanine's passion for Inspired Wellness and how you can live a healthier, more meaningful life at: www.inspiredwellness4life.com.

GOD-INSPIRED MONEY MASTERY

Snowe Saxman

My name is Snowe, and I believe that we can change the world. We create more freedom and happiness in our lives when we put God first, our families second, and our careers third. When you work for someone else, in most business models or until you master your business, you live career first, career second, and everything else third. I believe that when you put God first, you will have it all: more money, more choices, and more time with your family!

I am a Success, Wealth & Women's Expert. I am known as The Money Oracle. I teach women God-inspired success and financial/business strategies.

With God's help, I have been able to channel a painful past into a purposeful future and teach other women how to create, manage, and multiply money so that they can have a profitable business. I can show you how to master your money because I have done it myself.

I am originally from Virginia Beach, Virginia. I grew up in a "well-to-do" home in the best part of town. My father had an executive, nine-to-five career. My mother was a stay-at-home mom, gourmet cook, and socialite. I have one older brother. We lived in a big house, my parents drove luxury cars, we went to the best schools, we took family vacations every year, and I had everything a child could "want."

But, I also had a secret.

My earliest memories are of a male family member sexually abusing me. I was so young when it began that I didn't even know it was wrong. It's kind of like growing up and learning your name. You just somehow "know" it. I knew that I didn't really like it, and I didn't really want it to happen, but I couldn't stop it. There are a lot of memories I have in pieces and parts of time that I just don't recall.

By the time I was a teenager, I was living as two separate people. In public, I tried to be as happy as I could be, but in private, I was just trying to survive the regular sexual abuse. I remember having a lot of fears, doubts, and unanswered questions.

I was so excited to go away to college. For the first time ever, I felt a sense of freedom even though I had not dealt with all the years of abuse. I had no idea what I wanted to study when I started college; I was just happy to be away. I was always really good at math and managing my money. Often, as a young girl, my friends wanted to play teacher, but I wanted to play banker or Monopoly. So, when someone told me about their father's job as an accountant, I thought it was a good fit for my natural abilities. I decided to get a degree in accounting.

As I began to think about my long term career and take more courses in college, I loved the idea of managing a large company. When I graduated from college, I wanted to become a CFO of a large corporation, so I could work on the managerial side of accounting. I loved reviewing and preparing financial statements and looking for growth opportunities.

In my second year of college, I got married and pregnant. I thought I had found my one true love and we would be married forever. However, almost immediately after we were married, emotional and physical abuse began. The first incident happened in the first couple of months. I was pregnant. I do not remember what caused the confrontation. I remember being in our apartment, attempting to move down the hallway, and suddenly he pushed me violently against the wall. I remember feeling so much pain, hurt, and betrayal.

The emotional and physical abuse got worse with each new incident, and he began to beat me regularly. I found a way to stay in school, because I knew that was my best chance of making a better life for my daughter and myself.

In my third year of college, he left me for another woman. I had $20 in my pocket and a one-year-old baby. I cried myself to sleep for six months. I couldn't understand why I was so upset since he had been so abusive to me. I moved home with my parents and pressed through, finishing my degree in accounting. We never saw him again.

After I graduated from college, I decided my daughter and I needed a change in scenery, so we moved to Florida. I landed a job at Disney World as an accountant, which was really exciting! My daughter even went to pre-school on Disney World property. It seemed like *the* dream job. However, it only took a few months for me to realize that working for someone else was NOT for me because I wanted to control my time and my money. At age 23, I quit that "dream" job, enrolled in graduate school to get my MBA, and started my first business helping new business owners with accounting, money management, tax planning, and forming corporations.

One of my first clients was my future husband, Paul. We began dating almost as soon as we met. It seemed like the perfect connection. He had three boys from his first marriage and I had my daughter. Paul told me that he didn't want to get married again. He wanted to focus on his boys, and he DEFINITELY didn't want any more children. I thought, "That's FINE with me, because I feel the same way!" Ten months later, we were married, and eventually had three more amazing boys. (Truly, we make plans and God laughs!)

We built a multi-million dollar construction and real estate development company after giving a large investment to a man who took off with all of our money. He left us with three construction loans and three vacant pieces of property. We decided to turn lemons into lemonade. By the time I was 25, I was officially a millionaire. I was really enjoying being the CFO of our company and handling all the money, tax, and legal work, but I felt like something was missing. I ended up buying a salon and spa and a lady's fitness franchise in an attempt to fill the void. I didn't realize at the time that it was actually an underlying desire to help women that needed to be fulfilled.

At around the same time, we began to lead (what I call) somewhat of a "rock star" lifestyle! We had lots of connections in Orlando and we also had lots of money. Paul and I always loved to entertain and be entertained. Renting a limo for the weekend was a typical event for us. However, before we knew it, we were involved with drugs, strip clubs, underground swinger groups, and all night partying that sometimes lasted for days. We even hired a full time nanny to take care of the kids and the house, so that they weren't neglected. We saw things that most people would never understand. I was just trying to find anything that could fill the empty void and heal the pain that all the years of sexual, physical, and emotional abuse had left inside of me. At the time, I didn't know why I was doing all of these things, but deep down, I knew it wasn't right. All the partying left us with an emotional hangover, which was worse than the physical one. Since only God can fill that void, I went deeper and deeper into depression and post-traumatic stress. I was literally in an emotional prison.

One night, after partying and using cocaine, I came home and took half a bottle of my husband's pills in an attempt to kill myself. My husband woke up and somehow he knew what I had done. I was rushed to the hospital and I was involuntarily committed to a mental health institution for three days. While in the hospital, I finally admitted the sexual abuse I had suffered. It was the first time in my life I had told anyone about the abuse.

When I returned home, my husband said I needed to tell my parents about the abuse. I decided to tell them what happened. A few months later, I received a seven-page, handwritten "goodbye" letter from my mother and my "father." I didn't believe that my father really wanted to send this letter. When I told him about the abuse he was almost in tears and told me how sorry he was. He said if he had known, he would have stopped it. I told him that I didn't blame him; I just wanted our family to move past all of this. As of writing this book, we still haven't spoken. It has been almost 10 years.

When I first bought the ladies fitness franchise, I was supposed to break even. I soon realized it was losing about $2,000 a month. I was desperately trying everything I could to grow the business. I started going deeper into depression because I felt like I had already wasted so much of our resources on the salon and on buying the gym. Then, a buzz started among the other franchise owners. They were making more money selling skin care and makeup out of their gyms than with their gym memberships. I was really intrigued, because I needed to make additional income, but I was stuck in the gym during all operating hours. Since I was losing so much money each month, I couldn't afford to pay anyone to help me. Therefore, the only way that I could create more income would be to do something inside the gym.

I started researching cosmetics companies and that same week a Mary Kay consultant came into my gym. She shared information about the company and told me that she thought I would do really well selling the products. Even though I was already looking for something similar, I told her that I wasn't interested. I gave all of the most common objections, but the truth was, I was just scared to fail again. Since the economy was crashing, our construction and real estate company was falling apart, and I did have more free time to pursue something else. We also desperately needed additional income because the recession was growing stronger. I even knew from studying business that there are three things you look for when starting a business: a low ticket, consumable, and recession-proof product. It sounded like everything I had ever wanted in a business and life, but fear was holding me back. Even though I was scared to start, I was very intrigued with the numerous business awards Mary Kay Ash had earned during her lifetime and after. I finally decided to push past my fear because I was so impressed with Mary Kay Ash's accomplishments.

I thought that if I could just make $500 a month without leaving the gym, that would give me a little breathing room. Within six months, I earned my first free car and I became a Sales Director. Within the first year, I began making so much money part-time, and on my terms, that I decided to close the gym and only work on my Mary Kay business. I not only fell in love with the fact that I had unlimited earning potential and freedom through a proven business model, I fell in love with the principles on which Mary Kay was founded. God first, family second, and career third. Mary Kay Ash believed that, in this order, everything works, and outside of this order, nothing works.

When Mary Kay found me, I was so unbelievably lost and full of pain. God slowly started to draw me in and I began my healing journey through this incredible company. I met women who had literally earned millions and lived a life that truly exemplified God first, their family second, and their careers third. Through the model Mary Kay designed herself, I not only started a new business journey, but I also started a healing journey. To me, healing was more valuable than the potential to earn millions.

Even though I had a lot of success very quickly in Mary Kay, I still had a lot of "junk" to deal with from all the years of physical, emotional, and sexual abuse. I hit a brick wall within a year. From that point on, my business was literally like a roller coaster. One month, I would do really well, and one month I would do practically nothing. I was trying everything in my power to make things happen. I went to every training, event, conference, mastermind group, workshop, and retreat that was offered for years. I worked the numbers just like I was told, but I was STILL on a roller coaster. God had told me about my future and purpose in Mary Kay through prayer and messages from other people, and that was the only reason I didn't quit.

As I kept experiencing ups and downs in my Mary Kay business, I reverted back to building my business as an accounting consultant. I began to see a really unhealthy pattern with my consulting clients. All of my clients were frustrated with their accountants and CPAs. I heard the same things over and over again. They weren't asking enough questions, if any at all, they weren't offering money-saving tax strategies, they often would not "allow" them to write off legitimate business expenses, and they were just hard to deal with. I remember my housekeeper coming to me with her husband's business taxes. They had paid a CPA $1,500 and they owed $15,000 in taxes. She asked me if I would take a look at them. I asked two questions that her CPA had not asked and realized I could save her thousands with just those two things. They ended up only owing about $3,000. Out of this frustration, I created my first signature programs to help entrepreneurs save thousands of dollars using my signature tax strategies and financial management plans.

Things became increasingly worse financially for us as the economy completely crashed and we entered the height of the recession.

We began to literally sell off everything we had, bit by bit, over the next several years. We ended up with the bare minimum and we were living on food stamps. I still remember the day I looked into an empty pantry and thought to myself, "How are we going to feed our kids?" As a parent and a person, I felt unbearable failure. Even though my Mary Kay business had been doing fairly well, it had not yet replaced the income from our construction and real estate company. By the time I was 35, we had to file for bankruptcy. Going from millionaire to food stamps to bankruptcy was incredibly difficult. Not because I didn't want to give up the nice things, but because the loss of anything is devastating to your emotions and therefore your mindset.

Somewhere along the way, we got the idea that God was trying to teach us a lesson with money. For years, we kept praying and waiting on Him to JUST DO something. One day, I cried out to God, literally throwing myself on the ground! I asked Him what He was waiting on to bless us. What He said totally SHOCKED ME! I literally heard an audible voice, like a father in my ear say, **"Snowe, you're not waiting on Me, I am waiting on you!"** I remember saying, "WHAT?" I couldn't believe the answer. He was waiting on ME?

After that, I started asking myself what He meant. What was I doing or not doing that was blocking my blessings and the "flow" of money? God began to show me that I had fallen into the trap of negative fear and thoughts around money. After losing everything, I began to handle money in a way that was actually keeping it from me. And truthfully, I wasn't trusting Him as much as I thought I was. I was holding onto money so tightly that I couldn't make room for more. God literally showed me a vision of my hands stretched out and closed. He showed me that when my hands were closed, I was not "open" to receive more. This was such a powerful visual. I realized that I was indeed the problem, and I was ready for change.

So, I enrolled in an intensive group coaching program that was based on the science of the brain and how to move past your limiting beliefs. I was really excited because I had been studying the brain for years and I loved learning more. It was also so incredible to get a tangible answer to why my thoughts and feelings about money had become so bad. I finally learned why God said that HE WAS WAITING ON ME! I realized that I was actually holding myself back. Because I was not renewing my mindset daily and condition-ing it with God's promises for my life, my brain literally went into self-sabotage, creating its own reality. My negative self-talk created new, set ways of thinking and therefore beliefs which did not line up with God's word. Overcoming your past, negative self-talk and limiting beliefs is not an easy thing to do, but it is worth the end result. You will literally have to fight old beliefs that want to pull you back into your comfort zone and keep you stuck forever. In order to reprogram those old beliefs, you have to spend time every single day speaking new empowering statements over your life and yourself.

The longer you hold a thought, the stronger it becomes. Beliefs are just neural pathways in your mind that have solidified over time to the point that they become patterns. They are literally super highways of thoughts and patterns in your mind, most of which you are not aware. They control almost everything you do. In the coaching program I joined, I began to understand what I allowed to happen by not conditioning my mind daily and buying into the lie of there not being enough money. The truth is that there was more than enough money and resources for me to accomplish my purpose. I just needed to renew my mind daily and stay connected to God.

The group coaching program was really amazing. I learned a lot and even went one step further by studying to be a Master Coach, because I knew other women needed to be set free from limiting beliefs that were holding them back. However, there was still something missing for me. I was seeing a lot of improvement, but I could feel I was getting stuck again as I rebuilt my multiple streams of income. I was almost at six figures, but I wasn't able to push through.

I realized that I was stuck a lot sooner than I had previously, because I had already been down this path. I knew something wasn't feeling right and that, most likely, I was the key to change. The truth was that I was feeling very conflicted about my businesses, my passions, and my multiple gifts.

My passion has always been helping women. I fell so in love with Mary Kay because it was all about helping women. I loved teaching women how to have a profitable business while helping them grow personally. I was doing all of that through Mary Kay. Though I had a natural gift for finances and business, I would very quickly get frustrated when I was knee deep in money and numbers, because it is *so* not as feminine and fun. Mary Kay is feminine and fun, and that's why I loved it so much.

I was desperately trying to find a way to bridge the gap between my multiple gifts and talents. I even stopped marketing the money and tax business. I told God that I was just going to focus on my passion, Mary Kay. Without much effort of my own, He sent me more business in two days than I had all month, so I quickly got the message. He didn't want me to quit Mary Kay. I didn't understand why, so I just kept working the business as I attempted to get clarity.

I knew that I had to get crystal clear about who I was passionate about serving and why, or I would continue to be frustrated while not serving people at the highest level possible. I also realized that I would never find true happiness until I aligned with my soul's purpose. True success comes from being in complete alignment with your God-given purpose. It's not just about making more money; it's about why you are here.In order to get clear on these things, I had to understand how God made me. It's not just about what we want in life, it's about WHY God has put us on this earth and who we are meant to serve. God has given us all unique gifts, talents, personality, passions, and desires to help fulfill this purpose. Therefore, it is extremely important to understand all of these things so you can come into alignment with the purpose for your life.

I began to really think about the clients that I was serving. I started to ask myself which ones I really loved working with and why. I began reflecting on why I loved my Mary Kay business and the things that I knew God was intentionally bringing into my life. I also went back to my unique gifts, talents, personality, passions, and desires. I started to take an inventory of all of these things to bridge the gap between my frustration and purpose.

I knew that God had created me to be a spiritual leader for women, but I also knew I would serve well in business. I used to think that these things were separate, but then I began to realize they were one and the same. I was meant to be a business and spiritual leader for women entrepreneurs. After I realized this, I understood what God was trying to tell me. What I loved about Mary Kay, He wanted me to bring outside of the Mary Kay world.

There are women who do not have a business idea or gifts to monetize, but they desperately want to get back into the home with their families while still creating an executive income. There are women who do not want to sacrifice their family for a career, and women who will be stuck in low paying jobs with little or no opportunity for career advancement. For these women, I can help them start a Mary Kay business so that they can have it all: more money, more choices, and more time with their families. That was Mary Kay's mission and it is mine as well.

What I also began to realize, as I reflected on my business journey, was that a lot of women entrepreneurs were spinning their wheels because of their lack of business education, formal business training, money management training, and tax planning experience. Many of them were avoiding money and tax issues which caused even more problems. The ambitious ones were spending more time trying to make a business work, but they were still not realizing a profit. The women who were avoiding money and tax issues, or who had limiting beliefs, would get stuck and begin to think there was something wrong with them. This only made things worse.

The bottom line was that most women were not creating the type of success they really wanted. This kept them away from their families even more as they struggled to make a business work. Finally, I began to see the correlation between all of this and my life's purpose. As I began to think about the differences I wanted to make in this world to make it a better place, it finally all connected.

I realized that my passion and vision was to get women back into the home with their families. I realized that I wanted to teach women that they could build a six figure business and work SMART, not hard. Then women can truly have it all: more money, more choices, and more time with their families! I believe that when this happens, we will begin to see the change we want in this world as we pass on our values and not allow our children to be influenced by everyone else's. Once I understood this, I began to step into my divine purpose and that opened the door for more money to flow into my life. It wasn't just about making more money; it was about coming into alignment with my purpose.

Another reason I was able to move past what was holding me back was because I was committed to change. I was tired of struggling to make enough money and I began to see how I was the problem. God wasn't withholding something from me, I was.

Since then, I have talked to hundreds of women who are struggling to make enough money in their business and looking for help. For almost all of them, they are stuck because of one of three reasons, sometimes all three. The first reason is a lack of education or mentoring regarding a basic business and financial plan. Just like you cannot build a house without a plan, you cannot build a business without one. The second reason is that many women do not have clarity on their life's mission, so they are not in alignment with their soul's purpose. And the third is an unhealthy mindset or hidden success blocks. Mindset is simply a way of thinking. Unfortunately, most of us have been taught to think the wrong way from everything we experienced in life, and now we have hidden success blocks in our minds.I can teach you how to build a profitable business, how to create, manage and multiply money or how to have more success in your life, but if you have any limiting beliefs (which are learned behaviors that hold you back), emotional blocks or unresolved emotions, you will stay stuck.

The pain of remaining the same has to be far greater than making the changes to begin the journey. A lot of people say they want change, but they aren't willing to do the work. Change is not always easy, especially when you have to deal with junk deep within your heart and soul.

When I started to make changes in my life, I was ready. I did what was necessary every day so I could get the new results that I wanted. It's amazing how, in about a year, I went from bankruptcy to six figures. However, I know that I wasted years struggling and in pain when I didn't have to. I now help women learn from my mistakes, so that they can avoid unnecessary struggle and move years ahead in their journey.

Are you struggling with money when love and abundance are waiting for you? Are you tired of being stuck and frustrated? If so, change begins with you. You have a God-given purpose that only you can fulfill and everything you need, including money, is available for you. God has given you unique gifts and talents that you can exchange in this world for money, so you can fulfill your destiny. Money is just a tool that we use. But we must master this tool and not let it master us. We must learn to create, manage, and multiply money so that we can leverage this incredible resource everyone has access to. It is not an elusive object for a select few, something to be feared or avoided. It is a resource available to all who will learn to master it.

If you have negative thoughts about money or you fear or avoid it in any way, you must dig deep and press on so you can obtain that which you desire. The cave you fear to enter truly holds the treasure you seek. Do whatever it takes to learn how to master money, so that you can live the life God intended—emotionally, spiritually, AND financially free!!

Love and Belief,
Snowe

ABOUT SNOWE SAXMAN

Snowe Saxman is a Success, Wealth and Women's Expert. She has a degree in Accounting and studied for her MBA. She is a certified Tax and Neuro Coach and is known as the Money Oracle. She believes that we can change the world when we live our lives with God first, family second, and our careers third.

She is married to the love of her life, Paul. They have seven children and two grandchildren. Yes, Snowe is a Glamma (someone way too young and gorgeous to be called Grandma.)

Snowe was a millionaire at age 25, living on food stamps and bankrupt by age 35, and now she is earning multiple six figures and on her way to millions again. With God's help, she has been able to channel a painful past into a purposeful future and help other women with her unique gifts and talents.

Today she teaches women God-inspired success and financial + business strategies.

She can show you how to successfully improve your money mindset and create, manage, and multiply your money because she's done it herself. What makes her unique is that she is heart-centered but results-oriented. She uses a masterful combination of business savvy, money expertise, and a strong faith to improve your money mindset and a help you create, manage, and multiply money!

Snowe's approach is God-centered and faith-filled. Her mission is to empower women to live emotionally, spiritually and financially free. Her passion is to help you build a six figure business in a smart, soulful way that allows you to have more quality time at home with your family.

Snowe lives by the following belief: "It's not just about making more money, it's about helping more people."

You can connect with her at snowesaxman.com.

FINDING A WAY TO YES

Stephanie Sorrells

I sat sobbing uncontrollably with my forehead on my steering wheel. I had just pulled my car into the garage and closed the garage door. The heaviness and weight of the last three years came crashing down on me as if I was being buried alive under a rockslide. I couldn't breathe. Coming home from work and sitting in the dark garage triggered something in me and it was pouring out of every cell in body. My body was ferociously shaking. Thoughts bombarded my mind as they raced through my very essence and pierced my heart like darts.

I was overwhelmed emotionally and physically, and I was excruciatingly tired. I was tired of stress, tired of being a single mom, tired of not having enough, and tired of fighting with so many people. I just wanted it all to go away. If I just turned the car back on while in the closed garage, I would fall peacefully asleep forever, right? My life insurance money could be used to pay off debts, my kids' college education, and hopefully would help them get started in their own lives. The scar on my inner wrist from high school was a constant reminder that I had thought of this way out before. Helplessly, I languished in a pit of drowning sorrows as the darkness engulfed me and my thoughts.

Violently, a voice thundered at me as I felt the car shake. "Get out of your head. Your boys need a mom, not money."

In the moment, I couldn't tell if the voice I was hearing was fact or fiction. I peered into the darkness of my garage and even opened the car door to make sure no one was there.

What the hell is wrong with me? I thought. I had everything that I had envisioned and wanted out of this whole ugly divorce process.

Get your shit together! I screamed at myself.

Turning on the makeup mirror, I grabbed my purse off the floorboard to clean up my tear stained, snotty face as best I could. The genteel, southern women in my life taught me to always look my best and let no one see me cry. Besides, my youngest would know in an instant if I were upset. He was my empathetic one; he connected with others on a soul level and could sense things about others before anyone else. I dragged my briefcase, my purse, my cooler, and the groceries from the car and slowly trudged up the stairs and into the house.

Both boys bounded down from their rooms and into the kitchen with the most enormous hugs. "We missed you today mom!" they exclaimed.

It was all I could do not to cry, I felt like such a failure. Going through the motions of making dinner and absentmindedly reviewing homework, I felt like I was watching a movie rather than actually living my life. I couldn't eat; I couldn't even drink my nightly glass of wine I had poured for myself.

Finally, while the boys were taking their showers, I had time to sneak off to my room and change out of my work clothes and into my sweats. I just needed five minutes to myself. But as I hung my clothes in the closet, another wave of darkness and sobbing knocked me over. I fell to the closet floor, hugged my knees tight, put my head down, and just cried. I held myself so tight. I just wanted someone to hug me, someone to tell me I was making the right decisions, someone else to just take over. I was tired of being the strong one. I was tired of trying to be positive when I wasn't. I was tired of trying to be superwoman. I was tired of not shedding a tear. I was tired of working myself to pieces, not having enough, and keeping everything bottled inside me. I was so tired of listening to everyone else complain … I was tired. *Why won't this crazy merry-go-round stop?* My life was flying by at a million miles a minute. I just wanted off. Crying on my closet floor was the only place I could be alone in my tiny three-bedroom brownstone. It was the only place I could be where no one would see me.

THREE YEARS EARLIER

We were the epitome of the "white picket fence" family. We had a five-bedroom house in the suburbs, two boys who were stellar athletes with great grades, two cars in the garage, and my husband and I each had great jobs. We even had a golden retriever in the backyard. We did everything as a family: vacations, skiing on the weekends, and picking pumpkins. All of us were social. We had parties at our house and went out with friends. Our dance card was completely booked, as my grandmother used to say. To those looking in, we were the picture perfect family.

Funny thing is that when you are on the outside of the fish bowl, you truly have no idea what goes on behind closed doors. And if you are the one on the inside looking out, you may not have any idea what the others in the fishbowl are doing or thinking either. I know that was the case for both myself and my husband. Our "picket fence" family life mirrored itself on the inside, but deep down in our souls we didn't know what the other truly wanted. So our family life moved along as it was supposed to.

Because of my love of travel, I had built a company from the ground up and found a way to see the globe with my clients. I adored every minute of it. My company had become my third child, my life. I poured every ounce of love, heart, and soul into building Vibrant into a brand and attracting the clients that would believe in me. The more exotic the trip, the more excited I would become. I started attending conferences, speaking, being selected to join industry advisory boards, and traveling every other week. I relished my time on the road, seeing new places, and meeting new people. Even the long airport lines and crowded planes were exciting to me. I had created a life outside of my real one in Colorado. Vibrant ultimately became my happy place. And though I didn't realize it in the beginning, I had built my personal escape from reality. But deep in my soul, a question lingered. *What was so wrong with my reality that was making me run away?*

My husband had a job that allowed him to work from home, so he jumped into being the school mom, team mom, coach, and the school taxi driver. He loved every minute he got to be there for his kids. While I was away working insane hours, I would tell myself that being a school mom was never really my thing. But it was. I adored my kids and I felt alone and isolated when home. My travels took me to amazing, far away places and I had friends around the world. At home, I didn't know the parents on the football teams, swim teams, or at the schools. The seeds of resentment were being planted deep in my being while I berated myself because I wasn't a better mom, a more involved mom. The voice inside my head began as a low drumming, then over the course of time, it shouted at me continuously while my "mom guilt" continued to grow.

Working became my way of keeping my head in the sand while my reality at home slowly unwound. I tried everything to keep my marriage and myself together. If we were incredibly over-scheduled with parties, kids, activities, and social events, then I didn't have to be alone. I didn't have to talk about how this unsettling feeling within me was growing exponentially. I had the white picket fence life, the loving husband, and great kids. So what was wrong with me? If I wasn't home, things wouldn't get worse. I wouldn't have to face the things that were bottled up inside me and what was really going on in our little fishbowl. As my travel and business surged, arguments that we had never had started between me and my husband. I began blaming him for things that were wrong like finances, issues at our kids' schools, upkeep of the house, choice in cars, and purchases. I was finding fault with everything around me and blaming others rather than digging deep to find what was really wrong inside of me.

During the weeks I was at home, I would go through the motions of being a mom and wife. I made dinners, did the laundry, and helped with carpool when I could. But it didn't make me feel anymore fulfilled or happy. My joy of the day was waking my boys up in the morning or putting them to bed at night. It was my private time with them. I could snuggle up with them and laugh and talk. It felt like we were the only people on the planet. During the day, I would shelter myself inside my office and work at anything and everything that came across my desk to create trips or places I needed to go. My evenings were filled with mindless TV shows or movie reruns. My companion was my glass of wine. After the kids were in bed, sometimes I would drink the whole bottle and hope I could just sneak into bed without having to talk to or touch my husband.

This voice inside my head was getting louder. *What was wrong with me?* I had read every self-help book, met with therapists, tried to find hobbies and activities, joined gyms, and I had gone to see doctors. I even started taking Wellbutrin, thinking I had depression. I experienced postpartum depression with my oldest child, so maybe it was still lingering. Why was my husband always happy, and getting happier, when I seemed locked inside some prison that I couldn't escape? I began thinking about the "D" word, because I thought it had to be him or my marriage causing all this hell within me.

Hindsight is 20/20, so truthfully we were already there: divorced from a relationship with each other and divorced from a life together. I was gone every other week and he was usually traveling on the weeks I was home. There was nothing to share anymore except the kids and their routines and our friends. We didn't even like the same activities anymore; he adored the outdoors and mountain life and I yearned to be home in the south where my soul felt warmth and love, heat and humidity, the sand between my toes. It was our perfect suburban life that had overrun our marriage and the disengagement between us had dragged on for so long that I wasn't really sure I even wanted to work on us anymore.

But every time I would ask someone their opinion or seek some validation about my thoughts on divorce, the answers were the same. A friend that went through divorce told me, "That was the worst experience of my life." A dear loved one who had no idea what I was going through advised me that, "It will ruin your kids, you should stay together for the kids." My work colleagues said, "Are you crazy? How will you make a living for yourself?" And even my family warned, "The grass isn't always greener on the other side." The reactions would send me even further into a downward spiral that didn't seem to end. What was I going to do now if divorce wasn't an option?

The monotonous days at home turned into weeks away for work, and this went on for months and months. On the outside, we put on our happy faces and were the perfect couple. But the harder I worked to fix everything around me and find ways to make me happy, the worse I felt and the worse our marriage became. I was a "fixer,"

I liked to make everything OK. It wasn't until my mom emailed me a list of couple's therapists in Denver that I realized the "me" in "us" needed help to fix the "we." The list of therapists was long and overwhelming and I painstakingly went through each name reading the websites and reviews, interviewing and re-interviewing, asking for recommendations. Researching was my way of stalling so that I did not have to face what was in front of me. Finding a couple's therapist meant I wanted to work on us as a couple, but was that what I wanted? Could I not just find someone to listen to me, to help me find a better way back to myself?

Looking back now, my personal success coach, Kate Butler ,was correct in saying that the universe rewards inspired action. My research on therapists led me to Dr. Carole Brooks. She was my savior, my life raft in a turbulent sea of emotional messiness. Her office was my sanctuary, I could breathe there. Do you know what it feels like after you have had the breath knocked out of you? Finally inhaling and exhaling made me feel alive again. And even though my sessions lasted only an hour, I would feel revitalized again.

Patiently, she would listen, hour after hour, as I cried and sobbed out my story. There was no judgment, there was no opinion, there was just love. I learned so much about love of others, love of myself, love of the universe. She spoke of boundaries and gave me exercises and mind exercises. But most of all, there were assurances that everything would work out, as there is always a divinely crafted plan. She said something once, "God doesn't always give you what you want, but he gives you what you need. What you do with that need, whether to learn, or to grow, or to prosper, is up to you."

Dr. Brooks helped me realize that both me and my marriage had fallen by the wayside long ago. Everyone changes, it's inevitable in our life journey—nothing stays the same forever. As people change, a marriage or a relationship can grow to accommodate the changes if accepted by both people. But without the acknowledgement of the changes, the differences become little pebbles, dried leaves, and dead branches that, if ignored, over time will ultimately build a dam that stifles the energy flow in a relationship. A marriage is its own entity—like a puppy, a baby, or flower—it needs constant nurturing so that it will grow and prosper. Without love and growth, all things, including you, eventually find an end.

I was reminded of something an intuitive coach told me some five or six years earlier when I was dealing with my dad's passing. She said that a book is made up of many chapters, but just because a chapter ends it doesn't mean the story is over. A story is energy, a life is energy, a relationship is energy, and energy cannot be created or destroyed. It continues to exist by changing forms. That was one of my earlier "A-ha" moments from many years ago, and it came flying back to me in the moments with Dr. Brooks. Isn't it better to acknowledge that every ending leads to a new beginning? Don't we have a duty and a responsibility to teach our children when to recognize the end of a chapter and how to look forward to what is going to happen in the next one?

Dr. Brooks acted as a beacon of light that guided me through my thoughts and emotions. She taught me how to navigate back to certainty, back to a sliver of normal, and to recognize that, for me, divorce didn't have to be a bad word. Why did divorce have such a negative connotation? Was it just because others said so or their experiences were negative? When we change our perspective, the things around us change. We were already friends, we already shared most of the same values regarding raising our kids, and we did really want each other to be happy. I envisioned the end game, what it would be like when the divorce was final and all was settled. I focused on happiness; I focused on where I would live, what my life would look like, the happiness and centeredness of my children and their lives. Those became my goals, my intentions.

It's hard to meet with a couple's therapist by yourself. While I had many breakthroughs and realizations, those were only experienced by me. Now the reality was telling my husband and everyone else that I was OK, and that in order for me to grow, I wanted a divorce. And I believed that a cohesive divorce could be possible. I don't like conflict, I like making everyone happy. With my business I could make bold, boisterous decisions and be a badass entrepreneur. But creating waves at home, going against what someone else wanted, or hurting someone's feelings was a conflict I did not want to endure. And admittedly, I took the crappy way out; I let my therapist tell my husband while I was away on a trip. That didn't go so well. In fact, nothing in the months following went well.

Divorce was hard. Divorce was ugly. Divorce hurt. Divorce was sad. It was everything everyone had told me it would be. The dictionary refers to divorce as a separation, a dissolution, a cause to become disunited, disjointed, dislocated—the use of the prefix "dis-" always means bad news.

Feelings were hurt, words were said in anger, and wrongs were done by both of us. Yet, we kept it between us. Our children's happiness was our goal, our priority. I'm sure the boys felt tension, we all did. I was an emotional nutcase, I cried at the end of every day. I couldn't eat, couldn't sleep, and could barely keep my life together. The hardest thing was telling the boys, but for me the marriage was a commitment between "mom and dad" that was no longer serving the two people still in it. It was not the boys' fault and I didn't want them to suffer, carry emotional scars, or know later in life that we stayed together just for them. My vow to myself on that rainy afternoon in February was that a bad word would never be uttered about their father while they were present. That, in and of itself, changed the way we all viewed divorce.

I learned a lot about divorce and the resources available to couples. We filed all the paperwork ourselves and started the process of mediation. I wasn't a fan of our first mediator and I think because of that our negotiations disintegrated quickly, to the point that each of us had to hire lawyers. Though I think attorneys serve a purpose, the animosity that developed after hiring ours was unparalleled by anything I'd ever experienced. Our first family court date ended with my attorney yelling at me in the middle of the courthouse hallway because I wanted to do things my way, and submit documents that he had not reviewed. My husband and I had already agreed on the things we were splitting. It wasn't complicated. There wasn't a lot to be negotiated. Talk about an ego being rubbed the wrong way! The family court clerk asked the attorney to be removed from the property.

The kind woman brought us back into her office and I fell into a leather club chair, put my head down on her desk, and cried. I'm pretty sure my soon-to-be ex-husband wasn't sure if he should hug me, hold me, offer me a tissue, or laugh at me. But I didn't really care at that point. The clerk was so nice and gave us piles and stacks of booklets, paper work, business cards, and literally showed us a better, happier way. She said that was the purpose of their office, to make families stronger through divorce, not tear them apart.

That was another "A-ha" moment for me. We were still a family of four and would continue to be a family of four. No one or thing would change that. We would all be inexorably tied to each other and to our extended families and friends, forever. While I believe negative energetic ties can be cut, I also believe that once you are family, you are always family. My mother had always instilled the sense and importance of family in us. That was my turning point. Everything could be negotiated without the bad energy and negativity associated with divorce. As my youngest told me, "Mom, it's the creation of two households, not a separation."

By May of that year, after finding the perfect townhouse, I had moved out. I needed a fresh start, a new energy and purpose in my life. In September our divorce was final and all of this had only just started in February. Our new mediator was a true God-sent gift and the Family Court of Jefferson County, Colorado will always be on my gratitude list. In seven short months our lives were different. We were on our way to a friendly divorce.

THE CLOSET FLOOR

The heaving and quiet sobbing wouldn't stop. I hated this tiny closet. I had everything I wanted during my divorce: my freedom, my life, my finances, my business, my townhouse, and a very friendly divorce. In fact, we talked more now than when we were together. Was my family right, and the grass wasn't greener on the other side? What had I done to my life and to my boys? Regardless of how hard I worked or how much business I took on, there was never enough. Family and friends meant well, but the refrain was the same: "You shouldn't spend like that," "Put that towards the boys, not yourself," "What is your plan if you go through your money?" My favorite was, "You need to get a real job." I had constant fears of being a bag lady, losing my kids, and not being able to afford my townhouse or my car. The more I feared, the worse it got.

Bad habits crept back into my life. When the boys would go to their dad's, I wouldn't go to the grocery store because I didn't want to spend the money on food. I didn't want to go out with friends because I didn't want to spend the money. I stopped going to the gym and to yoga to save money. I bought a bathing suit to go on a trip with a girlfriend and felt huge amounts of guilt. Ironically, it was that same friend who said I needed help. I felt like the stress was going to kill me. Little did she know, I would drink a bottle or two of wine on the nights I was alone and lose myself in mindless television shows. To not think about my life, I would watch realities created by someone else.

By the end of that year I was stressed, overworked, and ended up needing an emergency hysterectomy right before Christmas. Ironically, I had just learned how menstrual and uterine problems arise from guilt and fear, rejection of creativity, and issues in home life. I adored the magic of the holidays and being with family, so to have a surgery interrupt that time of year made me angry with the doctors and everyone else. It should be no surprise then that every time I asked an opinion of someone, the feedback was negative: "You will be so miserable," "Your hormones will never be the same," "Did you research all options?" "Nothing is ever the same after surgery."

The universe was joyfully delivering feelings of guilt, anger, and fear, all neatly packaged with a bow for my Christmas gift that year. But by New Year's Eve, I was giving it all back.

During my recovery, I couldn't do anything but sit on the couch. I didn't take pain pills or drink, I just wanted to be better, and to be happy. I wanted more than what was happening on the outside of me. I wanted to help myself on the inside. The surgery and the recovery were my turning points. Slowly, I started remembering the things that made me happy. Playing board games and puzzles with the boys! Meditating and yoga made me happy—yoga was out for at least three months but I could meditate—so I found apps and music to download on my phone. An inspirational movie about the law of attraction had made me happy once many years ago, so I downloaded it and watched it religiously. I researched the speakers from the movie and found the ones that spoke to my soul. Writing made me happy, so I started journaling again. Reading made me happy. And somewhere in all of this I started finding myself and realizing only I can make myself happy.

FINDING MY WAY TO YES

When a person is driven to a ledge, it's usually for two very different reasons. The first is the more common, mainstream reason—they are drowning, drowning in negativity, drowning in fear. They are drowning in all that they see as wrong and this has forced them into a downward spiral. They have reached their breaking point.

The second reason a person is driven to a ledge is because she wants to spread her wings, shine her heart, and soar off the ledge in excitement to find out what is on the other side. She is inspired, confident, and wants the creative curiosity of what is out there.

Two very different feelings, two very different emotions, two very different ways of thinking can lead a person to a ledge. But it is the inbetween that matters most. It is inbetween those two stages where you MEET YOURSELF, find yourself, learn to love the vast expanse of your life. It is where you learn that, once you glide through the deep crevices and fields of life, you embrace the unknown and truly meet yourself.

When I finally found the courage to jump, I found my gift was my journey, including the fear and challenges along the way. My story is my way to share the gift, to show you the beginning, the inbetween, and that there is always the other side. It is finding a way to "Yes" even when you aren't really sure what your "Yes" is.

To meet your ME means that you know who you truly are at your core, at your heart center. You know what your downward spirals are and what brought you to the ledge. And you know how to talk yourself off the ledge and to look at it in a new light, a light that brings you to a "Yes." Yes is a word with a thousand connotations, but which one you claim for yourself is your determination. My gift is to show you three things: how to recognize a fear-spawned downward spiral, how to sit and stew (as a sweaty yoga teacher once called it) and take a predicated pause, and how to find the alluring inspiration lying on the other side.

I once saw the definition of the word spiral as "the path of a point in a plane moving around a central point while continuously receding from or approaching it." That definition struck me because my life is a moving plane, my journey is the path, and the central point is my heart center. When the death grip of a downward spiral lures me into its clutches, there can be no return as I steadily and almost violently recede from what my heart truly wants.

On the days when I didn't lead with my heart, it took one thought, one word, one action, one seemingly innocent experience or inter-action to cause the slip that allowed my head or my ego to takeover. Then I would feel the silent vise grip by some unseen force, and the negativity and fear slowly, and unceasingly, started their march to power within me. As with any revolution, it would start small—a quickening of my heart rate, my breath would become shorter and shallower, and my ego would sear one thought after another across my brain until the cascading waterfall of negativity turned into a violently churning wave and fear took over. I was lucky if this cycle would end in a couple of hours or even a day. In the last few years, my ego-demons would sit around for days, bullying my every move and thought. This was part one of my downward spiral.

The imagery and creativity inside me have always been lifelike in that I could create movie-like scenes playing on a reel in my head. I could see the colors, smell the scents in the air, and even feel emotions to my core. Everyone throughout my entire life has said I should be a writer because of what I could see only in my mind's eye. This power was great as a teenager on those rare occasions (well, not so rare to my family and friends) when I would rather lie to my dad than get caught doing something rebellious or wrong. I could recreate a scene in my head and live it so vividly, over and over again; lying became easy because my subconscious couldn't tell the difference. I had created an emotion that was tied to a feeling by a story and had thus altered my reality. This was part deux which led to a fear induced paralysis.

I learned through one of my mentors that a simple emotion or idea only lasts 90 seconds. So why do negative feelings like those of a breakup or lost loved one last so long? It is because we create stories tied to those emotions so that they become long lasting feelings that don't go away over time, unless we change the story. Changing the story changes the feelings and changes the emotions, so that the next time you have the same experience you can change your reaction. Many of our stories have been created over time or through many generations, which means changing them can take hard work, focus, effort, and time. This is when I sit and stew or take a very long predicated pause. If I can find what is causing my fear, then I can change the fear story.

My younger 20-something self usually didn't play in the short end of the fear pool very long before making a decision to change. And once I had made the decision, no one would be able to change my mind. I resembled a bull, charging after a matador's violently shaking red cape. There would be no conversation with myself, no time out. I would just decide the quickest route of escape. My emotions would get boxed up and put way high on a shelf, and I'd pull up my big girl panties and charge on. If I didn't get the answer I wanted, I either forced it on or turned somewhere else.

Effortless determination should have been my answer. When you take a predicated pause and look at fear from every angle you realize your fear is based on your perception of reality, your perception prison. Change your perception and you change your outcome.

When you mediate, pray, or put something out into the universe, you are asking for an answer and somewhere, somehow, you will receive it. But you have to be still enough to have the conversation and be open to hear the answer. Someone once said that when we are having a conversation, we are focusing on how we are going to reply instead of listening. In essence, we stop truly listening to what a loved one is asking, a family member needs, an employee is saying, a customer is requesting or what our soul wants because our minds are already formulating the reply. Our minds base their answers off of past experiences. As I tell my boys, "Get out of your head and into your heart!"

Your heart holds the answers to what makes your soul happy. Just visualizing, imagining, or focusing on what you want and what makes you happy brings joy and love into your heart. Your head is a wonderfully created analytical machine that usually tells you all the reasons why your dreams aren't possible. Your heart holds your center of gratitude and everyone has a reason to be thankful. Between my bed and the shower, I say five things I'm grateful for in my life. Every day I challenge myself to find something different. I play this game with my boys on the way to school. It will bring a smile to your face. It will show you that all is not lost and that it will provide your heart with hope. I journal and visualize my happily ever after—to be the "she-ro" of my own story. In order to visualize this, I have to get out of my head and ego. Be thankful of life's busy-ness, enjoy the pitfalls, the fears, the problems, and all the inbetween, because if you get to the stage of regret, you will have missed the point and opportunity of gratitude.

Every situation, every problem, every fear requires us to learn why we are here, unlearn the behavior or the story that brought us here, and then relearn a new way. Do you know how many times a child hears the word "no" by the age of 18? More than 250,000.

I don't believe in "No." Unless you are bleeding, walking into a burning building or some other dire situation. Actually, I've never told a client, "No." "No" is a negative and I'm in a customer service based industry.

"Let me work on that for a while and let me get back to you, will that work?" That is my standard reply, so much so that a client recently called me out on it and thanked me for it.

"Hey Steph, you know that thing you do when I ask you some wacky, bizarre, off the wall, request?"

I looked slyly at him and slowly shook my head and said, "What?" as a smile crossed my lips.

"You never tell me 'No.' You never do what I asked, but you come back with so many other options that we always do it a different way that makes me more happy than what I wanted in the first place."

Always remember that finding your "Yes" is often not the "Yes" you were looking for in the beginning. Sometimes you find your "Yes" in that inbetween, messy, middle part of the journey that requires you to jump off that ledge of fear. Challenges with any question or fear will always present themselves. Roadblocks are a normal part of the process and it's ok to be dejected and down when faced with the bumps. During times like this, take a pause … is a door truly shutting, or can you creatively find a "Yes?" My coach, Kate Butler, says it's because the universe wants to know if what you are looking for is truly what your heart desires.

Realizing I wanted a divorce wasn't the "Yes" I was originally looking for. Instead, I thought I needed to change myself or I needed to find something that would make me happy. It took someone else questioning my beliefs and offering different potential outcomes for me to see and then believe in the possibilities. The middle was a messy, hot, squalor-filled emotional volcano, but once I made the decision to focus on myself, my wings blossomed and my heart soared to happiness I didn't think could be possible. Find your fear and you find your way to "Yes."

ABOUT STEPHANIE SORRELLS

Stephanie Sorrells is the owner and Experience Creator of Vibrant Incentives. With 25 years of experience, Vibrant focuses on creating exclusive, luxurious, and authentic appreciation experiences for its clients. Top Fortune 500 companies call Stephanie their "secret weapon" when it comes to wowing their most important clients.

Stephanie is currently a member of the Northstar Media Advisory Board and the Leading Hotel of the World's Advisory Board, and she is a former member of Saveur's Culinary Travel Board. She was also a recently featured speaker for the Association of Destination Management Executives. Prior to opening Vibrant in 2008, Stephanie worked in the meetings and incentive industry across many sectors, including politics on Capitol Hill, the international automobile industry, manufacturing, and a luxury leisure travel service.

Stephanie is dedicated to creating a worldwide culture focused on appreciation and finding a way to "yes", both personally and in revolutionizing the customer service industry. Her first book will be published later this year on "Finding a Way to Yes" and will guide readers through finding their fears to a yes, both personally and professionally.

Stephanie Sorrells is a speaker, consultant, and writer in the meetings and incentives industry, elevating customer service and personally helping others find their way to yes. She can be reached through her website: www.stephaniesorrells.com.

THE VIEW FROM 38,000 FEET

Lee Tkachuk

November 20, 2011. What an amazing trip it was! Over 100 of us were finishing up one of the best vacations EVER—seven days in Puerto Vallarta, Mexico, with 22 in our actual group of friends. Perfect weather, sandy beaches, country music, delicious food, and too many blender drinks to count. Oh, Mexico. We weren't ready to leave you, but it was time to get back to our real lives, to our kids and pets and jobs and businesses. Time to get back to reality with bills to pay, deadlines to meet, and dentist appointments to schedule. But not yet! We still had 15 hours until we had to be back at our desks, in our kitchens, driving car pool. Fifteen hours to have fun and laugh and make more memories. Fifteen more hours to forget our responsibilities and spend time with this great group of people.

This was our eighth year at Country on the Beach, an annual gathering of country music fans, always somewhere tropical and always insanely fun with each one more fun andmore wild than the one before. We all meet up once a year for this wonderful break from the real world. We hang out with old friends and make new ones, year after year, and this year was one of the best so far.

Heading to the airport was still part of the adventure—a driver who was friendly, a road that wasn't quite paved, full of dips and bumps, but it didn't matter. We were all suntanned and happy and laughing all the way to the airport, through customs and on to the plane.

The flight attendants were smiling as we all got in our seats, still calling out to each other across the aisles, and they were probably thinking that we all had done some morning drinking before getting to the airport.

As my husband, Jeff, and I settled into our seats—me in my usual seat, 5B, and him right next to me—we smiled sleepily at each other and got ready for the flight. Pillows, blankets, headphones. Check, check, check. Phones off. Check.

Not quite 20 minutes later, everything changed. There was a weird feeling in the air, and the plane's air masks dropped down from above. Jeff and I looked at each other for a few seconds, not sure what was going on, and then put our masks on. (You know that part of the flight attendant's spiel about oxygen will be moving even if your mask doesn't inflate? It's true! Jeff's inflated, mine stayed flat. I was still getting air, but that wasn't what held my attention.)

Instead, I looked around for the flight attendants to see how they were reacting. I fly a lot and when we hit bad turbulence, I'm always reassured by the flight attendants sitting in their jump seats, legs crossed, flipping nonchalantly through magazines. Not this time!

One flight attendant was sitting and crying. Another one was praying. The third—trying not to get hysterical—was struggling to get her portable oxygen mask out of the overhead bin, but it was stuck. She was crying, and pulling, and starting to panic when it finally came free. What a relief! But only for a second.

We started to realize that this was real. This was not a drill. This was not a test. This was not a joke. *This was real.* The plane smelled like smoke. No one was saying a word. Even the baby that had been crying at takeoff was silent.

We all just sat there with our yellow masks on, not really sure what to do. I, too, just sat there, gripping Jeff's hand like it was a lifeline. The pilot came on the speaker and told us not to panic, to remain calm, that we were too far from the airport in Puerto Vallarta to turn around but that we were going to make an emergency landing in Monterrey, Mexico. He told us that we were going to descend pretty rapidly from 38,000 feet to 5,000 feet and to hang on.

Then he told us to pray.

I can't tell you what was going through the heads of everyone else on the plane, but I can tell you what was going through mine. And it sure wasn't what you, or I for that matter, would have expected.

As we were flying through the mountains of Mexico—not above them but literally through them, I didn't worry about leaving our only son, Jeffrey, then 20 years old, as an orphan. I didn't think about how devastated my parents would be if we crashed. I didn't think about who would take care of our dogs or straighten out our finances. I didn't even pray. At least not right away.

Instead, the only thing that went through my head, the only thing I was thinking about was … *I have a meeting with my biggest client on Tuesday, and I can't miss it.* Yup. Not my family, myself, or a movie clip of my life. All I could think about was work.

Since I'm telling you this, you've already figured out that we landed safely. The landing was a little benign compared to the rapid descent and the fear we had been experiencing. We landed very smoothly; it was sort of anticlimactic because we had convinced ourselves that it was going to be a traumatic event. We didn't bounce or hop or spin, but instead landed softly, a better landing than many flights I've been on in the past.

Nothing dropped out of the overhead bins or flew around the plane. No one screamed. Actually, no one did anything. We didn't talk, didn't clap, didn't laugh, didn't cry. I don't even think that the pilots or flight attendants made any announcements. We were in shock and just happy to be alive.

Once on the ground, we were met on the tarmac by ambulances, fire trucks, and shuttle buses that took us from the plane to the terminal. We were all quiet as we looked at the plane with the black burn marks down its side, from the engine extending halfway down the plane and a few feet high. We didn't say a word, nothing at all, until we were safely in the terminal.

The airline put us all in a restaurant and told us to have whatever we wanted to eat and drink while they figured out what they were going to do with us. It wasn't easy for them because we had just had an emergency landing in one of the most dangerous places in Mexico at the time.

This was a place where even our American Embassy had been closed. A place that it was not safe to be, even if driving, much less walking around. So dangerous, even in the airport, that we had to have escorts to leave the restaurant and go to the restroom, even though we were in the airport terminal. But we didn't care … we were safe, and we had each other!

Friendships were strengthened that day, and new friends became family. We had all shared something so powerful and had made it through! We ate and drank, and ate and drank some more, and then all too soon we boarded a plane that they brought in for us and flew back to Chicago.

Were we nervous? Oh, you better believe it! Were we happy to land at O'Hare International Airport at 2 a.m.? We sure were! But more importantly, we all walked away from who we were earlier that same day. We'd all changed. We all had something to think about, to be grateful for, and to celebrate.

Me? I knew I had to make changes. I knew that day, that experience, was going to change the way I looked at things. It would slow me down and would make me put family and friends first, and to put work lower down on my list. I knew I would have to make some serious changes and to really dig deep to figure out how to set my own priorities differently. I had to figure out what had brought me to that point and how in the world was I going to make the necessary changes. I didn't have the answers right then, but I knew that I would down the road, that my true priorities needed to be reflected no matter the circumstances.

I decided to jump all in on this one, as I do most things. Instead of going back to life as it was before the plane scare, I decided to take a few days and figure out what to do. I took out a few pieces of paper and a bunch of brightly-colored markers, and I put a title on each of the pieces of paper, all in a different color, to represent the six areas of my life that were (supposed to be) my priorities: family, friends, work, home, faith, and obligations.

A couple of these were easy and I could get them out of the way fast—obligations (who likes paying bills or going to the doctor?) and faith—but four really needed my attention, and this was the time to give that attention, to fix what I could and move on, hopefully in a better place than before the vacation. It was obvious that I could not continue the way that I was living. Who could? I was unhappy all the time, stressed beyond belief, and marking time rather than living life. I needed to hit the reset button.

FAMILY

This one was going to be tough. I considered myself a good mom and good wife, but what was I really measuring? Sure, I was home a lot and never missed anything that my son was in. I was involved in his school, went to every play, attended every game. I had been married for 22 years, and Jeff and I still loved each other and actually liked each other, but was that enough? I saw my parents a few times a year, spent holidays with my brother and sister and their families, and rotated those holidays with spending time with my in-laws. I made sure to make birthday and anniversary calls and always, always wrapped presents so pretty that everyone commented on them. Wasn't that enough? Nope. It was all on the surface. I no longer knew what anyone liked or loved, and the only way I could do Christmas shopping was if everyone gave me a list of what they wanted. The only time I spent any time with my family was marked by holidays on a calendar and the few times a year that I felt guilty and stopped by my parents' house for half an hour. More often than not, those visits were because I needed to drop something off or pick something up, not just a random visit. I wasn't even sure where to begin to make the changes but I knew that I needed to do something.

I made a promise to myself to connect—really connect—more with my family and extended family. I started with evenings, being more available to Jeff and Jeffrey, going out to dinner and not talking about work, and even enjoying an occasional movie with them. Jeffrey was, and still is, living in South Florida, where he was attending the University of Miami. We have always been close but upon thinking about it, I was becoming a robot mom and a nagger. Every call centered around his grades and my money (my son can spend like no other!) and things he needed to do. We ended every call by saying that we loved each other, but it was usually after I spent 10 to 15 minutes nagging him. Not fun for him, and certainly not fun for me. I needed to change that and I started with the very next call. I told him how proud I was of him, how I admired him for going to school 1200 miles away from his friends and family. I asked him about his friends, what he was learning, and what he did in his free time. Being a typical college student, he was a little hesitant at first and gave me a lot of one and two-word answers, but as the call progressed and with calls that followed, he started to open up and we talked—really talked—about everything. He told me about how scared he was when he first got down there, how much harder the classes were than he expected, how it was hard to not procrastinate. I was able to give him stories of me in college and things I went through, and both of us were amazed at how little things have changed in 30 years. Of course, I left some things out, wanting him to still believe I was a perfect student who spent evenings at the library and went to bed every night by 10 p.m.! Some things are best kept secret from our kids, right?

My husband was a little tougher. He's an awesome guy, but we'd grown apart. We've always had separate interests (let's face it ... I am NOT an outdoors person, so I was never going to share a love of hunting, fishing, or camping) and some shared ones (hockey, football, and music), but we had gotten to the point that we were doing most things apart. That's not a good place to be. I was working a million hours a week, and he was playing a million hours a week, nothing bad, but it was building resentment inside of me. I couldn't understand why he wasn't as motivated as I was in my business and what the attraction was to playing video games, having a beer, and watching bad (in my opinion) television. He wasn't hanging out in bars or running around with rough people; he was home, but we were not doing anything together. So I tried to make some big changes and to spend more time doing things together every day. The first night, I fell asleep watching a movie that he loved and I found boring. The second night, I sat on a stool in our basement and watched him shoot pool and have drinks with his sister and her husband. I'm surprised I didn't fall asleep during that; I was bored out of my mind. The third night, he asked me what the heck was up, so I told him. He laughed and thought about it a second and then listed everything we do together, the things we both love to do together and the fact that we eat dinner together and sleep in the same bed most nights. The only exception was when he was at our camper, a place I avoid at all costs. (If you could see our camper, you'd laugh. It's not exactly roughing it. It has an upstairs, hardwood floors, a big-screen T.V., and a fireplace! But it's still camping, and not my thing.) He was right! We do a lot together, but we're not glued at the hip, and it works for us. I was creating problems where there were none, but we would try to do a few more things together, just not things that would seem like torture for the other person. The best thing to come out of all of that was the decision to take up ballroom dancing and get lessons. Hmmm … still working on scheduling that!

FRIENDS

My husband and I have a huge group of mutual friends, many since high school, and I have others that I have made throughout the years—college, work, neighbors, sports moms, mutual hobbies and interests, through other friends—the usual ways we make friends as adults. I'm lucky that making friends comes easily to me, but what kind of friend was I? Not very good. Again, I was always good with remembering birthdays and anniversaries and everyone can expect my holiday card to arrive first every year, but that doesn't equal being a good friend. I made a decision to reach out to a different friend (or family member) at least three nights a week while taking my evening walk. I walk for an hour five or six times a week, and some nights I can talk to two people. Funny thing is, a few others have started doing the same thing, and we have weekly walk-and-talk calls, a great way to catch up AND to get our steps in. I sometimes invite people to walk with me, another great way to catch up with each other. I made a few breakfast dates with girlfriends on the weekends when Jeff is at the camper. I'm grateful to have girl time, and he's grateful to not be included! I also made it a point to start going to important milestones for our friends—birthdays, graduations, sporting events. It's easy to get caught up in our own lives, but we are all enjoying seeing each other more often and making the effort, well worth it. It's crazy how often you can see your friends when you make the effort. And even if it's just something you would be doing anyway (think BBQ on a summer night), it's amazing how much fun it can be!

HOME

We have a beautiful home, but we'd been there for 7 years already, and there were things that needed to be changed or finished, and we were WAY overdue for a decluttering. My honey-do list was getting longer by the second, but we had ignored it all, thinking that there would be a better time to get to it, a time that was less busy and less hectic. Never happened. Now the list was long and overwhelming but not impossible. I went room to room and made a list of everything from "fix the paint chips" to "hang the pictures leaning against the wall" to "call someone to fix our smoke alarms". We've knocked out quite a few of those things now but there's always something that needs to be done. We do them as needed now, as we decide they need to be done, rather than letting them pile up. It's MUCH less stressful. It's also quite satisfying to go through clothes and books and donate them. Double bonus—decluttered my house and helped someone else.

BUSINESS

The last and final thing combines work and personal, and, in my opinion, was the hardest to tackle as I had fallen into habits that needed to be changed drastically. Have you ever heard the phrase "Ain't no one happy if mama ain't happy"? That applies here. I wasn't happy, not at all.

I had spent the last 15 years building Keystrokes (my business) from a one-man show at my dining room table to an eight-figure corporation with more than 400 employees, but I was miserable most of the time. I was working around the clock. I had gained a lot of weight, was not healthy, and snapped at everyone. And not occasionally, but all the time.

Even when on vacation, I was spending a good portion of every day on my laptop, checking emails and getting updates from my staff, then telling them what I needed them to do. I had my phone glued to my hand, even at school functions with Jeffrey or dinner with my family. I could not sit through one of Jeffrey's football games or wrestling meets without taking glances at email or sneaking off to make a phone call.

I was under the mistaken impression that I had to answer every email immediately, to pick up the phone the second it rang, to check office messages every 20 minutes. It was a reactive, not proactive, way of running a business, and no one was having a good time. I was always stressed and rarely happy.

More. I was always trying for more. More everything. Money. Time. Customers. Employees. Numbers were more important than the people behind them. I needed to change that, but first I needed to figure out what would be a better place for me. What did I really want to do? What was my passion?

I sat down with yet another clean sheet of paper (I love clean sheets of paper, can you tell?) and a pen and just brainstormed. What did I enjoy about my business? What did I dislike? What would I love to do if money were no object and time was unlimited? What would I WANT to do if I didn't HAVE to do anything?

The words came easier than I imagined, and what I saw on the paper energized me. The things that I loved to do were no surprise—giving presentations, teaching others, learning new things, closing sales and forming relationships. If I could be a professional speaker and train others to be better speakers, I could combine my skills and passions into a happier life. I could constantly learn new skills that I could pass on to others. I could help others become successful in their businesses and their lives.

However, I still had a business, and a pretty big one, to run, and it was taking all of my time—while awake and asleep! I needed to figure out how my dreams could work with my reality, and I came up with a way to do both. I delegated most of my daily, weekly, and monthly work obligations and decided to concentrate on speaking.

I started with our internal sales presentations, something I had always done but never considered speaking. Crazy but true! I started giving webinars to potential customers and speaking at industry conferences. All of a sudden, I realized that six months had passed and I was ENJOYING life again. I had successfully transformed from a workaholic—stressed, not enjoying life, unhappy, and un-healthy—to a person who was playing as hard as she was working. And even when working, I was ENJOYING myself.

What a difference! Was it easy? Actually, it was easier than I thought it would be, but I believe that the changes were born of necessity. I still work hard and still have a passion for growing my business, but I take time to enjoy life, too. When I do something with my friends or family, I'm all in. I've even left my phone at home while out for the evening, something I never, ever, ever would have done five years ago. I've gone on vacation without a laptop, more than once! And now I have time to do things I love with people I love, all because of a scare in the air.

Looking back on that fateful November day, I'm embarrassed to admit that my thoughts centered around work. In fact, it took me a few years to tell anyone that—even my husband and closest friends, but I've decided there's a reason that happened to me.

Put yourself in my place. What will be at the top of your mind in an emergency? Will it be your spouse? Your kids? Your parents? Your siblings? Your pets? Your friends? Your job or company? What is most important to you? I have my answers, but it took a serious scare to get me where I needed to be. I'm there now. You have a chance to evaluate your priorities without such trauma.

What will you do when the air masks come down?

ABOUT LEE TKACHUK

Lee Tkachuk is a serial entrepreneurand the founder of Keystrokes Transcription Service, Ellipsys, SpeechCheck, Girly-Girls Know Sports and Lee Tkachuk – Limitless! She is a professional speaker, a born entertainer, a knowledgeable teacher and avid Chicago sports fan. She and her husband, Jeff, live part of the year in the far west suburbs of Chicago and part of the year in South Florida, a short drive from their son, Jeffrey, who goes to school and lives in nearby Miami.

With a passion for teaching others and a love for travel, you can find Lee speaking at conferences and meetings, coaching others on improving their presentations and speaking skills, and sharing her knowledge while helping fellow entrepreneurs avoid the speed bumps, potholes and brick walls that often come with starting and growing a business! You can contact Lee by phone at (630)385-7504 or via her websites at:

www.LeeTkachuk.com or www.GirlyGirlsKnowSports.com.

CAREFUL WHAT YOU WISH FOR ...
YOU JUST MIGHT GET IT

Erin Whalen

*(AKA, How to Get Clear On Your Vision and
Manifest a Life You Love.)*

I have a confession to make: I'm not that into "woo."
  I don't read my horoscope, consult tarot cards, speak to angels, or wear crystals in my bra. No disrespect to those who do—whatever fills your life with purpose, magic and meaning and helps you feel like you're connected to something larger than yourself is a good thing in my book.

But I'm more of a seeing is believing kind of person. That's why I am such a huge believer in manifestation—the idea that once we get clear on what we want, we will "attract" it into our lives. I've seen the force of this principle at work in my life too many times for me NOT to believe in it.

WHEN A DOOR OPENS, WALK ON THROUGH

Nine years ago, I was living with my husband and two-year-old son in a tiny shoebox of a house in Vancouver, the most expensive city in all of North America. My husband Rob and I worked for the same marketing company as copywriters and content developers. We were grateful for our jobs but didn't love them. Rob had gone to school to be an elementary school teacher but hadn't been able to find a job in Vancouver, and it was my lifelong dream to be a successful author. To achieve that goal I spent all of my free time working on a young adult novel that I hoped would allow me to quit my job and spend all my time writing fiction.

We were stressed out from our jobs and tired all the time but couldn't afford to work fewer hours—not with the cost of living in Vancouver. The thought of moving out into the suburbs, so far away from Vancouver's beautiful mountains, beaches, and forests, made us sad. And we dreaded the idea of making the hour-plus commute to work every day and losing even more precious time with our fast-growing toddler.

To make matters worse, we really wanted to give our son a younger brother or sister close to him in age, but our shoebox was too small for four people. We were reluctant to move, though. The rent was so cheap, moving meant we would have way less money in the bank.

I desperately wanted our situation to change, but I couldn't see how it could possibly happen.

Then one day, when I was feeling especially frustrated with my family's work/life situation, a former colleague stopped by the office to say hi. I felt a surge of envy as soon as I saw him. Mike had managed to escape the corporate world a couple of years earlier and was living what I considered "the dream." He was a copywriter and content developer who had used his talents to create a successful online business and grow it to the point where he was able to quit his job and become his own boss. Soon afterward, he and his family had moved from the city to the Sunshine Coast, a beautiful stretch of coastline 40 minutes north of Vancouver and accessible only by ferry.

I had visited the Sunshine Coast once, years earlier, and remembered how beautiful it was—a string of small coastal communities nestled in the rainforest, bordered by snow-capped mountains on one side and the Pacific Ocean on the other. Trees, ocean, mountains, wildlife: it was my idea of paradise. Rob and I often daydreamed of retiring there someday when we were finally free from our jobs in the city.

So yes, I was just a wee bit jealous of Mike and his family. When he stopped by the office that day, I told him how lucky I thought he was, and how much I wished I could follow in his footsteps.

"Why don't you?" he asked. "You could go freelance and work from anywhere you want."

"I can't afford to quit and go into business for myself," I told him. For years that had been my worst nightmare. I couldn't imagine dealing with all that uncertainty and risk. Where would I find clients? What if no one wanted to hire me? What if I failed?

"You could always ask the boss if he'd let you work remotely," he suggested.

I hesitated. My manager had agreed to let me and Rob work a four-day week (at 10 hours a day) and take separate days off so our young son only had to go to daycare three days a week. It was possible he would agree to let us work from home. Not very likely, I thought, but possible.

Mike must have seen the flicker of hope in my eyes. He insisted on inviting me and my family to spend the night at his place on the Coast the following weekend, so we could check out the area for ourselves and see if we liked it.

The funny thing is, I didn't even know Mike very well at the time. He had quit six months after I started and the idea of spending the night with people I didn't know very well made me feel shy. But something inside me knew I needed to accept the invitation. So I swallowed my fear and said yes.

That weekend getaway changed the course of my life.

Mike and his family were lovely hosts. They had a beautiful home with a gorgeous backyard that bordered a forest, and their living room windows looked out over the ocean. Mike took us on a ride in his speedboat and we caught crabs that we boiled and ate for dinner that night.

It was paradise.

On the ferry ride back to Vancouver the next afternoon, Rob and I were already plotting to return the following weekend to start looking at houses for sale. But first, we had to talk to our manager and see if such a move was even possible. If he didn't agree to let us work from home, there was no way we'd be able to make the move.

When I went to bed that night, I dreamed of forests and oceans. I woke up the next morning filled with powerful conviction and the certain knowledge that I wanted to move to the Sunshine Coast and build a life for my family there.

That day, I swallowed my nervousness and walked into my boss's office to present my plan. I explained that my husband and I wanted to move to the Sunshine Coast, and asked if it would be possible for us to work remotely three days a week and come into the office on the fourth.

To my complete and everlasting surprise, my boss said yes. (It just goes to show you—it never hurts to ask, and you never know which helpers in your life will give you what you need to make your dreams come true.) Rob and I were so ecstatic that we celebrated that night by trying for baby number two. When we returned to the Coast the following weekend to start looking at houses, I was already pregnant.

We fell in love with one of the houses we looked at that day, and less than a month after asking, "Is this even possible?" we bought our first-ever home in the rainforest paradise of our dreams.

HAPPILY EVER AFTER? GUESS AGAIN

Life on the Sunshine Coast was amazing. Making the weekly commute into the city was not. Sure, it was only one day a week, but it was a long day that started at five in the morning and didn't see us getting home until seven at night. And I was pregnant with our second child, which made the commute even more exhausting. I counted down the number of weeks until I'd finally be able to go on my yearlong maternity leave (props to Canada, yo.)

"Lucky you," my husband would grumble. "I wish I could take more than just a couple weeks off to stay home and enjoy the baby."

Then he got laid off.

The year was 2008 and our company had been hit hard by the financial crisis. My husband was one of the last writers hired by the company, and as sales continued to plummet, he ended up being one of the first to get fired.

Be careful what you wish for.

There we were, living in a remote coastal community and paying a hefty mortgage for our first-ever home, and my husband had no job. What were the chances of him being able to find another company in Vancouver that would be willing to let him work from home? Not so good, we figured. But the idea of him commuting five days a week into the city and never seeing his family was too horrible to contemplate. So I begged him to try looking for a job locally.

By some miracle, a local company had posted an ad in the local paper looking for an experienced online marketer. My husband applied for the job and was hired. The position paid considerably less than what he had been earning in Vancouver, but at least he would be able to spend more time with us at home.

Money was tight but we managed to make ends meet. As the end of my maternity leave approached, I began to dread my impending return to work.

My coworkers who had kept in touch during my year off told me that the company's sales had continued to plummet. People were getting laid off every month, and the company had moved from its downtown location to cheaper offices near the outskirts of the city. The move added an extra 30-40 minutes onto my commute. I couldn't stomach the thought of making that long journey every week, so I negotiated a new deal with my new manager (the old one had been a victim of one of the many rounds of layoffs) that allowed me to go into the office just one day a month instead of one day a week.

To my surprise, like his predecessor, he agreed. (Once again, it never hurts to ask.)

When I went back to work, I was startled to discover how depressingly toxic the workplace had become. No one had any faith in the company and people were sick of seeing their friends lose their jobs. My coworkers were jumping ship one after the other. I yearned to follow their lead and escape—but what company would hire me and let me work from home? There were a lot of out-of-work marketing specialists at the time and I didn't think any company would hire someone who worked from home when they could have their pick of people willing to go into the office every day. Once again, I felt trapped.

Then the company went belly up, forcing me to escape whether I was ready or not.

Like I said, be careful what you wish for.

SERENDIPITY SIGNALS THE WAY

There I was, newly jobless, living in my small coastal town in the rainforest with my husband and two young boys—and faced with an impossible choice: Do I find another job in the city and spend zero time with my young children Monday through Friday, thanks to the two-plus hour commute, or do I go into business for myself?

Aaaiiiieeeee! Talk about a Catch-22.

There was no way I was going to miss out on seeing my kids five days a week. But starting my own business was the scariest idea in the world to me. Even though I was a seasoned marketing professional, I hated the idea of having to market myself. I was used to plying my trade incognito. As lead copywriter, I was the voice of the company, selling its products and services. I wasn't the voice of "Erin," selling my own services. The idea made me feel naked and vulnerable.

With the alternative being never getting to see my kids, however, I had no choice but to bite the bullet.

"Please don't let me fail," I remember thinking. "Please let me get clients ASAP and make enough money to ensure we don't go bankrupt and get forced out onto the streets!"

Seriously. I worried that might happen.

Within days of making the conscious decision to start my own business, I learned there was a government program here on the Coast that helped people create and launch their own small business.

"How serendipitous!" I thought.

I applied and was accepted into the program, which started a couple of weeks later (serendipity at work again.) The main reason I was so excited about the program is because it provided me with a year of guaranteed income as I went through the process of launching and growing my business. It wasn't a lot of money, but it was enough to pay the bills and ensure my family wouldn't get kicked out onto the streets.

To make things even better, I started getting consistent client work before I had even launched my business. Through the program

I had the opportunity to meet a number of local businesses, many of whom wanted to hire me.

"Well, that's certainly fortuitous," I thought.

When the yearlong program ended, I had to say goodbye to my government-funded financial safety net.

And I got scared.

Sure, I was getting consistent client work, but there were many times when I had no idea what I'd be working on the following week. A week without income made me anxious. What if it stretched into two weeks? Or three?

Looking back, I can see that I never had anything to be concerned about. Despite the fact that I never really bothered to market myself, a new client opportunity always seemed to come along at just the right time.

BUT, I cautioned myself, over and over. Just because I had been lucky so far, that didn't mean the work wouldn't dry up in the near future. I couldn't allow myself to trust that my luck would hold. The fact that it wasn't "luck" at all, but a testament to my ability to provide excellent work, never occurred to me.

So I developed a very grasping mentality about client projects and said yes to every single one that came my way.

THE CLEARER YOUR VISION, THE EASIER IT IS TO MAKE IT A REALITY

I wrote sales pages for hardcore Internet marketers—website copy for a model rocket builder and an auto parts manufacturer, search-optimized product pages for a company selling high-end organic children's wear, and newsletters for knitters and quilters.

I wrote artist statements for local painters and email-marketing campaigns for baby sleep consultants. I created media kits for a children's author, an essential oils company, and a traditional black-smith. I designed websites for my son's daycare and a local arborist.

All of these were valuable experiences that taught me a lot, and my clients were all lovely people. But, juggling dozens of small jobs for very different audiences and industries was exhausting. I was working seven days a week, morning to night most days, and was still barely making enough to make ends meet. This was mostly my fault. I kept my rates deliberately low because the majority of my clients were local businesses with small marketing budgets. On top of that, I felt guilty charging them for the full amount of time I worked on each project. I worked a lot of hours that I never got paid for.

I was working seven days a week and barrelling towards burnout. On top of that, I spent almost every night working on my young adult novel and was feeling more pressure than ever to finish it so I could find a publisher and finally start making money with my fiction writing. I had frequent crying jags because I felt like I never got to hang out with my family and was missing out on key moments in my sons' childhood.

I couldn't go on like that.

So I did something I never thought I'd do: I started working with a coach to help me bring more order and sanity into my business and my life. With her support, I made the uncomfortable decision to pursue a different kind of client. Instead of saying yes to whatever came my way and working for dozens of clients who all had small jobs for me, I decided I wanted to find one or two clients who would give me a large amount of regular ongoing work. Juggling two clients seemed like it would be way easier than juggling twenty!

Lo and behold, just a few weeks after getting clear on what kind of client I wanted, I was approached by a local start-up in need of an experienced online marketer. They hired me to write all of their website and online store copy and set up an email marketing program that would allow them to sell their products to an online audience. They also wanted me to do PR and content development.

I felt like I had won the lottery.

Well. Once again, be careful what you wish for.

Everything seemed great for the first few months. The company gave me a decent amount of ongoing monthly work, which allowed me to shrink the number of clients I worked for at any given time. For the first time since going out on my own, my schedule had a semblance of sanity to it. I started taking weekends off to chill with my family. I went to sleep before midnight. I began to feel human again.

But then the owner took off on a series of back-to-back business trips and fell behind on paying my invoices. After almost two months of avoiding the situation, he finally admitted that he couldn't pay me the thousands of dollars he owed me. He'd run out of funds. He assured me that he'd have the money soon, but couldn't tell me when.

Um … what?

This was money I desperately needed to pay my mortgage and feed my family. I couldn't be content with receiving it "whenever." Suddenly I had blinding clarity on what kind of client I wanted to work for, and it wasn't someone who thought that paying me was optional.

After that experience, I knew I had to get much, much clearer about who my ideal client was. For the first time, I asked myself what I needed in a client to make me feel secure, happy, and motivated in my business. I enjoyed working for local clients. It's an awesome feeling to help your neighbours. But, I'd always felt guilty charging them my full value, or the full number of hours I worked, and that led to me working long hours for little pay.

I enjoyed the simplicity of working for just one or two clients at a time, but I wanted those clients to have established businesses and a strong understanding of what I offered, and to pay me promptly without any nudging.

I also realized that I was done saying "yes" to jobs I hated. No more PR work. No more search engine optimization. No more creating media kits or designing websites. Sure, I could do those things, and I was good at them, but I wasn't great at them. I didn't love them. They weren't my area of expertise—writing online copy and content was. And that was what I loved doing most. So I vowed I would start declining anything that wasn't a strict copywriting or content job.

This was a scary leap of faith for me. The idea of saying no to potential work was terrifying. But my coach had repeatedly told me that I had to get rid of what I didn't want in my life in order to make space for what I DID want. I decided to put her advice to good use and see what happened. I did three things:

1. I told all of my clients that I would only be offering copywriting and content development services from then on.

2. I raised my rates to attract a higher calibre of client. This meant that a lot of local clients stopped calling, which made me sad because they are awesome people, but it simplified my schedule and restored sanity to my life.

3. I approached a Vancouver marketing agency that had been contracting me to write one or two articles a month and asked if they had any more work for me. They were delighted to hear I had more time to give them and offered me a consistent number of hours each month – more than enough to pay the monthly bills.

Suddenly, my life seemed so much easier. I had a decent amount of financial security, the clients loved my writing, and they paid me promptly at the end of every month, no questions asked. If I could attract one or two more big clients like them, I figured I would be set.

DO YOU REALLY WANT WHAT YOU THINK YOU WANT?

A couple of months later, I went on a weekend business retreat and had an epiphany that completely transformed my business.

At the time, I regarded my business as a "necessary inconvenience"—a way to make money until I published my young adult novel and started making enough money to live the life of my dreams. I was still spending almost every night working on my young adult novel, and felt like I was trying to push my life in different directions while going nowhere fast.

At that time, I belonged to a writing group that included several published authors and editors who worked for local publishing companies. Through them, I began to realize that the vast majority of published authors didn't make enough money to support themselves on their book sales. They all had day jobs just like me, even the ones whose books had won literary awards. They were teachers, coffee-shop baristas, mill workers, or they were retired and living on their pensions.

The more I learned about the book publishing industry, the more I realized my chances of achieving financial freedom by publishing my young adult book were almost nil. I'd have to write many books and devote myself to marketing them day and night before I would ever make enough money to quit my day job.

The thought was too depressing for words.

I was tired of working all the time, either for my clients or myself. I did love writing, but it was still work. I wanted more time to do other things, such as hang out with my family, do more yoga, and learn how to kayak. I wanted to hang out with friends and go camping more often. And I wanted to be able to travel and go on adventures in different countries with my boys. But despite all my hard work, my dream life seemed to be receding further than ever beyond my grasp.

When I went to the business retreat that weekend, I vowed to myself that I would figure out a way to bring more joy and freedom into my life.

The first day there, I was asked to create a detailed vision of my ideal future. As always, I imagined myself making great money as a successful bestselling author. But this time, I went deeper and asked myself why I wanted to become a bestselling author so badly.

First of all, I flat-out loved writing, and I loved the idea of using my words to make a lasting positive impact on people's lives. I wanted to be my own boss and work from home—or wherever else I wanted—and have total control over my own schedule. I wanted to research interesting topics and learn more about whatever subject piqued my curiosity. I wanted a job that allowed me to go traveling whenever I wanted, and once I became a mother, to be at home with my kids as much as possible. And I wanted to be paid good money while doing it.

Imagine my surprise when I realized that I had already manifested almost every aspect of my dream life and was actively living it at that moment!

LOOK FOR THE TRUTHS THAT ARE STARING YOU IN THE FACE

I WAS my own boss. I worked from home and had total control over my schedule. I got paid good money to research and write about all sorts of interesting things. My "necessary inconvenience" was earning more money than I'd ever make writing fiction, unless I happened to hit the bestseller jackpot, which wasn't going to happen anytime soon. And I was enjoying myself! Even though I worked too much, I still woke up every morning happy to start my day.

Because, as I mentioned, I flat-out love writing.

On top of that, I was living in the rainforest paradise of my dreams, just a 10-minute walk from the ocean.

That epiphany was a huge eye-opener. I had progressed so far toward creating my ideal life without even realizing it! But I had been so hung up on the idea of needing my fiction writing to be my primary source of income that I hadn't seen the path that was blinking in neon lights right in front of me the whole time.

For the first time, I saw my copywriting business not as a necessary inconvenience, but the source of huge good in my life. And I began to consider its full potential and explore the ways I could grow it to make my ideal vision a reality—AND create the time and financial freedom I needed to spend more time writing fiction as a fun hobby, instead of trying to force it into the impossible situation of becoming my primary source of income.

I asked myself: how could I grow my business in a way that feeds my soul and makes me proud to share my work with others? What clients do I need to attract in order to make my vision a reality?

I realized that I wanted an established client with a large audience who was doing great good in the world. Someone whom I was proud to write for, who had the marketing budget to provide me with a lot of consistent work, and who could help me make the connections I needed to grow my own business in ways that would help me achieve my vision.

Less than two weeks after I came home from that business retreat, I received an email from a former marketing director of mine. He had a client who was looking for a copywriter – did I have time to take on anyone new?

Having become so clear on the kind of client I wanted to work for, I was cautious to say yes. "I'm pretty booked these days," I responded, which was true. "Who's the client?"

"You'll want to make room in your schedule for this guy," my old boss replied. "It's Jack Canfield."

Yeah. THE Jack Canfield. The creator of the Chicken Soup for the Soul series and author of The Success Principles. A man who, during the course of his career, has actively helped millions of people change their lives for the better. And with my copywriting skills, I could help him positively impact millions more.

Needless to say, I said yes. And I've been writing the majority of his copy and content ever since.

Since writing for Jack, I've become much more familiar with the idea of manifestation and how we are able to attract the things we want into our lives once we get clear on what they are. And I've learned to recognize the role that manifestation has played in shaping my life. It has steered me to take the necessary actions and attract the kind of clients who will help me create the lifestyle I've always wanted.

I'm not saying that I snap my fingers and "the Universe provides". I've put a lot of my own time and energy into making it happen. But it seems like the perfect person or resource or opportunity shows up at exactly the right time SO OFTEN that it's hard not to read it as so much more than a coincidence.

And yeah, it feels a little like magic.

That said, there are some specific lessons I've learned in life that have greatly increased my ability to manifest the things I need when I need them. Here are six of my favorites:

1. GET REALLY (AND I MEAN REALLY) CLEAR ON WHAT YOU WANT

If you only have a fuzzy idea of what you want, the results you manifest will be fuzzy as well. When I first started out, I thought, "I want to be able to make enough money to pay the mortgage and the bills and not go bankrupt." And I achieved that with no problem. But I was working around the clock and doing a lot of jobs I didn't enjoy. It wasn't until I got clear on exactly what kind of work I wanted to do, and why, that I really began to love my job.

2. GET CLEAR ON WHO YOU WANT TO SERVE

In the early days of my business, I decided I wanted to serve local clients. And I got local clients – lots of them! But I always felt I had to undercharge them, which meant that I worked far more hours than I got paid for, and that made me miserable. When I finally got clear on the exact kind of client who could help me grow my business in the way I wanted, I managed to land Jack Canfield as a client!

'Nuff said.

3. ASK FOR WHAT YOU WANT

It took me a long time to get comfortable asking for what I wanted. When I worked in the corporate world, I never imagined my manager would be okay with letting me work from home – and yet he was. If I hadn't worked up the courage to ask, I never would have known, and we never would have made the move to the Sunshine Coast.

When I needed more work, I asked for it, and the marketing agency that had been sending me one or two blog posts a month to edit was happy to give me all the work I wanted. But it never would have happened if I hadn't asked.

4. LISTEN TO FEEDBACK

It took me a long time, but I finally began listening to the feedback the world had been giving me in response to my dream of becoming a bestselling fiction author. All the writers who I would have described as "successful" (in terms of getting their novels published and receiving positive critical reviews) weren't able to support themselves on their fiction writing alone. If they couldn't, what were the chances that I could? It was crazy for me to keep chasing a dream that would take years for me to catch, when a great source of freedom and opportunity was staring me in the face.

5. TRUST IN YOURSELF & THE UNIVERSE

Growing beyond your current circumstances—whatever they may be—involves risk. If you wait until your plan is 100 percent guaranteed to be successful, you will never get started. So get clear on what you want, create a workable plan to make your vision a reality, and take the leap! Even if you don't hit the bull's-eye right away, you're certain to end up closer to your goal.

I spent years working in a job I didn't enjoy because I was afraid to leave the security it offered. The idea of going into business for myself terrified me, even though it was what I had to do to create the life I always dreamed of. Sometimes I wonder what would have happened if the company I had been working for hadn't gone bankrupt. Would I still be working for them, bored and unhappy but terrified of pursuing a better opportunity?

I shudder to imagine.

So even when things seemingly go bad, look for the positive and figure out what you need to do to turn the situation to your advantage. There's always a way. You just have to look for it with clear eyes and an open heart, and trust that you have the skills and expertise to make it happen.

6. MANIFESTATION WORKS WHEN YOU HAVE CLEAR VISION AND THE WILL TO ACT

I absolutely believe it's possible to manifest the life of your dreams. I have seen the power of manifestation happen in my own life again and again.

It's not a matter of sitting on a yoga mat and meditating on what you want until it falls into your lap. Manifestation is a far more active and practical process than that.

But when you get laser clear on what you want, and do the work needed to become the kind of person who is capable of creating your

283

ideal life, you will make it happen.

Just be aware it might not unfold the way you expect, and keep your eyes open. The key to achieving your dreams might be staring you in the face at this very moment.

ABOUT ERIN WHALEN

Erin Whalen has a bachelor's degree in journalism and a Master of Arts in English Literature and has been a professional copywriter and content developer since 2004. In 2010 she started her own business, Made You Look Online, and now writes copy and content for inspiring entrepreneurs and best-selling authors—including Jack Canfield, America's #1 success coach.

Erin is passionate about helping awesome entrepreneurs and small business owners get their message out in a way that attracts their ideal clients and inspires them to take action. You can tap into her knowledge and expertise by signing up for her free 7-day copywriting course, "Write the Real You"—and learn how to develop an unforgettable voice for your business that captures the attention of your ideal customers and inspires them to take action.

You can sign up for this powerful free writing course at:
http://erinwhalen.com/write-the-real-you/

MIDLIFE MIRACLE

Eve Wittenmeyer

A week before Christmas 2014 I turned 41. Like all winter days in Southern California, the day was sunny and bright. But, to me, it appeared unremarkable, vague and indistinguishable. Behind that brilliant and beautiful façade the air seemed brittle, fragile, as though it might shatter and break apart. I felt the weakness of that illusion inside me. I was the one in danger of splintering apart.

Throughout the day I endured a few birthday wishes at work. Once home, my family knew not to fuss. The thought of celebrating the passing of another year exhausted me. It was Friday night. I went to bed early.

The following weekend I turned on a Los Angeles Kings hockey game, a matchup against a division rival that promised to be exciting, but it was hard to focus. I couldn't concentrate. A familiar, hazy bleakness filled my thoughts. Something did creep through my mind, though. I imagined I did feel something, the unwanted remnants of that birthday, cracks in the façade, widening, splitting me open from the inside out.

The players rushed onto the ice to warm up for the second period and I struggled to engage. As one of the young forwards gave an interview to the sideline reporter, I fidgeted from my seat on the floor in front of the couch while the camera showed the rookie's parents in the stands. I stared at the screen, a thought suddenly ambushing my mind with an abruptness I didn't have time to block.

I was too old to date any of the players. Even the older ones.

It was a meaningless, inconsequential thought, but one that carried with it a painful and devastating realization. I was old. Me. Old. The words looped through me with an irrefutable and inescapable resonance. When had this happened? How?

Questions flooded my brain, overwhelmed me as they followed the lines of all those cracks inside me. I was powerless to stop them. Was this really my life? What was I doing? How could I be this person? I wasn't proud of where I lived, where I worked, or who I shared my life with. My dreams remained unrealized.

Awareness, which I had carefully avoided for years, surged through me. I hated the way I ate, the way I felt, the way I looked, the way I dressed. I hated going to work and I hated coming home. Worst of all, my life was statistically half over.

It didn't make sense to me that I was a sad, stagnant person, but I had to admit it was true. The air in my lungs crowded my chest. I wanted to gasp, cry, choke, scream. I got up quietly and went into the bathroom to stand before the mirror. I *looked* sad and stagnant. Did I look like this all the time? I didn't recognize myself.

I had been disengaged from my boyfriend for years. Our decade long relationship was a negative habit, deteriorated and withered away due to his emotionally abusive behavior brought about by his struggles to deal with massive anger issues. Despite this, I raised his two kids. Not surprisingly, they grappled with anger problems of their own. We all attended family therapy off and on to manage the problem, but merely coping with negativity is a universe away from being happy.

Over the years, living with such despair made me disappear. I was never able to solve the problem, no matter what I did. I never found a way to change the anger. It was a bottomless pit that I threw kind words or patient actions into every day. It devoured my once sunny disposition and stole my identity, robbed me of my confidence and self-worth.

It's not in my nature to be angry. I just became sadder and more withdrawn as time passed. My disappointment in my failures to fix what was wrong deepened, and as I internalized that grief, I abused myself more and more. I abandoned friendships. I stopped eating real food and instead lived off of soda and not much else. The more my sadness grew, the further I turned away from my health.

Exhaustion filled my days. No matter how long I slept, every morning I hit snooze for an hour before finally getting up just to feel more drained than when I'd gone to bed. And I was cold all the time. Not chilly, I was bone-numbing freezing every second of every day. I was so cold my body hurt.

At work I wore an undershirt, a t-shirt, a regular shirt, and a sweater just to survive. My nose ran while I sat at my desk and my hands and feet ached, my skin icy to the touch. During lunch, I often sat in my car after it baked in the Los Angeles sun all morning, without even cracking the windows. The brutally stifling air barely sunk into me.

My doctor diagnosed me with adrenal fatigue and pre-diabetic blood sugar levels. I chose to ignore his warnings, even though I was puffy and becoming overweight. I hated being puffy—even more than I hated being cold. I also suffered from ADHD. Sugar was one of the primary causes of all these problems, but sugar had become the way I coped with the stress in my life. I couldn't give it up.

As I started to face these truths, they played through my mind on endless repetition. Even the hockey games I loved so much couldn't distract me. Being a sports fan had always been a special part of my life. I loved the competition and achievement, the sense of community and bonding it fostered. But suddenly that wasn't enough. This season meant more. I wanted to see my team win. I needed my team to win. I was losing, but maybe they could win.

December rolled into January, the New Year came and went, and it was time for the NHL All Star game. The Kings were having an awful year. I knew how they felt, each game a defeat, an opportunity lost. The knowledge that so much time was passing, disappearing forever, crushed me. The idea of doing something, anything, to change this consumed me.

Based on a recommendation, I started listening to a podcast while walking my dog and the podcast, it turns out, was the "something" I was looking for. It was the first podcast I'd ever listened to and I was immediately hooked. Every day I enjoyed beautiful interviews of people dedicated to changing the world for the better, stories of men and women overcoming obstacles to achieve phenomenal success. Some of those people were younger than me. But others were my age or older. Many, including the host, described experiencing times of intense doubt and despair. They all shared how they overcame that adversity to create a sense of purpose, to develop lives of impact and service. Inspiration rushed through me for the first time in years. I thought, "What makes me so special that I can't face and overcome the challenges and wrong turns that life throws at all of us?" Maybe I hadn't wasted too much time.

The podcast's endless positivity and enthusiasm motivated me to seek therapy. Although I now admitted to myself that I needed things to change, I had no idea how to actually begin. So I found a therapist and snuck off to my appointments without telling anyone.

At first, I found therapy empowering as I started to voice the things I wasn't even saying to my best girlfriends. I admitted I was in a harmful relationship, I alluded to my health problems. As each appointment passed, though, the answers I sought failed to materialize. I was still stuck. And now growing impatient.

But I didn't give up. It might have been silly, but I didn't want to let the host of the podcast down. Many of the people interviewed talked about nutrition and exercise routines. I got out some unused workout videos and browsed the diet book that accompanied them. The recipes were incredibly simple. It seemed pretty easy, actually. The plan was to just eat fresh, whole food. Maybe I could try it? I was hesitant.

Around this time I started using (I mean lurking on) social media, trying to find a way to reconnect with the world. Posts written by an acquaintance of mine started popping up in my Facebook feed, linking to her inspirational articles for women on health, wellness, and sexuality. In one article she shared the story of her recovery from anorexia. The day she realized she was ill she suffered a fall while running, and her first thought as she came to was to wonder if dirt contained any calories. She was face down in a ditch.

Empathy constricted my chest. How could the beautiful, powerful woman I knew have suffered so much? I held my breath as the story continued, as she revealed her self-doubt and loneliness, her lack of fulfillment, her unhealthy relationship with food.

For the second time since my birthday, truth slammed into me, ricocheting around my mind until it forced me to stop reading. I was dizzy. I flew to the library shelves to confirm what I suddenly suspected. After finishing the first two chapters of a book on eating disorders for middle-aged women, I sat still, stunned. I had BED, binge eating disorder.

In one sense it was terrifying to come to this realization, but it was also liberating. I was desperate to understand myself and suddenly I not only knew what was wrong, there were people telling me I could fix it.

My heart actually raced as I burned through the book. How could I be on these pages? My failings, my sorrows, my secrets. All there in print, right in front of me. Recurring episodes of overeating, feeling a loss of control while binging, feeling a great deal of distress afterward. Yes, I experienced it all. Anxiety, stress, low self-esteem, feelings of a lack of control in life. It was *my* story, there, in those chapters.

For me, the eating disorder was a strange mix of trying to self-medicate while also punishing myself for being unhappy. I knew I was harming my body, but I couldn't stop. I drank soda and paired it with popcorn, corn chips, or corn nuts every day. But I wasn't just having a snack. I had to eat the entire bag every time. And fill the biggest cup available. I could never get enough. I didn't want to eat anything else—and many days I didn't.

Binging was like plugging the holes, like stuffing everything in that I lacked in my life. It soothed away all the emotions I didn't express, all the needs that went unfilled, the stress I couldn't control. But it was a fleeting, momentary reprieve that vanished painfully, leaving me vacant again as soon as it was over. And afterward I felt physically sick, not only because I was putting poison in my body, but also because I overfilled myself. Mentally, I agonized over binging. Every. Single. Time. It was utterly exhausting. More than anything, I wanted to stop. Sometimes I bought the soda and immediately threw it away. But within an hour or two I would return to the store and buy it again.

As I finished the book, I committed to healing myself, to stopping this painful cycle. The recommended treatment required learning how to use food as fuel only, not as an emotional substitute for everything that was missing from my life. I told myself I could do this.

The tiny diet booklet that came with the workout videos was still sitting on my kitchen counter and it seemed like the perfect place to start. Within twelve hours of making the first meal I felt a drastic change. My body rejoiced. I had forgotten you could nourish your body and eat from a place of loving yourself. Eating was a time of failure for me, a time of stress and guilt and shame, but I realized that could change.

Inspired by my newfound dedication to improve my health, I decided I needed to leave the toxicity of my relationship as well. I wanted a "divorce." My boyfriend and I weren't technically married but we'd lived together for ten years. My "stepdaughter" was finishing high school in four months and would go off to college. The timing was right. I could stay until she graduated and then go. I told my boyfriend I wanted to leave but he asked me to work on things, at least for a while, before breaking up. So I got a second therapist, a couple's therapist.

Months passed. The Kings crashed and burned spectacularly at the end of the season. It was a ridiculous embarrassment. They won the Stanley cup the year before (I went to game two of the finals when they beat the New York Rangers 5-4 in double overtime) and this year they missed the playoffs entirely. It was time for the Kings to reassess. I knew how they felt. All the effort I had put into moving forward hadn't gotten me anywhere yet.

Although my body relished the improved nourishment I was giving it, the sugar cravings and the ADHD brain fog continued to plague me. I thought about drinking soda at least once every five minutes and it drove me mad. It was impossible to concentrate. When I caved in to the temptation I was angry and frustrated with myself for being weak. I did the best I could to distract myself with research. I followed health podcasts, bought books, read blogs.

I studied health almost five hours per day. Two hours in the morning before work, again at lunch, and a couple hours more after work. It was hard, really hard. For every theory there were a dozen opposing theories, all with "studies" to back them up. But slowly, I began to piece a story together. Sharing my research with my acupuncturist prompted her to run some tests and she diagnosed me with leaky gut syndrome, a condition that is almost always associated with autoimmune disease. Finding a solution to my health problems became critical.

Finally, I put all my knowledge together and came up with a plan. In July 2015, I quit gluten, sugar, and dairy. Months of research convinced me that the most important key to good health is nutrition, and quitting these foods was the first step in creating a healthy life. Within two weeks of putting this plan into action, the sugar cravings stopped, exactly what I hoped would happen. I knew I'd done it. My health was changed for good.

Shortly after, the day came that I didn't think about soda at all. I rejoiced. Alone in my office at work, I laughed and cried and celebrated. I was free. I felt like a new person. By the end of the month I stopped thinking about my addiction completely.

For the first time in years energy and enthusiasm radiated through me. Revitalized, I adopted a sprint exercise program, started drinking Bulletproof coffee, and began practicing intermittent fasting. I bought new clothes. I was successful at meditating every day.

A miracle happened. I lost weight, I wasn't puffy any more. I wasn't tired. And I wasn't cold. My mind cleared and the brain fog that had afflicted me for years ended. I could think. I could feel.

Now: who was I?

Did I still want a "divorce?" I agonized over this question. One day I would decide I was firmly committed to leaving, the next I was firmly committed to staying. I wasn't happy, but we had shared so much of our lives together. We'd been a family together.

I pressed my personal therapist for a solution until finally she said, "You know the dream that every little girl has about a happily-ever-after with a handsome prince? It's time to grow up. You're an adult now. You have to deal with the relationship you have." The couple's therapist seemed to agree—my boyfriend was willing to attend therapy, so therefore I should stay with him. That was the definition of a keeper. But I didn't know if I could accept such a bleak ending to the fairy tale.

Like all relationships, ours was a complicated web of shared experiences. There were positive aspects, and the fact that we shared so much in common confused me. I wondered if maybe the therapists were right, I should stay—because we liked the same things.

The moment this thought occurred to me, I knew it was over, the choice made. I realized that staying in a relationship because we shared the same tastes was a fear-based decision. I was afraid I wouldn't find anyone else I had so much in common with. But I was no longer going to allow fear to make my decisions. It was a risk I was going to have to take. I refused to settle any longer. I would give myself the opportunity to find my handsome prince. And if I didn't, well, then I'd be happy alone.

It was time. I was going to set myself free.

The new hockey season started. My relationship ended. The Kings had blown up their roster. It was a fresh start. For me too. For the first time in years I could breathe.

The day I left the relationship I hired a life coach. I resolved to walk away from something negative that no longer served me while stepping toward something positive that would empower me. It was the best decision I could have made. It changed my life in countless profound ways. And the therapists who told me my dreams of a fulfilling relationship were childish nonsense? I walked, actually ran, away from them to dedicate myself to creating my "happily-ever-after" every day.

Recently one of my very wise friends expressed the concept of change this way: making progress is taking one tiny step at a time until suddenly you make a giant leap and you don't even notice how big it is. The steps I took every day started out so small! I listened to a podcast. I downloaded an app. I read an article. But they were movement and they were persistent.

When I made the leap to move out on my own and started making decisions from a place of love for myself, I woke up early every day filled with joy. I liked going to work again. Everyone I encountered told me I glowed. In fact, I even started to look younger. I connected with new people, powerful women on missions to change the world. I believed I could find my mission too.

Every day I still think of new small steps to take and some of them are terrifying, but I take them anyway. I'm proud of all those little steps and every once in a while I take another big leap.

My "health journey" as I call it, was actually just the beginning of my transformation. It was the foundation I needed to be able to build the life I was really meant to live. A few days after I set myself free, I started a gratitude journal. It's just a simple entry I write every night before going to sleep, a list of all the things I have to be thankful for. There is nothing too small to include, and certainly nothing too great. I offer thanks for my coffee, my work, my comfortable bed, my friends, my health, the massive abundance of love I have in my life now. I feel immense gratitude for the path I'm on and all the lessons I've learned that have led me to this life that I truly love. Yes, even the painful ones.

Gratitude has become one of my greatest tools and highest priorities. I discovered that gratitude is a skill, a daily choice, as is taking responsibility for your life and practicing forgiveness. I know the importance of all these things now, as well as the fact that mindset is the key to achievement. Our thoughts create our lives. We don't get what we want, we get what we believe. And we create what we focus on.

Women are often taught to put themselves last while taking care of everyone and everything else, but that can backfire. Middle age can arrive with a sense that something is wrong, something is off or unfulfilled. It might be vague at first but it's persistent. When it arrived for me, I didn't know what to do about it, but I thought maybe if I could get healthy something good would happen. Now my health is sacred, because once I found my health, I found myself.

I learned that self-love is the greatest priority, it is not something to feel guilty about or put behind the needs of others. Now that I take care of myself first, I have so much more to give. I have more time to connect to the world, not less. My relationships are better and stronger than ever, including those with my "step kids". My "stepdaughter" is thriving in college and proud of who she is and how hard she works in school and at her job. Experiencing her as a beautiful, productive adult has helped me view my time with them as a success, not the dismal failure I once feared it would turn out to be.

I remain dedicated to my self-care routine. I do acupressure on myself, talk into the mirror, make bone broth, take detox baths, balance my checking account, meditate, visualize, say affirmations, attend events for female entrepreneurs, invest in coaching, take supplements … and there's more, much more. It sounds like a lot in list form, but it's not a bunch of tasks I do, it's how I live my life, how I choose to show up for myself every day.

It is a lot of work and sometimes I fall short. I still have to manage the challenge of emotional eating. My self-care is both an accomplishment and a goal every day. But, through the counsel of another of my brilliant friends, I've come to understand that it's not the "destination" or the "journey" that matter—it's the person you are along the way that counts.

As I write this, the hockey season is winding down. Only nine games are left. I don't know what will happen, but the Kings are having a killer year. Will they be in the Stanley Cup finals again? I don't know. But if they are, I'll be there. Either way, this year has been a win.

I have a future to work toward now that I'm proud of. One of my favorite things to think about is what my life will be like in six months or a year. I can't even imagine all the possibilities, but what I can imagine is how I'm going to *feel*. And that, without doubt, is spectacular.

ABOUT EVE WITTENMEYER

Eve is a writer, mentor, and librarian. She believes in "happily-ever-afters," finding handsome princes, and is certain there can never be too much glitter.

Since her midlife crisis turned midlife miracle, Eve has been on a soul-sparkling and joy-filled journey of gratitude and authentic living. She is currently pursuing her dream of founding a nonprofit ranch where she will host retreats, rescue horses, and provide a restorative sanctuary for artists in the mountains. Eve's mission is to construct a haven where writers can acquire the skills they need to achieve their creative dreams while learning how to support their passion by manifesting prosperity and abundance in their lives.

Intentional joy is Eve's daily approach to a radiant life and successful entrepreneurship, the happy result of combining her twelve years of professional research and management skills with her mindset and health expertise to develop practices that cultivate a healthy mind and body in alignment with the soul's highest purpose.

Growing up in the woods of upstate New York instilled in Eve that being in nature provides the most joy and nourishment for the soul. She loves hiking and kayaking, stargazing, evenings by the fire pit, and making love under the stars.

Please connect with Eve at intentionaljoy.today@gmail.com.

NEVER LOSE HOPE

Hope Zvara

I often tell people that I didn't find yoga, yoga found me. Yoga came into my life at a time I needed it most—at a time when I was desperate, alone, scared, and frantically clinging to my life because it felt so out of control.

I had an eating disorder and it was ruining my life. I yoyoed through high school, bouncing between anorexia and bulimia, but to be honest that was only the surface issue. Throughout most of my late grade school and teenage years I felt like an outsider, like people didn't get me and I didn't fit in. So many of my school memories are laced with the feeling of trying so hard to fit in, to be liked, and fearing that tomorrow I would suddenly not be good enough.

My parents loved me and my sisters, but sometimes just loving someone isn't enough. I lived in an emotionally tense environment, one parent a dry alcoholic most of my life (with little outside help to understand the issues at hand), and the other unable to take a stand and speak up on my and my sisters' and behalf. We grew up in an emotionally unhealthy environment. And as a result, I was deeply broken, hurt, and alone. I had no self-worth and felt like a failure the second I woke up each day. I would often lie in bed at night and ask God, "Why me? Why are you punishing me?" I felt it was unfair that my three sisters got to be normal and I wasn't. Why was I the bad egg? It was unfair and no one understood me—not my friends, not my school counselors, not even my parents.

Like an answer from God (and I didn't even know it) a friend suggested that I try yoga, simply because I looked like someone who would practice. Something inside me pushed me to persue her request, and a few weeks later, accompanied by my mom (she wanted to come too), we showed up for our first yoga class. As I waited for the previous class to clear out of the room, I thought how uncomfortable I felt and how nervous I was. I felt slightly paranoid at what others thought about me when they looked at me. And truthfully, if my mom had not been there with me I probably would have never gone in—too many unknowns, too stressful, too different, too new. For all those reasons and more are why so many are stuck and frozen with anxiety. It's hard to step out of the "safe" box, no matter how unsafe that space truly is. Thank God my mom came with me that day!

I remember my first yoga class like it was yesterday. The instructor, Sharon, led us from one posture to the next. I was clueless as to what they all were and was more distracted with seeing myself in a full wall-length mirror at every twist and fold. It was a challenge to keep myself from looking at every imperfection on my body, despite the fact that I was rail-thin and thinking about how everyone else was probably looking at me too.

Every pose felt like forever—five breaths felt like fifty, my wrists were killing me, and I could barely hold Plank for 10 seconds without shaking. I felt weak, but at the same time I didn't. The dynamic of the class was strange, and not because I was the youngest student by about 25 years, but rather because of the dualistic nature of my feelings.

And before I knew it, the hour long class was over. I rolled up my yoga mat and walked out of the room feeling slight relief. There was a small moment in time where I, for once in a very long time, did not feel the urge or thoughts that often went with my addiction. It felt like freedom, however shortlived. And those few moments that I had with no urges to binge and purge, I felt at peace in my own skin.

Every Wednesday became "my day." At barely 18 years old, I was desperate and hopeful at the same time. I was binging and purging up to eight times per day and greatly wanted out of the hell I called my life. I was ashamed that I had let it get so bad and even more ashamed that my parents thought I was in recovery, considering the multiple past attempts at such a milestone. Again, it was another thing I couldn't do right. Again, another failure. Again, another screw up. I was a burden to my family and I had been slowly slipping away for years. My entire life revolved around my eating disorder—I was no longer living, I was merely surviving. When I practiced yoga and lay in relaxation pose, it was simultaneously scary and hopeful, because being still in my thoughts and body was new to me. I never liked my thoughts, and I hated my body, but I was able to lie there and be with my thoughts and be in my skin. It was all new for me. Nothing in my life felt hopeful, nothing in my life was honest or truthful. But in that moment, and the moments after, I rolled up my mat and felt a small glimmer of hope, a small space of freedom where my mind and body weren't shackled to my addiction. My eating disorder, that had once given me a sense of control and accomplishment in life, was no longer controlling me.

As Wednesday would roll around each week, I would look at that 7 p.m. class as my second chance. Because every time I stepped onto the yoga mat, I wasn't the girl with the eating disorder. To my surprise, no one was staring at me and no one was judging me. For one hour, it was just me and my mat.

The combination of feeling physically weak coupled with the slow development of strength was empowering. The hour long class would give me about thirty minutes of clarity; time when I wasn't bombarded with eating disorder thoughts; something that I had to deal with from the moment I woke up to the moment I fell asleep each night.

There were plenty of Wednesdays that I had severe anxiety (and if you know anything about anxiety, then anything different, new, or out of order can bring it on.) Like an alcoholic having a drink to take the edge off, I binged and purged prior to going to class, and then during class I prayed to God that He would help me leave feeling healed. I prayed that I could go home and not do it again. One would think that since I got home slightly before 9 p.m. it would be easy to abstain from binging and purging and just go to bed. But my addiction had full reign over me, it was no longer my choice whether I did or did not do anything in my life anymore.

Every night I wrote in my journal and prayed—prayed to God to heal me, to let me wake up normal. I prayed about how sorry I was to be failing over and over. But, oddly enough, I also prayed about how grateful I was for what I did have, the people in my life, the little things. And maybe my nightly ritual was part of what kept my head just out of the water for so many years. As much as I didn't understand why, I did believe that God does not do anything without purpose. Aside from prayer most nights, it was sheer luck if I made it to bed without purging. Like an old record player stuck on repeat, I'd say to myself, "This is my last time, tomorrow I'll stop, tomorrow I'm going to get better." As addicts, we say that because we need that last purge, last drink, last fix to take the edge off. Tomorrow it will be easier to "get better," but today it just ain't happening.

Yoga had literally become my life line, and I think my mom saw it as a way to help me. I am pretty certain she wasn't sure to what extent I was struggling, but she knew I was. As time went on, we seldom missed a Wednesday class, and I did physically feel stronger. Though it was slow, I do believe there was a mindset shift that was taking place.

It was April and I was almost finished with my first year of college. One night, after our Wednesday yoga session, our teacher Sharon commented that I was pretty good at yoga and asked me if I ever considered teaching.

It had never crossed my mind, but that night something switched on for me. I still can't explain exactly what inspired me to take her advice and pack my bags for a month to go to Colorado and learn to teach yoga. But something inside me said do it, and a part of me was hoping it might also help me find hope again and stop my self-destructive lifestyle. The thought of going 30 days without binging and purging felt like a far out of reach dream. Heck, it had been such a long time since I had gone one day! This last minute trip felt like the next step in the right direction for me.

May 1st came and I packed up my things and was off for the month to Colorado. That experience was everything I needed at that time in my life. It pushed all my buttons and brought out deep discomforts, but I knew I had finally found something I was good at. I wasn't a perfectly polished teacher, but I had a knack for it. Teaching yoga fed my soul in a way it had never been fed before, and this was after eighteen-plus years raised in the church.

I left there after a month, hopeful to have put my addiction behind me, but sadly that was not the case. For every three steps forward, there were surely two steps back.

I had been living in the valley of darkness for so long that peeking out, even for just a moment, was liberating, but also saddening because I still couldn't do one thing right: eat food like a normal person. I found myself, yet again, questioning why God was punishing me.

What did I ever do to deserve this?

As fall rolled around, something told me not to go back to school. I had enrolled in college mainly because that was what we were told to do in school, and at the time I knew of no other options. My eating disorder made me socially awkward and my anxiety made it difficult to interact socially, not to mention deal with any situation I felt I had no control over. But more than anything, I finally felt like I was good at something. When I was on the yoga mat, when I was teaching, I wasn't "Hope with the eating disorder", I was the me I was dying to be but didn't know how. And that me was a yoga teacher.

With addiction still having full reign over my life, I dove deeper into yoga and understanding the nature of the practice and lifestyle. Faith was not new to me, but yoga was like faith—belief in action. I tell my students now that, to me and many others, yoga is like the 13th step in AA. It is where you take all the internal work, thought, and prayer you've done and practice it in action in a safe place called your yoga mat.

I used the mat, both personally and as a teacher, to feel my own feelings. This was something I had spent half my life trying not to do: feel. Yoga is all about being in your body, being in the moment, and feeling. The continuous request to be in each breath and focus on nothing else but the current moment in time is a necessary piece for everyone in order to live fully and experience all that life has to offer.

On the mat, if I could just take one breath and be calm, then two, then five, then twenty and sit with whatever I was feeling, to my initial surprise those feelings that I spent my entire life running from would surface but then pass. Yoga became an incubator for life, a place where I could go and feel in a safe environment, work on what faced me at that time, and then go out and try it in life. We've all been there in some way, shape, or form: At the end of a stressful day we eat cake; We're annoyed about work so we go for a run; We fight with the spouse and we have a drink. What makes yoga different is that when you are on the mat, you are asked to get quiet andbe still. With that comes the opportunity to see what is actually there, why you were upset, angry, sad, happy or even joyous. You can't see, feel, or deal with those inner experiences without fully and completely being in your body, your breath, and the moment.

It was a love/hate feeling that I was willing to dance with.

As time went on, it became more and more apparent to me that I couldn't fully recover from an eating disorder on my own, that I didn't want to live like this, and that I didn't deserve to. I wanted a future, a family, and kids. But I most certainly didn't want kids if I continued living this way. I told myself that, in order to have a family and a future, I first needed to get well. I was an adult child of an alcoholic and I refused to raise my future children in an unhealthy environment.Exactly two years after enrolling in my first yoga intensive, I had finally had enough failed attempts and asked for help. I whispered to my mom that I needed to tell her something. I pulled her out to the back deck and before I knew it I was crying so hard that I couldn't even speak. I could tell my mom was worried as she was asking me what was wrong and what I needed. Part of me was already boycotting the mission—it was too much for me to take. But this time was different. I was so sick and tired of being sick and tired. I so deeply wanted to live a normal life.

I finally caught my breath and, with my eyes shut tightly, I told her I needed help, that I wasn't in recovery, and that I couldn't do it on my own. I felt I let her down. She had told me so many times that I could do this, to just pray to God to help me and He would. But prayer wasn't enough. I had been on a course moving towards a slow death for quite some time, and if I didn't jump ship soon, I wouldn't be crying with my mom: she would be crying over me.

She kept asking me what kind of help I needed and I just said

I didn't know. Deep down, I knew I needed and wanted to be put in some sort of treatment. I was so sick of struggling, lying, and hiding. I had calculated my time spent in addictive behaviors and it topped the scales at 16 hours per day. I spent this time thinking about binging and purging, sleeping because I was so exhausted after engaging in those behaviors, having stop-me-in-my-tracks anxiety, and constantly thinking about how much of a failure I was. It was like having a nightmare that I lived out day after day after day. There was no waking up. I was at a point where I looked at sleep as safety. I couldn't harm myself if I was sleeping.

It wasn't long before I had the number for Roger's Memorial Hospital in my hand. For years, my mom had been my enabler. When things got hard she would step in and do them for me. I had mastered the art of utilizing the people around me to keep me sick, because sick was familiar, it was a state I could control. But there was no turning back now. As luck would have it, the next week my mom was leaving for Colorado, as she too was going to take the very same yoga teacher training as I had (interesting how life works out that way.) My only choice was to call the hospital myself, or it would be only a matter of time before I damaged my body so much that I wouldn't wake up from one of those nights that had made me feel so safe.

That was the first time that I had ever taken the steps on my own to get the life that I deserved, the life that God had planned for me.

Outpatient treatment was one of the best experiences of my life. Being there with other women who were struggling with the same thing was both comforting and eye opening. I came to realize just how many people didn't truly want to get better. They weren't ready, and sadly they were there spending thousands of dollars per day. Some had been there two or even three times already, only to wait for their insurance money to run out so they could go back to their eating disorder stricken lives.

I was sad for these women, but also thankful for the insight. I had done a lot more work than I had thought. I wanted it. I wanted to get better. I wanted to succeed. And I realized that I did have a choice. I had yoga to thank for much of my growth and I had faith in God that I had a purpose. I had come to see that there was a plan for me, but I couldn't do it living the way I was.

Outpatient treatment was not the end, there was still an uphill battle. But this time was different, this time I had real tools and saw that I could, in fact, do it. I could manage my urges and yoga was a huge component to that. Each time I stepped onto the yoga mat was another opportunity to remind myself to never lose hope. I learned, like others who have walked through recovery, that I would forever be in recovery. Treatment gave me even more tools to forge on fully toward what looked like a hopeful future. The stretches between binging and purging slowly got larger. I used my experiences of learning to breathe in moments of anxiety and sit with the feelings until they will pass. And then I learned to just let go (or at least I told myself that until I actually was able to.) I developed an affirmation: *What can I learn from this?* I would say this affirmation, or mantra, to myself as I looked in the bathroom mirror after eating my feelings and then puking them back up again. I started to challenge myself to see that I wasn't failing each time I had a small fall. Then, in my mind I would say "I forgive you," and in time my heart caught up.

In my home life I felt left behind, unnoticed. My parents joked that my name was spoken most often in the house, as I had a tendency to say what was on my mind. Sadly, their joke damaged my spirit and I internalized that as "nothing I do is right and nothing I say is worthy." My older twin sisters were the pretty ones—they were twins, who doesn't love that? And my litter sister was "Bear" (a nickname given to her by my father.) She could do no wrong, she too was cute, sweet, and perfect. So where did that leave me? I was a nobody: I wasn't pretty, I wasn't smart, I wasn't cute, so what was I? I felt like a lost soul, like I didn't fit into my own family.

But despite being a wreck on the inside, I had Brian. Brian and I met in the seventh grade and from there on our friendship developed, and eventually we both felt drawn to each other for reasons we weren't even sure of. Brian loved me when I didn't love myself. He loved me even when I was slowly killing myself. He never judged me and it was with him that I experienced true unconditional love.

We are high school sweethearts and soul mates. Six months after I went through outpatient treatment, he asked me to marry him. The light at the end of the tunnel was slowly becoming brighter. The dark valley was slowly gaining light. He loved me. He loved me when I didn't even love myself. I asked him why he loved me, and he always replied, "I just do." I told him that I didn't deserve him and he replied, "I don't deserve you." He *saw* me. When I was with him I felt safe and I didn't feel judged. This was something I was deeply in need of.

Most men would have run. Who wants a girlfriend with an eating disorder? Who wants someone with baggage like that? He did. We had been dating seriously for five straight years, but honestly, we had loved each other for over a decade.

When my husband and I got married I wasn't even sure I could get pregnant with all the damage I had done to my body, but three months later and shocked as all hell, I was pregnant. Having a baby at that time was not part of the plan. I had just opened up my own yoga studio, and now I was having a baby?

It took almost eight months for me to accept that I was having a baby and get excited about it. And then my worst nightmare happened.

My husband and I were attending the wedding of a friend from high school. That night we danced, played cards, and conversed with friends. After several dances in a row, I went to the bathroom, stood up in the stall, and looked down to see blood in my urine. Something triggered inside of me and I knew something wasn't right. I ran out of the bathroom, fighting back tears, and fled to find Brian. Pulling at his arm, I told him we needed to go to the hospital NOW. We said goodbye to no one and ran out to the truck. This was the one week my obstetrician was not in the office and we were unable to get a hold of the doctor on call, so we drove to the nearest hospital.

The check-in process and waiting for the ultra sound tech and on-call doctor took hours. After an hour long ultra sound and then waiting for what seemed like forever for the doctor to arrive, we got the worst news of our lives.

It appeared our innocent, unborn child had severe abnormalities. They noticed that there was little amniotic fluid surrounding my baby due to underdeveloped lungs and cysts in the kidneys. In addition, it looked like our child's head was abnormally shaped. The worst news of all was that it appeared that our precious little baby had no legs.

I screamed a scream only a mother knows. I can still remember thrashing at the bed while my husband held me down. "Why me," I thought, "what did I ever do to deserve this?"

I was numb. I had been numb for most of my life, but this numbness was nothing I had ever experienced before. Broken and devastated, I walked to the bathroom to change to go home. I closed the door, slid down the wall, and fell to the floor sobbing. My throat was dry, my face puffy, and my eyes red. I could barely move. I felt paralyzed. The sobbing eventually turned into hysteria and soon my husband came in and scooped me up. He had to dress me, put me into the wheel chair, and then into the car. I couldn't move. I couldn't speak. I was lifeless.

After learning all of this heartbreaking news, we were sent home.

There was nothing they could do for us in the wee hours of Sunday morning. We would have to wait until Monday to see a specialist at Children's Hospital in Milwaukee.

Once at home, we both cried all night long. We cried so much we had no tears left to cry. And as day broke, reality struck; this sick joke, this terrible nightmare, wasn't one at all.

Monday came and though I prayed to God that this was all a mistake, this prayer was not answered. Sadly, the outcome was fatal. Our baby was not going to live. A two hour long ultra sound did show our baby had legs, but everything else was as bad as it could be. We had to decide whether to have the baby early or wait until I went into labor on my own. If I had the baby early, there would be a 50/50 chance the baby would be born alive, and would likely only live for a few minutes, at most. If I waited to go into labor naturally, I would most likely deliver a stillborn.

We chose to deliver early and that Wednesday at 5 am, we were back at the hospital. I experienced the most painful labor imaginable, all for a child I wouldn't even get to keep. I was on an emotional roller coaster during the four hours of labor, but at 12:59 pm our daughter was born. I was in so much shock. All I remember feeling was sadness and despair. She lived for nineteen minutes and she died in my arms. The only pain in the room was what my husband and I were feeling, she had none. And just like that, my baby was gone. That night I refused to sleep at the hospital. I felt like a fraud in the maternity ward with no baby. And once the wheel chair was brought up to take me to the truck, I refused to sit in it. That was for mothers, and I wasn't one.

Those following weeks were dark for me. Darker than anything I had ever experienced in my life. Darker than the hundreds of rock bottoms I had experienced before. I was newly in recovery and uncertain about what my future would be like after this. The following two weeks I only left the house to go for walks, which often turned into runs. I would run and feel the pains of the physical recovery. Deep down, I knew I pushed through the pain to punish myself. I had no baby. I deserved to feel pain.

But after those two weeks, something happened. I realized I couldn't go on living like that. I had a business that needed me and a husband who had no idea how to help me, not to mention deal with his own grief. When everyone was waiting for me to relapse, to breakdown, I did the opposite. My daily affirmation became: *There has to be something good in this.* I took this to my mat. Yoga had been a saving grace for me, not once, but twice now. Every day I had to choose to move forward. I had to choose life when my daughter couldn't choose hers.

We named her Faith, and that is what she gave me: faith.

I would never wish what I went through on my worst enemy. To have your child ripped from you and to never to see them again is a life shattering thing. And I survived.

I had to make a mindset change. I had to make a choice to see things differently, because I knew that if I didn't I would slowly wither away. God had a purpose for me; I had to believe that now, more than ever. To this day, I believe that my daughter gave up her own life so that I could have one. A debt I will forever be repaying, a debt I am forever grateful for. I dove even deeper into my yoga practice. Each time I step onto my mat, I would fearlessly feel whatever surfaced, reminding myself that my mat was a safe place. My own practice would often be a combination of pushing myself physically to feel strength I had never felt before, and allowing myself to be emotionally vulnerable as I got into a deep pose like Pigeon or seated forward bend. Next to my puddles of sweat would be pools of tears; for months I relived the loss of my daughter. I was grieving, and my yoga mat was a safe and expressive place to grieve.

Her death forced me to face life each and every day. I'm not going to lie, it wasn't a walk in the park. The thought of falling backwards into the eating disorder I desperately clawed my way out of seemed like an easy way to stop feeling what I was feeling.

My addiction, my recovery, and my feelings all needed to be faced, now, alongside the loss of my daughter. Though it seemed like such an uphill battle, I started to walk it. There had to be purpose for me if I was still here and she was not. There had to be good in this somewhere.My yoga practice again became a safe place, a place where it was OK to cry, it was OK to be angry, it was OK to feel like I failed. And I can't totally explain it, but fully and consciously breathing, feeling my body move, feeling every sensation, every emotion and every space between the moments gave me hope, gave me a small window of promise that this wasn't the end, but rather just the beginning.

It's been nine years now since she's been gone, and a lot has changed. I now have three more beautiful children. Without her short life, I believe they would never have life themselves. Without her selfless act, I wouldn't be where I am today writing about this very experience. If my story helps just one person, then it wasn't all for nothing.

My mission is clear; I don't wonder why I am here anymore. Using my gifts and talents, and sharing my experiences, I can help those who, like me, are in the darkness and looking for the light. Or maybe those who have clawed their way out but are still wondering, "Where do I go now?"

For all of you, never lose hope. Believe there is something good that will come from even the most dire situation. Because if I can find life after a life-strangling addiction and my daughter's death, never lose hope that you can too.

Never lose hope …

Namaste,
Hope

ABOUT HOPE ZVARA

Hope works with people who are sick and tired of being sick and tired, people who are looking for a little "HOPE" to light their way. She is an innovator, yoga leader, and life guide. She inspires and assists willing and ready individuals to break through barriers in their bodies, minds, and businesses to help them become the best damn versions of themselves ever!

She has been teaching yoga for the past fifteen years and has owned and operated her home base yoga studio, Copper Tree Yoga Studio & Wellness Center, in Hartford, WI. Hope has used the yoga mat for half of her life to reach people and guide them to go deeper into their lives and into their hearts, to work on themselves on the mat, and to better themselves off of it.

She loves creating, sharing, and inspiring in every way she can. Her passion in life has always been writing and speaking, and she has created dozens of products for people from all walks of life.

You can catch her on the yoga mat at her local studio, teaching at conferences, and teaching teachers the tricks of the trade. When she's not there, she's sharing her life story and talking to others about why they, too, should never lose hope.

Find Hope at:

www.HopeZvara.com or www.HopeCoreFitness.com

Facebook: Hope Zvara

Instagram: @HopeZvara

#DailyDoseOfHope

YouTube: Hope Zvara

info@hopezvara.com

Studio contact information:

1364 E. Sumner Street, Hartford, WI 53027, 262-670-6688,

info@coppertreewellnessstudio.com

www.CopperTreeWellnessStudio.com

PERMISSIONS

Kellie Adkins. Reprinted with permission.
Lucette Beall. Reprinted with permission.
Donna Nudel Brown. Reprinted with permission.
Kate Butler. Reprinted with permission.
Melissa Camilleri. Reprinted with permission.
Michelle Simkiss Dunk. Reprinted with permission.
Anjela Ford. Reprinted with permission.
Belinda Ginter. Reprinted with permission.
Jennifer Granger. Reprinted with permission.
Colleen Hauk. Reprinted with permission.
Shelly Hodges. Reprinted with permission.
Teresa Huggins. Reprinted with permission.
Faith Leuschen. Reprinted with permission.
Jeanine Mihalak. Reprinted with permission.
Dina Proctor. Reprinted with permission.
Snowe Saxman. Reprinted with permission.
Stephanie Sorrells. Reprinted with permission.
Lee Tkachuk. Reprinted with permission.
Erin Whalen. Reprinted with permission.
Eve Wittenmeyer. Reprinted with permission.
Hope Zvara. Reprinted with permission.

Are you a Woman Who Ignites?

Do you wish to share your story to serve the world?

Have you dreamed of publishing a book?

Share your story with us and learn about how you can become
part of the next volume of the Women Who Ignite Series!

info@katebutlerbooks.com

May you find the spark that ignites your soul.

With love, gratitude, and admiration,

the women who ignite

Made in the USA
San Bernardino, CA
31 December 2019